Digital Entrepreneurship

A comprehensive guide to digital entrepreneurship, bridging academic research and industry practice. Morabito provides a strategic overview of the main challenges and trends related to digital entrepreneurship, structured in three parts. Part I focuses on strategy and management issues, guiding readers through the theory and practice of building, implementing and growing new digital ventures and outlining the skills that are necessary for digital entrepreneurs to succeed and lead. Part II focuses on digital business systems, describing the main technological aspects that support and comprise the core infrastructure for digital entrepreneurship, including social media and the Internet of Things. Finally, Part III provides analyses of three core industries in which digital ventures are particularly important: fintech, manufacturing and fashion. Digital Entrepreneurship will appeal to students and researchers in the areas of digital strategy/innovation and information systems management. It will also be of interest to practitioners looking to develop or innovate digital ventures.

Vincenzo Morabito is Associate Professor at the Management & Technology Department, Bocconi University (Università Commerciale Luigi Bocconi), Milan, Italy. He has participated in various research projects, many financed by Italian Ministry of University and Scientific Research (Ministero dell'Università e della Ricerca Scientifica e Tecnologica).

Digital Entrepreneurship

Management, Systems and Practice

Vincenzo Morabito

Bocconi University

CAMBRIDGE
UNIVERSITY PRESS

CAMBRIDGE
UNIVERSITY PRESS

University Printing House, Cambridge CB2 8BS, United Kingdom

One Liberty Plaza, 20th Floor, New York, NY 10006, USA

477 Williamstown Road, Port Melbourne, VIC 3207, Australia

314–321, 3rd Floor, Plot 3, Splendor Forum, Jasola District Centre, New Delhi – 110025, India

103 Penang Road, #05–06/07, Visioncrest Commercial, Singapore 238467

Cambridge University Press is part of the University of Cambridge.

It furthers the University's mission by disseminating knowledge in the pursuit of education, learning, and research at the highest international levels of excellence.

www.cambridge.org
Information on this title: www.cambridge.org/9781108845519
DOI: 10.1017/9781108979917

First published 2022

Printed in the United Kingdom by TJ Books Limited, Padstow Cornwall

A catalogue record for this publication is available from the British Library.

Library of Congress Cataloging-in-Publication Data
Names: Morabito, Vincenzo, author.
Title: Digital entrepreneurship : management, systems and practice / Vincenzo Morabito, Bocconi University.
Description: 1 Edition. | New York : Cambridge University Press, 2022. | Includes index.
Identifiers: LCCN 2021001941 | ISBN 9781108845519 (hardback) | ISBN 9781108969857 (paperback) | ISBN 9781108979917 (ebook)
Subjects: LCSH: Information technology – Economic aspects. | Entrepreneurship. | Information technology – Management. | Strategic planning.
Classification: LCC HC79.I55 M67 2021 | DDC 658/.05–dc23
LC record available at https://lccn.loc.gov/2021001941

ISBN 978-1-108-84551-9 Hardback
ISBN 978-1-108-96985-7 Paperback

Contents

vi   Contents

Figures

Tables

Acknowledgments

This book has been written over the last two years, and I want to acknowledge a number of people for their support, useful comments and cooperation during that time. Special mentions go to Professor Vincenzo Perrone at Bocconi University, Professor Vallabh Sambamurthy at Wisconsin School of Business and Professor Franco Fontana at LUISS University as main inspirations and mentors. Moreover, I acknowledge Professor Giuseppe Soda at Bocconi University and the rest of the department colleagues, in particular Professor Arnaldo Camuffo, Professor Anna Grandori, Professor Severino Salvemini and Professor Giuseppe Airoldi, all formerly at the Institute of Organization and Information Systems at Bocconi University, who have created a rich and rigorous research environment where I am proud to work.

I also acknowledge some colleagues from other universities with whom I've had the pleasure of working and conversing and from whom I've received useful comments as well as valuable insights for this book: among others, Anindya Ghose, Heinz Riehl Chair and Professor of Business at New York University Leonard N. Stern School of Business; Vijay Gurbaxani, Professor of Business and Computer Science at Paul Merage School of Business, University of California Irvine; Saby Mitra, Associate Director of Risk for the Institute for Information Security and Privacy at the Georgia Institute of Technology; Ravi Bapna, Board of Overseers Professor in the Information and Decision Sciences at the University of Minnesota Carlson School of Management; Stephanie Woerner, Research Scientist at MIT Center for Information Systems Research; Sam Ransbotham, Professor of Information Systems in the Carroll School of Management at Boston College; Tobias Kretschmer, Head of Institute for Strategy, Technology and Organization at Ludwig Maximilian University, Munich; Jan Mendling, Professor at the Institute for Information Business at Vienna University of Economics and Business; Christopher L Tucci, Professor of Digital Strategy and Innovation at the Imperial College Business School; Garrick Hileman, Head of Research at Blockchain; Marinos Themistocleous, Director of the Institute for the Future at the University of Nicosia; Federico Pigni, Professor at Grenoble School of Management; Vincent Mangematin, Dean and Chief Academic Officer at KEDGE Business School; Antonio de Amescua and Román López-Cortijo, Professors of Computer Science at Carlos III University, Madrid; Paolo Aversa, Senior Lecturer in Strategy and MBA Director at Cass Business School; Stefano Zanero, Computer Engineering Associate Professor at the Polytechnic University of Milan; Angela Sasse from University College London; and Ferdinando Ametrano, Bitcoin and Blockchain Technologies Lecturer at the Polytechnic University of Milan and Bicocca University.

Furthermore, I want to gratefully acknowledge all the companies that have participated in research interviews, case studies and surveys.

Financial institutions: Agos Ducato, Aldermore Bank, Banca Carige, Banca Credito Trevigiano (BCT), Banca d'Italia, Banca Euromobiliare, Banca Fideuram, Banca Mediolanum, Banca Monte dei Paschi, Banca Passadore, Banca Popolare dell'Emilia Romagna, Banca Popolare di Bari, Banca Popolare di Sondrio, Banca Popolare di Vicenza, Banca Sistema, BancoBPM, Bancomat, Barclays, BAWAG, BCC Roma, BNL-BNP Paribas, Borsa Italiana, BPER, Cariparma, Cassa Depositi e Prestiti, Cassa di Risparmio di Firenze, Cedacri, Che Banca!, Compass, Corner Bank, Credem, Credit Agricole, Crédit Agricole Life Insurance Europe, Credito Emiliano, Deutsche Bank, Dexia, FCA Bank, Istituto Centrale delle Banche Popolari Italiane, ING Direct, Intesa SanPaolo, Intesa SanPaolo Luxembourg, Intesa SanPaolo Servitia, Istituto per le Opere Religiose, JP Morgan Chase, Key Client, Luxemburg Stock Exchange, Mediobanca, Monte Titoli, Nexi, Poste Italiane, Profamily, Raiffeisen Bank, Royal Bank of Scotland, SEC Servizi, Société Européene de Banque, Standard Chartered, UBI Banca, UBS, Veneto Banca, Volksbank Wien, WeBank and Widiba.

Insurance: Allianz, Aspe Re, Assicurazioni Generali, Assimoco, Aviva, Cardif, Cattolica Assicurazioni, Coface, Europe Assistance, Eurovita Assicurazioni, Foyer, Groupama, Munich RE, Novae, Poste Vita, PRUDENTIAL, Reale Mutua, Sara Assicurazioni, Standard Life Aberdeen, Tysers, UnipolSai, Uniqa Assicurazioni, Vittoria Assicurazioni and Zurich.

Industrial: A1 Telekom, A2A, ABB, Accenture, Acea, Aci, Aci Informatica, Acqua Minerale S. Benedetto, Adidas, Aeroporti di Roma, Alitalia, Alliance Boots, Alpitour, Amadori, Amazon, Amplifon, Anas, Angelini, ArcelorMittal, Areti, Armani, Arval, Astaldi, AstraZeneca, ATAC, ATM, Auchan, Audi, Augusta Westland, Autogrill, Autostrade per l'Italia, Avio, Baglioni Hotels, Barilla, BASF, BasicNet, Bayer

Pharmaceuticals, Be Consulting, Benetton, Between, BMW, Boeing Defence, Bormioli, BOSH, Bottega Veneta, Bravo Fly, Brembo, Brunello Cucinelli, BSH, Business Integration Partners, Calzedonia, Cementir, Centrica Energy, Cerved, Chiesi Farmaceutici, CIA Agricoltori Italiani, CNH Industrial, Coca Cola HBC, Comau, Coop Italia, Costa Crociere, Daimler, Dainese, D'Amico, Danieli, Danone, De Agostini, Diesel, Dimar, Dolce & Gabbana, Ducati, EDF, Edipower, Edison, Elettronica, Elica, ENAV, Enel, Enel-X, Engie, Eni, ENRC, E. ON, ERG, Ermenegildo Zegna, Eurobet, Fastweb, FCA, Fendi, Ferrari, Ferretti, Ferrovie dello Stato, Ferservizi, Fincantieri, G4S, GE Capital, General Electric, GFT, GlaxosmithKline, Glencore, Grandi Navi Veloci, Grimaldi, Gruppo API, Gruppo Coin, Gruppo De Agostini, Gruppo Hera, GVC Holdings PLC, H3GWind, Hupac, IGT, Il Sole24Ore, Ingenico, Infineon, Interoll, IREN, Istituto Europeo Oncologico, Istituto Poligrafico e Zecca dello Stato, ItalGas, ITV, Jaguar Land Rover, Kuwait Petroleum, Labelux Group, Lamborghini, La Perla, Lastminute Group, Lavazza, LBBW, Leaseplan, Leonardo-Finmeccanica, Levi's, Linde, Linkem, L'Oreal, Loro Piana, Lottomatica, Lucite International, Luxottica, Magneti Marelli, Mail Boxes Etc, MAN, Mapei, Marcegaglia, Maserati, Mediaset, Menarini, Mercedes, Messaggerie Libri, Metaenergia, Metro Italia Cash & Carry, Miroglio, MM S.p.A., Mondelez International, Mossi & Ghisolfi, Natuzzi, NH Hotel, Novartis, Octo Telematics, Oerlikon Graziano, Olivetti, OSRAM, PAX Italia, Perfetti, Pernod Ricard, Peroni, Pfizer, Philip Morris Int., Philips, Piaggio, Pinko, Pirelli, Poliform, Pomellato, Porsche, Postel, Prada, Premier Oil, Procter & Gamble, ProSiebenSat1, Prysmian, RAI, Retonkil Initial, Rexam, RFI, RHI, Rizoma, Roche, Rolex, RWE, Saipem, Sandoz, Sanofi Aventis, Schindler Electroca, SEA, Seat PG, Selex, SIAE, Sigma-Tau, Sisal, SisalPay, Sky Italia, Snaitech, Snam, Sorgenia, Suzuki, Teksid, Telefonica, Tenaris, Terna, TIM, Tods, Trenitalia, Trussardi, TuevSued, Tyco, Uber, Unicoop Firenze, Unilever, Valentino, Virgin Atlantic, Vodafone, Volkswagen and Whirlpool.

ICT: Almaviva, Cabel Holding, Engineering, Ericsson and Oasi Servizi.

Public: Agenzia per l'Italia Digitale, Comune di Milano, Consip and Regione Lombardia.

Others who participated in research interviews, case studies and surveys for this book include: Silvio Fraternali, Paolo Cederle, Massimo Milanta, Massimo Schiattarella, Diego Donisi, Marco Sesana, Mario Di Mauro, Giovanni Damiani, Gianluigi Castelli, Salvatore Poloni, Milo Gusmeroli, Pierangelo Rigamoti, Danilo Augugliaro, Ranieri De

Marchis, Francesco Giordano, Nazzareno Gregori, Edoardo Romeo, Elvio Sonnino, Pierangelo Mortara, Massimo Messina, Mario Collari, Giuseppe Capponcelli, Massimo Castagnini, Pier Luigi Curcuruto, Giovanni Sordello, Maurizio Montagnese, Massimo Tessitore, Alberto Sferch, Enrico Bagnasco, David Cis, Bruce Hodges, Carlo Brezigia, Massimo Malagoli, Riccardo Sfondrini, Fabio Ugoste, Giuseppe Virano, Domenico Fileppo, Giovanni Mori, Roberto Di Fonzo, Umberto Angelucci, Giuseppe Dallona, Davide Tesoro Tess, Gilberto Ceresa, Rene Keller, Jesus Marin Rodriguez, Fabio Momola, Rafael Lopez Rueda, Eike Wahl, Marco Cecchella, Carmine Artone, Maria-Louise Arscott, Antonella Ambriola, Andrea Rigoni, Giovanni Rando Mazzarino, Paolo Martella, Alfredo Altavilla, Silvio Sperzani, Samuele Sorato, Alessandro Preda, Andrea Cardamone, Salvatore Molè, Alberto Ripepi, Alfredo Montalbano, Cristina Porzio, Gloria Gazzano, Massimo Basso Ricci, Giuseppe De Iaco, Isabella Fumagalli, Riccardo Amidei, Davide Ferina, Massimo Ferriani, Roberto Burlo, Cristina Bianchini, Dario Scagliotti, Ettore Corsi, Luciano Bartoli, Stewart Alexander, Luca Ghirardi, Francesca Gandini, Francesco Del Pizzo, Vincenzo Tortis, Agostino Ragosa, Sandro Tucci, Vittorio Mondo, Giangaddo Prati, Andrea Agosti, Roberto Fonso, Federico Gentili, Nino Lo Banco, Fabio Troiani, Federico Niero, Sebastiano Marulli, Gianluca Zanutto, Mario Bocca, Marco Zaccanti, Anna Pia Sassano, Fabrizio Lugli, Alessandro Garofalo, Marco Bertazzoni, Vittorio Boero, Francesco Maldari, Francesco Durante, Carlo Achermann, David Cis, Stefano Achermann, Jean-Claude Krieger, Mario Martinelli, Reinhold Grassl, François de Brabant, Maria Cristina Spagnoli, Pietro Amorusi, Alessandra Testa, Anna Miseferi, Matteo Attrovio, Giorgio Mosca, Roberto Saracino, Nikos Angelopoulos, Igor Bailo, Stefano Levi, Luciano Romeo, Alfio Puglisi, Gennaro Della Valle, Massimo Paltrinieri, Luca Vanetti, Pierantonio Azzalini, Carlo Garuccio, Enzo Contento, Marco Fedi, Fiore Della Rosa, Dario Tizzanini, Francesca Durì, Gabriele Scarponi, Carlo Capalbo, Bruce Hodges, Pietro Maranzana, Vittorio Giusti, Piera Fasoli, Carlo di Lello, Gian Enrico Paglia, George Sifnios, Francesco Varchetta, Gianfranco Casati, Fabio Benasso, Angela Gemma, Alessandro Marin, Gianluca Guidotti, Fabrizio Virtuani, Luca Verducci, Marco Valioni, Luca Falco, Francesco Pedrielli, Riccardo Riccobene, Roberto Scolastici, Paola Formenti, Stefano Malvicini, Nicoletta Rocca, Emanuele Balisteri, Mario Breuer, Fabio Caressa, Simonetta Consiglio, Luca Gasparini, Mario Costantini, Matteo Colombo, Marco Lanza, Marco Poggi, Gianfranco Ardissono, Alex Eugenio Sala, Daniele Bianchi, Giambattista Piacentini, Daniele Savarè, Fabio Cesaretti, Marcello

Ronco, Tommaso Pellizzari, Filipe Teixeira, Andrea Giovanni Mugnai, Roberto Riccardi, Barbara Monfredini, Luigi Zanardi, Valerio Momoni, Daniele Panigati, Christian Ciceri, Maurizio Pescarini, Ermes Franchini, Francesco Mastrandrea, Vincenzo Cervino, Federico Boni, Vincenzo Pensa, Roberto D'Attili, Ernesto Ciorra, Fabio Veronese, Mauro Minenna, Giampiero Astuti, Massimo Romagnoli, Vasco Tomaselli, Nicola Grassi, Alessandro Capitani, Mauro Frassetto, Bruno Cocchi, Marco Tempra, Martin Brannigan, Alessandro Guidotti, Monica Colleoni, Gianni Leone, Stefano Signani, Domenico Casalino, Fabrizio Lugoboni, Giorgio Piotti, Roberto Ghislanzoni, Giuliano Capizzi, Fabrizio Rocchio, Mauro Bernareggi, Claudio Sorano, Marcus Heidmann, Paolo Crovetti, Antonio Perrotti, Alberto Ricchiari, Alessandro Musumeci, Luana Barba, Pierluigi Berlucchi, Matthias Schlapp, Ugo Salvi, Giovanni Paolo Bruno, Elisabetta Torri, Daniela Manuello, Danilo Gismondi, Elisabetta Nobile, Patrick Vandenberghe, Daniele Balbo, Claudio Colombatto, Massimiliano Ciferri, Danilo Ughetto, Tiberio Strati, Massimo Nichetti, Fabio Maini, Stefano Firenze, Remo Nadali, Vahe Ter Nikogosyan, Giorgio Voltolini, Franco Caraffi, Andrea Maraventano, Martin Giersich, Michela Scovazzo, Massimo Bertolotti, Guido Oppizzi, Alessandro Bruni, Marco Franzi, Stefano Gentili, Guido Albertini, Massimiliano De Gregorio, Chiara Pellistri, Vincenzo Russi, Franco Collautti, Massimo Dall'Ora, Fabio De Ferrari, Giuseppe Alibrandi, Marco Moretti, Mauro Ferrari, Domenico Solano, Pier Paolo Tamma, Susanna Nardi, Massimo Amato, Alberto Grigoletto, Nunzio Calì, Arturo Baldo, Fabio De Santis, Gianfilippo Pandolfini, Guido Rindi, Cristiano Cannarsa, Fabio Degli Esposti, Riccardo Scattaretico, Claudio Basso, Mauro Pianezzola, Piergiorgio Grossi, Marco Zanussi, Alberto Fenzi, Davide Carteri, Simonetta Iarlori, Marco Prampolini, Luca Terzaghi, Christian Altomare, Paolo Gasparato, Pasquale Tedesco, Fabio Boschiero, Franco Colzani, Elisabetta Castro, Maria Dentamaro, Roberta Crispino, Carlo Castiglioni, Nicoletta Carlomagno, Francesco Modesti, Isabel Castillo, Aldo Borrione, Paolo Beatini, Maurizio Pellicano, Ottavio Rigodanza, Angelo D'Alessandro, Marcello Guerrini, Stefano Torcello, Francesco Germini, Michela Quitadamo, Massimo Severin, Salvatore Rocco, Chiara Galli, Dario Castello, Giorgio Degli Abbati, Giuseppe Bramante, Marco Casati, Stefano Boscolo, Fabio Boschiero, Silvia Zanni, Fabio Cestola, Roberto Mondonico, Alberto Alberini, Pierluca Ferrari, Umberto Stefani, Elvira Fabrizio, Salvatore Impallomeni, Dario Pagani, Eric Peyer, Jean-Luc Martino, Marino Vignati, Giuseppe Rossini, Paolo Calvi, Francesco Genovese, Alfio Puglisi, Renzo Di Antonio, Maurizio Galli, Filippo Vadda, Roberto Casula, Marco De

Paoli, Paolo Cesa, Armando Gervasi, Riccardo Delleani, Luigi Di Tria, Marco Gallibariggio, David Alfieri, Graziano Cavallo, Mirco Carriglio, Pier Francesco Gavagni, Maurizio Castelletti, Gaetano Scebba, Roberto Andreoli, Barbara Monfrini, Vincenzo Campana, Marco Ravasi, Antonella Cirina, Fabio Grassi, Mauro Viacava, Giacomo Carelli, Flavio Glorio, Alessio Pomasan, Salvatore Stefanelli, Roberto Scaramuzza, Marco Zaffaroni, Giuseppe Langer, Francesco Bardelli, Davide Barbavara, Daniele Rizzo, Silvia De Fina, Gabriele Raineri, Paulo Morais, Massimiliano Gerli, Andrea Facchini, Massimo Zara, Luca Paleari, Alessandra Ardrizzoia, Andrea Dupplicato, Alberto Maldino, Carlo Bozzoli, Luigi Borrelli, Marco Iacomussi, Enrico Senatore, Marco Tendas, Stefano Ceravolo, Mario Dio, Giulio Mattietti, Alessandro Poerio, Fabrizio Frustaci, Roberto Zaccaro, Maurizio Quattrociocchi, Gianluca Giovannetti, Francesco Frau, Massimo Alberti, Andrea Lippi, Pierangelo Colacicco, Paolo Lissoni, Silvio Sassatelli, Filippo Passerini, Mario Rech, Claudio Sordi, Tomas Blazquez De La Cruz, Elia Mariani, Paolo Torazzo, Diego Ceresa, Matteo Arpini, Luca Spagnoli, Fabio Oggioni, Dante Buccelloni, Luca Severini, Roberto Conte, Federica Dall'Ora, Alessandro Tintori, Giovanni Ferretti, Patrizia Tedesco, Antonio Rainò, Claudio Beveroni, Chiara Manzini, Simone Macelloni, Francesco Del Greco, Luca Sacchi, Alessandro Sala, Miriam Imperato, Lorenzo Tanganelli, Ivano Bosisio, Alessandro Campanini, Pietro Donati, Matteo Ortenzi, Giovanni Pietrobelli, Pietro Pacini, Vittorio Padovani, Luciano Dalla Riva, Grazia Campanile, Jarvis Macchi, Gabriele Lunati, Lucinda Spera, Paolo Pecchiari, Francesco Donatelli, Massimo Palmieri, Rossana Barzizza, Giovanni Rossi, Alessandro Cucchi, Riccardo Pagnanelli, Raffaella Mastrofilippo, Roberto Coretti, Alessandra Grendele, Ruggero Platolino, Stefano Smareglia, Roberto Corradini, Luca Del Din, Marianna Pepe, Massimo Rigobon, Antonina Tornabene, Matteo Dell'Orto, Sonia Aidani, Gabriele De Villa, Myrtille Clement Fromentel, Matteo Nube, Daniele Galleani, Andrea Arrigoni, Davide Casagrande, Lucia Gerini, Filippo Cecchi, Silvia Spadaccini, Massimilano Spadini, Gianlorenzo Magnani, Antonio Chiappara, Marzio Bonelli, Giovanni Gurioli, Roberto Privitera, Fabio De Maron, Alberto Peralta, Stefano Sala, Massimo Pernigotti, Massimo Rama, Francisco Souto, Oscar Grignolio, Gianni Rumi, Mario Mella, Massimo Rosso, Mauro Restelli, Filippo Onorato, Stefan Caballo, Ennio Bernardi, Gianluigi Zarantonello, Matteo Formenti, Aldo Croci, Giuseppe Genovesi, Gianrico Sirocchi, Maurizio Romanese, Daniele Pagani, Derek Barwise, Luca Ingrao, Guido Vetere, Christophe Pierron, Pietro Giardina, Guenter Lutgen, Lorenzo Marietti, Domenico Porto,

Alessandro Di Fonzo, Carlo Romagnoli, Claudio Luongo, Riccardo Angeli, Giovanni Bagnoli, Andreas Weinberger, Luca Martis, Stefano Levi, Paola Benatti, Massimiliano Baga, Matteo Baido, Marco Campi, Laura Wegher, Sebastiano Cannella, Diego Pogliani, Gianpiero Pepino, Rosy Bellan, Alessandro Marzi, Simona Tonella, Thomas Steinich, Barbara Karuth-Zelle, Ralf Schneider, Rüdiger Schmidt, Wolfgang Gärtner, Alfred Spill, Marco Damiano Bosco, Mauro Di Pietro Paolo, Paolo Brusegan, Giovanni Cialariello, Stefano Mander, Arnold Aschbauer, Ralph Karliczek, Robert Wittgen, Peter Kempf, Wilfried Reimann, Abel Archundia Pineda, Jürgen Sturm, Stefan Gaus, Peter Rampling, Elke Knobloch, Andrea Weierich, Andreas Luber, Heinz Laber, Sandra Betocchi, Daniel Besse, Michael Hesse, Markus Lohmann, Andreas König, Herby Marchetti, Marcell Assan, Klaus Straub, Robert Blackburn, Wiebe Van der Horst, Mattias Ulbrich, Matthias Schlapp, Jan Brecht, Enzo Contento, Michael Pretz, Gerd Friedrich, Florian Forst, Robert Leindl, Wolfgang Keichel, Stephan Fingerling, Sven Lorenz, Martin Hofmann, Nicola Benvegnù, Nicolas Burdkhardt, Armin Pfoh, Kian Mossanen, Anthony Roberts, John Knowles, Lisa Gibbard, John Hiskett, Richard Wainwright, David Madigan, Adam Ewell, James Freeborough, Matt Hopkins, Gill Lungley, Simon Jobson, Glyn Hughes, John Herd, Mark Smith, Jeremy Vincent, Guy Lammert, Steve Blackledge, Mark Lichfield, Jacky Lamb, Simon McNamara, Kevin Hanley, Anthony Meadows, Rod Hefford, Stephen Miller, Giovanni Leone, David Edwards, David Edwards, Stuart Lawson, Dean Eaves, Paul Johnson, Martin Beaver, Diana Medeiros-Placido, Jeremy Waters, Parker Humbert, Rob Lankey, Chris Michael, Willem Eelman, David Bulman, Neil Brown, Alistair Hadfield, Carsten Poetzschke, Andrey Martovoy, Marc Hotton, Neil Dyke, Tod McKenna, Andy Wilson, Kerry Grinham, Simon Hogg, Daniele Vigna, Roberta Rossi, Edoardo Anzani, Enrico Cagnin, Enrico Masoero, Cristian Pistamiglio, Davide Collavizza, Marco Triozzi, Antonia Casamassima, Daniele Valesani, Roberto Catto, Manuel Vanzetti, Francesco Baldi, Alessandro Ghio, Ivan Pavesio, Fabrizio Andrisani, Azzurra Ciraci, Francesco Maldotti, Francesco Mannaioli, Christophe Salomon, Giovanni Ballotta, Alexander Heinrich, Andrea Molteni, Michel Vukusic, Alexander Angebrandt, Christoph Auerbach, Rainer Kiel, Sherin Abraham, Arianna Paiella, Umberto Costanzini, Alessandro Caridi, Andrea Della Vedova, Fabian Topp, Andrea Pettinelli, Eckart Pech, Olaf Frank, Silviu Popescu, Tina Pogacic, Wolfgang Hanzl, Alexander Stock, Gerald Prangl, Alexander Bockelmann, Antonio Bergalio, Peter Novak, Melanie Kehr, Sven Laue, Joerg Benischke, Michele Fioravanti, Silvia Morabito, Marina

Morabito, Enzo Greco, Andrea Arancio, Daniele Pedrazzi, Angelo Parente, Alessandro Gentili, Fabio Potenza, Alessandro Linguanti, Giuseppe Napolitano, Federica Susanna Beretta, Alessandra Faranda, Ivano Di Lauro, Alessio Taruffi, Giulio Capacchione, Francesca Cavallari, Alessandro Fiumara, Giuseppe Portoricco, Emiliano Muroni, Alberto Giaccone, Maria Rosaria Carlesimo, Paolo Bazzocchi, Andrea Mori, Emiliano Sorrenti, Marco Rizzoli, Priscila Bossi, Michele Panigada, Ivano Gatti, Fabrizio Rigolio, Gennaro Bisesti and Francesco Bianco Marino.

I would especially like to gratefully acknowledge Gianluigi Viscusi and Alan Serrano-Rico at Brunel University who provided me with valuable suggestions and precious support in the coordination of the production process of this book.

Furthermore, I acknowledge the support of Business Technology Foundation (Fondazione Business Technology) and all the bright researchers at the Business Technology Organization (BTO) Research Program who supported me in carrying out interviews, surveys and data analysis: Giuseppe Pugliese, Antonio Attinà, Marco Castelli, Umberto Bosisio, Alessandro Poli, Roberta Raimondi, Federico Latella, Alessia Bonanno, Luigi Scipioni, Lorenzo Chiara, Andrea Della Rocca, Francesco Schipa, Fabio Formosa and Roberto Valerio. Among my research partners, I would like to especially acknowledge Florenzo, Fabrizio, and Martino who made this journey possible.

A special acknowledgment goes to the memory of Professor Antonino Intrieri who provided precious comments and suggestions throughout the years.

Finally, I acknowledge my daughters Vittoria and Angela whose constant support, patience and understanding made this book happen as well as Hanaa for the positive energy that she transferred to me.

Abbreviations

3D	three-dimensional
AI	artificial intelligence
API	application programming interface
AR	augmented reality
BBC	British Broadcasting Corporation
CA	California
CEO	chief executive officer
CIC	community interest company
CIO	chief information officer
CMO	chief marketing officer
CRM	customer relationship management
CTO	chief technology officer
e-commerce	electronic commerce
EHS	environment, health and safety
FDA	Food and Drug Administration
EU	European Union
GDP	gross domestic product
GPS	Global Positioning System
H1	First Half
HTML	Hypertext Markup Language
HTTP	Hypertext Transfer Protocol
ICT	information and communication technologies
IoT	Internet of Things
IP	Internet Protocol address
IPO	initial public offering
IPR	intellectual property rights
IT	information technology
KPI	key performance indicator
m-commerce	mobile commerce
MPEG	Moving Picture Experts Group
NGOs	nongovernmental organizations
OEE	overall equipment effectiveness

OLED	organic light-emitting diode
PC	personal computer
PDF	Portable Document Format
PPC	pay-per-click
Q&A	questions and answers
R&D	research and development
RFID	radio-frequency identification
ROI	return on investment
RSS	rich site summary | really simple syndication
SEO	search engine optimization
SME	small to medium-sized enterprise
SMS	short message service
STEM	science, technology, engineering and mathematics
TV	television
UK	United Kingdom
URL	Uniform Resource Locator
US	United States
USA	United States of America
USD	United States dollar(s)
VC	venture capital
VIP	very important person
VP	vice president

Introduction

Digitalization has been a driver of transformation in business and society, leading to radical changes in the ideas and shapes of what work is, what organizations are and how value can be captured and created. One of the key issues of digitalization has been its capacity to enforce new ecosystems and the consequent rise of a new breed of entrepreneurs and ventures exploiting the opportunity of digital business. Therefore, this book discusses and presents the main challenges and trends related to digital entrepreneurship to an audience of managers and scholars. Moreover, this volume aims to provide a unified survey of both practice and current scientific work on the topic, considering the key issues for strategy and management as well as the role of technology in developing new digital ventures. Thus, as in my previous volumes, I will consider different perspectives, from information systems, technology management and innovation research to strategy and marketing, among others. Accordingly, this volume aims to create a bridge between industry and academia, presenting practices that are suitable for use by established businesses and digital entrepreneurs through the lens of academic work. This book continues the mission of my former published volumes in providing practitioners with a toolbox and "food for thought," too. So, as in previous work, each theme will be analyzed in its technical and managerial aspects, also through the use of case studies and examples.

Outline of the Book

The book argument is developed along three main axes, following a structure similar to the one adopted in my previous books [1–3], considering, first (Part I), strategy and management issues for digital entrepreneurship; subsequently (Part II), the role of technology, focusing on key digital business systems suitable to enable and for consideration by digital entrepreneurs and ventures; and, finally (Part III), the challenges and development of digital entrepreneurship in *three* key industries (fintech, manufacturing and fashion), through presentation and review of case studies at a global level.

In Part I, I first discuss digital entrepreneurship's main characteristics and types (Chapter 1) before considering its relationship with innovation and the related challenges for new ventures as well as different kinds of organization apart from start-ups (Chapter 2). I focus specifically on digital marketing as a key aspect for digital entrepreneurs wanting to successfully target and manage their customers (Chapter 3). I conclude the first part of the volume by analyzing the education and skills required for digital entrepreneurship (Chapter 4). I begin Part II by exploring the key challenges of digital information and communication technologies (ICT) for digital entrepreneurship (Chapter 5). I then consider in detail three key digital technologies for digital entrepreneurship: social media (Chapter 6), the Internet of Things (Chapter 7) and blockchain (Chapter 8). Finally, as already mentioned, I investigate, in Part III, the challenges and development of digital entrepreneurship in the fintech, manufacturing and fashion industries alongside discussion and analysis of case studies at a global level.

As in my previous volumes [1–4], I adopt both a scientific approach and a concrete stance to introduce the characteristics, challenges and opportunities of digital entrepreneurship with the goal of providing insights and "tools" for understanding and acting through new ventures in the current digital competitive environment. Thus, this book is ideally connected to my former volumes on digital challenges and trends as well as Big Data and analytics [1–3], aiming to synthesize the issues and be a ready-to-consult guide to the key topics of digital business innovation for both managers and scholars.

References

1. Morabito V. *The Future of Digital Business Innovation*. Springer (2016).
2. Morabito V. *Big Data and Analytics*. Springer (2015).
3. Morabito V. *Trends and Challenges in Digital Business Innovation*. Springer (2014).
4. Morabito V. *Business Technology Organization – Managing Digital Information Technology for Value Creation – The SIGMA Approach*. Springer (2013).

Part I

Strategy and Management

1   Digital Entrepreneurship and Digital Business

1.1   Introduction

The digital revolution, brought about by the wide adoption and use of numerous technological tools such as smartphones, the Internet, social media and cloud technology, has created explosive changes in the economies and markets in which businesses operate. By 2020, it was estimated that there will be 50 billion Internet enabled devices, which in the entrepreneurial world is translated into more potential customers for businesses to reach. Offering billions of emerging opportunities, the digital disruption has transformed businesses as well as their processes and activities, reinventing their relationships with stakeholders such as suppliers, vendors and customers. In the era of digital trends, entrepreneurs are exploiting the dynamics of digital technologies in order to create value, expand their business and ultimately achieve high revenues that translate into the success of the firm [1]. "Software is eating the world" was the phrase used by famous Internet pioneer Mark Andreessen when trying to describe the extent of the digital phenomenon, with more and more businesses in almost every industry being run online and offering their products and services through the Internet. From movies to agriculture and defense, firms around the world have embraced the digital disruption [2].

1.2   Defining Digital Entrepreneurship and Digital Business

Over the last few decades, the concept of entrepreneurship has received significant attention from extant literature, where academic consensus on an equivocal definition has not been achieved yet.

In the early twentieth century, Joseph Schumpeter, who is considered the father of the contemporary version of entrepreneurship, in his seminal work described entrepreneurship as a process that involves the creation of new opportunities through "creative destruction," by breaking the equilibrium and embracing change [11]. In other words, an entrepreneur is an individual who introduces innovations, in the form of processes, products and services, into the existing system, and is willing to take the risk as well as the responsibility involved in creating and implementing a new business strategy for an existing firm or in starting up a new business. Several studies in the literature try to define the concept of entrepreneurship and contribute additional value.

Table 1.1 presents some of the various definitions that have been proposed by authors in extant literature. It can be observed that some definitions omit the aspect of innovation while others tend to focus on the outcomes of entrepreneurship, with some concentrating on different instances of it such as "international" entrepreneurship. Overall, although there has been no mutual consensus on a global definition, studies seem to agree that at the core of entrepreneurship lie the aspects of innovation, risk-taking, seeking of new opportunities and creation of

Table 1.1 *Definitions of entrepreneurship*

Author	Definition
Shane and Venkataraman 2000 [3]	"We define the field of entrepreneurship as the scholarly examination of how, by whom, and with what effects opportunities to create future goods and services are discovered, evaluated, and exploited ... Consequently, the field involves the study of sources of opportunities; the *processes* of discovery, evaluation, and exploitation of opportunities; and the set of *individuals* who discover, evaluate, and exploit them" (p. 218).
Casson 1982 [4]	"An entrepreneur is someone who specializes in taking judgmental decisions about the coordination of scarce resources" (p. 20).
Cuervo et al. 2007 [5]	"Entrepreneurship includes the identification and assessment of opportunities, the decision to exploit them oneself or sell them, efforts to obtain resources and the development of the strategy and organization of the new business project" (p. 3).
Frank Knight 1921 [7]	"Universal foreknowledge would leave no place for an 'entrepreneur.' His role is to improve knowledge, especially foresight, and bear the incidence of its limitations" (p. lix). "Let us consider first the simple case of unique and undivided exercise of the function, the control and uncertainty-bearing being all concentrated in the same individual, under the assumption that outsiders[,] whether employed by him or not [,] have neither opinions upon nor interest in the question of his competence. It will further simplify the problem if we begin by assuming that this is the only type of entrepreneurship in our society" (p. 280).

Table 1.1 *(cont.)*

Author	Definition
Reynolds 1999 [8]	"Any attempt at new business or new venture creation, such as self-employment, a new business organization, or the expansion of an existing business, by an individual, a team of individuals, or an established business" (p. 3).
Ruiz 2016 [9]	"Entrepreneurship means an undertaking by an individual, a team of individuals, or an established private or public entity in any of the following activities or areas. Any attempt at new business or new venture creation such as self-employment, founding a new business organization, or expanding an existing business. Any attempt at creating a new public initiative such as a new public organism, or expanding an existing organism. Any attempt at innovation, such as launching new products or services, new strategic development, new organization of resources (including human), entering new markets (including internationalization), creating new sectors, social development, or any other action that adds economic or social value" (p. 1029).
Oviatt and McDougall 2005 [10]	"International entrepreneurship is the discovery, enactment, evaluation, and exploitation of opportunities – across national borders – to create future goods and services" (p. 540).

new business activity as well as management of the new business and value creation [6].

Similar to the concept of entrepreneurship and taking into account its core aspects, digital entrepreneurship entails pursuing opportunities by utilizing information communication technologies (ICT) such as cloud computing, mobile computing and social media, providing entrepreneurial innovation in order to create value and gain competitive advantage over operations as well as competitors [6, 12].

Digital entrepreneurship can be defined as "the pursuit of the generation of value through the creation or expansion of economic activity by identifying and exploiting new ICT or ICT enabled products, processes and corresponding markets"[6]. If we considering digital enterprise to be the intersection of physical and digital economy, as depicted in Figure 1.1, as well as the intersection of digital technologies and entrepreneurship [14], we can differentiate digital entrepreneurship from traditional venturing in the following respects:

• **Focus.** Digital entrepreneurship is focused on technology innovations that are inspired by developments in science and engineering,

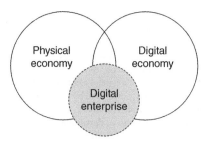

Figure 1.1 Digital enterprise as the intersection of physical and digital economy
Source: Adapted from [13].

promoting the emergence of novel entrepreneurial opportunities including promising markets, novel products and even new customer segments and industries [15].

- **Activity form.** In a digital firm, some or all of the entrepreneurial activities happen digitally instead of via traditional forms. This includes not only firms that have embraced digitization as an endeavor to reduce their costs and improve their customer service, for example through the adoption of a website, or to aid in the distribution of physical goods and services, such as with Amazon or eBay, but also digital enterprises that sell completely digitized products or services, such as music and applications [12, 16].
- **Business strategy and model.** Digital ventures use different business models from those favored by traditional ventures as well as different marketing strategies to promote their products and reach their customers [12, 17].

According to [18], a digital business is defined as an organization that uses a combination of two or more digital technologies in order to create new revenue opportunities, boost customer engagement, penetrate into new markets and increase product or service development speed to market. By harnessing the power of digital technologies such as mobile computing, cloud computing and social media, the digital enterprise achieves mobility by bringing teams of people together regardless of their location, enabling face-to-face interaction among different parties dispersed around the world via social collaboration tools. By leveraging digital technologies to create virtual offices, digitize its business processes or create an e-commerce platform, the digital venture is able to achieve international expansion by introducing its products into the world's most promising markets while at the same time reducing the costs of internationalizing its business activities and operations [19].

The infusion of new digital technologies into the entrepreneurial era has provided digital ventures with a vast amount of business innovative opportunities to explore as well as novel market segments to enter. These digital technologies, which enhance entrepreneurial pursuit as well as play a crucial role in shaping entrepreneurial actions and outcomes, manifest in three interrelated elements, according to [14]:

- **Digital artifacts**. Digital artifacts are digital components or applications embedded into physical objects, providing specific functionality to users. They can be in the form of either stand-alone software and hardware components on physical devices, such as applications in smartphones or fitness watches, or parts of products such as home appliances and personal products (Amazon Virtual Dash Button, Oral-B connected toothbrush). Characterized by reprogrammability and recombinability, digital artifacts are open, flexible, easily modifiable and expansible, enabling the entrepreneur to infuse new functionalities into the object thus generating new entrepreneurial opportunities. For example, drones, digital devices that were originally invented for military services, have been recently modified and adopted by several industries, such as agriculture, logistics and real estate, which are exploiting their functionality in new purposes [14].

- **Digital platforms**. A digital platform is a technology business model that enables exchanges among different groups such as producers and consumers. The most popular example is the Apple iOS platform, otherwise known as Apple Store, where users can buy applications for their smartphones and developers can contribute to the ecosystem with innovative ideas translated into applications. Another example is the Android platform, which operates on similar lines. Emphasizing variability and agility, then, digital platforms create a wealth of opportunities for entrepreneurs, among other things, to develop apps [14, 20].

- **Digital infrastructures**. Digital infrastructures are digital tools, systems and technology structures – such as cloud computing, social media, analytics, 3D printing and digital marketplaces – that offer the necessary collaboration, communication and computing capabilities in order for a digital enterprise to function [14, 21]. Assisting in the digitization of the entrepreneurial process, digital infrastructures are open, dynamic, extremely flexible as well as scalable, as their components can be easily updated or replaced; they therefore promote generation of entrepreneurial ideas that can be translated into development of successful products and services [21].

Overall, digital technologies have been embraced by digital ventures as they lie at the heart of every entrepreneur's powers of innovation and economic competitiveness. Two of these technologies, namely social media and the Internet of Things (IoT), will be discussed in greater detail in Chapters 6 and 7, respectively.

1.3   Types of Digital Venture

Digital ventures range from large enterprises, already established in several industries, to small businesses or start-ups that use ICTs in order to create value and carry out business activities targeted toward their customers.

Academics and industry experts agree that start-ups can been defined as organizations that have been designed to scale very quickly into large companies [22, 23]. Although there is no timescale that determines how long a company can be considered a start-up, reaching certain thresholds – for example achieving revenue of more than $20 million, employing more than 80 people, having a high growth rate, founders being able to sell their shares, acquiring endeavors from larger companies – can signal the end of its "start-uphood." All in all, when a start-up starts becoming profitable, it means that it will cease being a start-up very soon [23].

While start-ups are considered to represent a big percentage of today's digital firms, small and medium-sized enterprises (SMEs) have long dominated the markets, characterized as the "backbone" of every economy. More specifically, SMEs represent 99.8 percent of the European economy; almost all European businesses can be considered as SMEs [24]. But how do start-ups and SMEs differ? Some key differences are listed here [25, 26]:

- **Growth:** As already mentioned, start-ups are designed to scale quickly and evolve into big companies; they are eager to reach their aspirations and disrupt the market. A small business, on the other hand, usually offers traditional products and services and is mostly focused on making profit within controllable boundaries with a set number of customers; it does not have high expectations in terms of scaling and growth.
- **Innovation:** A small business is usually not something new in the industry, while start-ups are infused with innovation, trying to translate novel ideas into products and services in ways that have never been done before, thus disrupting the industry. A very well-known example is Uber, which will be discussed in greater detail in Section 1.7.
- **Focus:** While small businesses are focused on their profit with low operational costs, start-ups are more concerned about scaling fast and growing quickly by bringing innovative ideas into the market.

- **Funding:** Small businesses usually rely on personal savings, bank loans and friends or family funds, while start-ups usually receive funding from investors and venture capitalists.
- **Exit strategy:** For a small business, future aspirations involve passing the company to the next generations such as family members or a large company that is interested in buying it. However, start-ups aim much higher, to sell big to a large corporation or go public (initial public offering (IPO)).

That covered some of the main differences between start-ups and SMEs. The next sections provide a deeper look at digital ventures: both start-ups (Section 1.3.1) and spin-off companies (Section 1.3.2).

1.3.1   Start-Ups: Big Ideas from Small Businesses

Focused on growth with no geographical boundaries, a start-up team works with excitement to solve existing critical problems by introducing innovative ideas, ultimately aiming to make an immediate impact in the market [23]. One of the central characteristics of a start-up is innovativeness: "[T]o be a startup is to claim a freshness that suggests a finger on the pulse of the future" [23].

Lying at the heart of entrepreneurship, innovation constitutes a key value for the success as well as the longevity of a business. An innovative company constantly keeps up with trends and demands and seizes arising opportunities to fulfill the ever-changing needs of customers by coming up with novel ways to produce products or services. In the entrepreneurial world, open innovation refers to the notion that ideas and resources should be shared among a wide range of players such as large firms and start-ups. Open innovation, which will be discussed in greater depth in Chapter 2, is facilitated through several digital technologies that offer tremendous opportunities for a firm's growth and success. As shown in Figure 1.2, in the open innovation ecosystem, the demand and supply sides of innovation are connected through bridge-makers, who constitute the "glue" between the two actors of the ecosystem. For example, Singularity University, founded by Peter Diamandis and Ray Kurzweil in the NASA research park in California, is characterized as a one-of-its-kind hybrid accelerator; it serves as a bridge-maker connecting the demand and supply sides of innovation, offering both educational programs to potential students and innovative partnerships within a business incubator to start-up companies, to help them in their entrepreneurship endeavors [19].

Small start-ups tend to collaborate with large established enterprises, with benefits accruing to both sides: on the one hand, start-ups are eager to enter the market and present themselves as a "best of breed" product provider choice; on the other hand, large firms gain access to new technologies and highly skilled talents while at the same time decreasing their research and development (R&D) costs [19].

Most young entrepreneurs – founders of small start-ups who embrace innovation and are eager to succeed – choose to establish collaborations with a variety of different large organizations, such as governments, nonprofit organizations, academic institutions and researchers as well as incubators or accelerators, in order both to speed up the process of translating their ideas into products and to accelerate their entrance into the relevant markets. Through these partnerships and collaborations with business incubators or multinational companies, start-ups gain the opportunity to leverage a wide range of resources including access to finance as well as foreign investment, mentoring services, efficient marketing strategies, robust sales resources and greater production scale [19].

More specifically, in the case of business incubators and accelerator programs, start-ups benefit from several advantages such as office space and professional services, business advice and even early-stage funding in order to get the initial "boost up." In some cases, large-company accelerators even

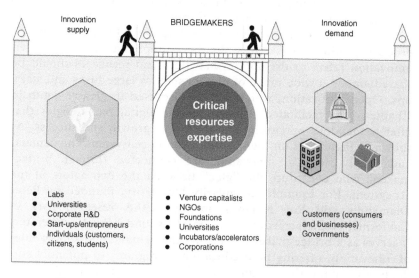

Figure 1.2 Open innovation and bridge-makers
Source: Adapted from [19].

end up buying the start-ups they have been working with. Establishing a connection with a large enterprise gives start-ups the opportunity to exploit the market recognition of the enterprise-partner and to benefit from an already established brand name, thus gaining credibility and increasing their potential to create enhanced revenue as an outcome of their business activities [19].

Corporate-led accelerators are gaining public attention; one example is the recently established Microsoft Ventures, which invests in early-stage start-ups that are developing products and services using technologies such as cloud, security and machine learning. Furthermore, Microsoft Accelerator has a number of accelerator programs worldwide, which offer to late-stage start-ups a variety of workshops as well as access to funding and connections with customers and other venture capital investors [19, 27, 28].

1.3.2 Spin-Offs from Large Enterprises

Although acquisitions of small start-ups by large corporations such as Microsoft, Apple and Facebook are very popular these days, another trend in the market is de-merging, that is, spin-off companies being created as offspring of large enterprises [29]. Gareth Wilson, an executive at Fog Creek, a software development company, who participated in the spinning off of Trello and StackOverflow, highlights that spin-offs from an established company constitute a high risk but at the same time a great opportunity to create a successful new business. Although customers tend to associate one thing with a name, a spin-off is preferred by investors as it shows a focused company perspective and offers financial benefits and attractive returns to stakeholders [30–32].

While in the USA every year only around fifty companies emerge from the de-merging of large business corporations' key assets as separate legal entities, academic institutions are considered a very fruitful source of spin-offs. Recent research has shown that in today's business environment, university spin-offs have shown outstanding performance as they are 108 times more likely to go public than any other average company [31]. As intellectual property of the academic institution, including the active involvement of the inventor, a university spin-off is a new company that exploits the university's scientific and technological knowledge as well as the outcomes of university research. Critical steps for developing a university spin-off include [33]:
- generating the business idea
- translating the idea into the business process
- creating the firm
- contributing value to the stakeholders, customers and employees.

By commercializing the university's technology, a university spin-off is translating research ideas and results into market solutions, thus contributing to the economic development of the academic institution while at the same time creating opportunities for the local economic community too. NaturalMotion, a digital animation company created by a PhD zoology student, is a brilliant example of how academic research can lead to huge success. A spin-off company from Oxford University, focused on animation technology in the film and game industries, NaturalMotion was recently acquired by NASDAQ-listed Zynga for $527 million, making it the highest university spin-off sale in years [34].

1.4   Setting Up an Online Business

In today's global economy, emerging technologies have penetrated into the processes and services of nearly all organizations with e-business as well as e-commerce, becoming an integral part of their business strategy. Both e-business and e-commerce have facilitated easier and quicker business transactions while at the same time increasing competition among vendors. E-commerce is becoming bigger every year, with estimates for worldwide e-commerce retail sales reaching $4 trillion in 2020 [35]. Digital entrepreneurs need to understand, follow and implement a series of critical steps in order to set up an online business [36, 37]:

- **Decide the business**: The first important step for a digital entrepreneur when planning an e-business is selecting the product(s) or service(s) that will be offered to customers. By thoroughly investigating the market and understanding the current competition, the digital entrepreneur is able to identify a niche to enter and set a business strategy and future goals.
- **Create the business plan**: Developing a business plan constitutes the most critical step for the success of any digital business. It includes defining the needs of the online business, its aims and objectives as well as its viability. Although it is crucial to undertake this planning process at the starting point of setting up a company, however, entrepreneurs should not get too bogged down with it and should instead keep their business plan flexible and capable of evolving around their mission, vision and values.
- **Design and build the website**: A successful digital business includes a well-considered and thorough plan that accounts for elements such as programming capabilities and design skills as well as sales and marketing abilities. Even when a company has the most innovative product in the market, if its website application does not provide ease of use, intuitive navigation and flexible processes, the digital endeavor will

eventually fail. Multiple technologies can be used in order to develop an e-commerce website – for instance HTML, Java, PHP, SQL – depending on the preferences and skills of the digital team. As the website is the only storefront of the business, ensuring that it is customer friendly by paying attention to critical elements such as web content, ease of use and site navigation will contribute to achieving high customer satisfaction, which will in turn lead to customer retention and attraction of new customers from competitors [37–39].

- **Develop the marketing strategy**: After the online business has been set up, the next critical step is to attract customers. Developing a digital marketing strategy, which will be discussed further in Chapter 3, is a crucial component of the success of any online business. Search engine optimization (SEO), pay-per-click advertising (PPC), email marketing, content marketing and web analytics are only a few of the wide range of options that a digital business can deploy in order to increase traffic to its website and attract buyers. Identifying the right online marketing tools to deploy as well as evaluating existing media channels and assets for utilization enables a digital business to build up effective online marketing campaigns that will incrementally lead it to accomplish its overarching goals [40].

1.5   The Role of E-commerce

While e-business refers to businesses that run their operations online or use Internet technology in order to improve their productivity and profitability, e-commerce describes the activities of marketing, buying as well as selling products and services to customers using Internet technologies. The difference between the two terms lies in the fact that the first one is broader, encompassing use of technologies not only to buy and sell goods and services but also to collaborate with business partners, process e-transactions and run internal processes such as inventory management, human resources and finance [41].

E-commerce is used by businesses in order to execute transactions (i.e. sales) facilitated by modern technology (i.e. the Internet, computer, online, email) to provide customers (i.e. selling, shopping, buying) products and services (i.e. shop, web store, delivery). E-commerce automates enterprises' business processes, providing twenty-four-hour goods and services availability, thus making products and services available anytime and anywhere. It also provides faster and reliable communication with customers and partners and cuts down operational costs. Moreover, e-commerce websites provide a platform where all information is available online at one place, facilitating more shopping options to customers, who can easily compare products and prices, as well as expedited delivery of the product [42, 43]. A common classification of the several business models of e-commerce includes [44, 45]:

- **B2B (business-to-business)**: The B2B business model describes businesses that focus on selling their products to other businesses. Both the buyer and the seller constitute separate business entities. Prominent examples include Cisco, IBM and Hewlett Packard (HP).

- **B2C (business-to-consumer)**: Characterized as the second largest and earliest form of e-commerce, B2C is where a business sells its products, including physical goods, services and information goods, directly to consumers. By drastically reducing transaction costs for organizations, B2C increases customers' access to information, enabling them to choose from a wide range of products and find the most competitive price among many vendors.

- **C2C (customer-to-customer)**: This model describes transactions between private individuals selling or purchasing assets such as cars, residential property and motorcycles, personal services and new or used products. Online marketplaces such as eBay, Etsy and Craigslist facilitate the execution of these transactions by offering a space where sellers can pay to advertise products for sale, including images and descriptions. Furthermore, portals such as eBay offer online real-time bidding where consumers can participate in online auctions to bid for items being sold on the website.

- **B2G (business-to-government)**: B2G is an underdeveloped area of e-commerce but one that is steadily growing. It describes use of the Internet to execute various operations and transactions between organizations and the public sector, including procurement, licensing and filing of taxes.

- **C2B (customer-to-business)**: In this model, the opposite of B2C, a private individual, such as a blogger or a photographer, sells value to companies by offering to advertise those companies' products or services for a fee, for example through reviews or sharing on social media as in the case of current "influencers."

- **Mobile commerce**: M-commerce refers to the purchasing of goods and services by consumers through wireless technologies such as smartphones and tablets. As the penetration of smartphones has grown among consumers and rocketed with the introduction of the first iPhone in 2007, e-commerce is fast transforming to m-commerce. Rapid developments in mobile technologies along with the popularity of social media have created a habit shift such that consumers now tend to use their mobile phones rather than desktop applications [44–46].

Having acknowledged the main e-commerce business models that exist today, the digital entrepreneur is able to recognize the right niche to market as well as all the options at hand that can be exploited in order to create a successful online business.

1.6 Risks and Challenges

The wide adoption and deployment of digital technologies for entrepreneurial purposes offers tremendous opportunities to digital firms but, at the same time, includes several pitfalls and hazards. Digital opportunities and risks are two different sides of the same coin. In today's entrepreneurial world, already established digital firms, as well as entrepreneurs and managers that are interested in starting up a new digital business, need to understand the risks and challenges that are associated with digital entrepreneurship and its opportunities [26]. Some key challenges are:

- **Security**: Although the benefits of the digital revolution are undisputable, they are accompanied by important risks and challenges. Digital threats can result in a wide variety of implications for organizations such as operational, financial, legal, intellectual property and reputation risks [47]. Cybercrime-related risks are at the top of the list of five global business risks creating major concerns for digital entrepreneurs using digital platforms and infrastructures as means to offer their products and services to customers [48]. Protection of digital intellectual property and business information against cyber criminals constitutes one of the most critical challenges for today's digital entrepreneurs. While large enterprises may have the financial resources to implement strong security measures, small businesses and SMEs face a major threat regarding cyber security. Due to financial and management constraints, SMEs usually choose not to prioritize implementation of a digital security management strategy. Furthermore, deployment of certain digital technologies and more specifically cloud computing encompasses several critical concerns, such as lack of security control in the cloud as well as regulatory and compliance issues and lack of cloud usage visibility. Since most of the critical and personal data of customers, such as personal details and bank details, is stored in the cloud and several new security threats appear every day, a digital firm should ensure that a strong security strategy is followed in order to retain the trust of its current customers and not lose new ones [24, 48–50].

- **Financial challenges**: The recent financial crisis, resulting in a highly volatile business environment, contributed to banks becoming reluctant to provide loans to start-ups and small businesses. At the same time, venture capital funds have started following a less risky strategy, thus preferring to invest in late-stage start-ups. As a result, access to funding constitutes a major challenge for digital entrepreneurs [19, 51]. However, financial challenges will occur in different stages and in different time periods for every digital firm. Although, as discussed in Section 1.3.1, several accelerator and incubator programs exist in order to aid start-ups, digital firms should plan their funding strategy ahead of their launch. One very popular practice for raising business finance is crowdfunding, where start-ups can collect funds from many different people in exchange for shares in the company. While this has been characterized as a considerably efficient funding option for a new company and the future of fundraising, a digital business should be aware of some critical challenges [52]:

∘ *Planning the time frame and amount*: The start-up team should plan thoroughly and determine the specific amount they aim to raise through crowdfunding as well as the time frame for starting their campaign and reaching their goal amount.

∘ *Choosing the platform*: Today, there are several crowdfunding platforms available, all created for the same purpose but targeted at different audiences. Some platforms are targeted at individuals who can contribute small amounts, while other platforms are more focused on investors and entrepreneurs who are interested in investing millions. Early-stage start-ups that have decided to use crowdfunding as a means of raising business funds should research diligently in order to find the platform that best fits their needs.

• *Human resources*: In the very early stages of a start-up, the team usually comprises only the co-founders. As time goes by and the needs and demands of the company increase, more experts need to be hired, to complement the existing team, in order for the company to grow and reach its future goals. But finding the right talents that possess the right skills, expertise and mindsets is one of the most critical aspects of the success of a start-up. Not having the right team on board is one of the top reasons why start-ups fail today [51, 53]. Furthermore, digital ventures, either large enterprises or small businesses, are dealing with skills shortages as they all compete for the same underdeveloped pool of science, technology, engineering and mathematics (STEM) graduates who are in great demand from businesses around the world. At the same time, entrepreneurs are looking for "five-legged sheep" [19], as they are eager to recruit individuals who can successfully do almost everything. The success of any digital firm depends highly on the skills, expertise and knowledge of the workforce that it has employed; thus, the human capital management aspect of the company should be at the top of the list of priorities [19].

• *Piracy*: Having reached a worldwide rate of 35 percent with organizations' losses estimated at around $34 billion, piracy constitutes a tremendous challenge for today's digital entrepreneurs. Digital products, such as movies, music and software, being downloaded by thousands of individuals without payment and permission from the creator is a phenomenon that is spreading across many countries around the globe today. According to Siegfried's 2004 study [54], individuals who illegally downloaded digital goods did not recognize that anything about their actions was wrong, revealing that consumers perceive physical products differently from virtual ones [26]. As a result, digital firms need to be very cautious and undertake strong protective measures against this phenomenon, which can significantly affect their business.

- **Increased competition**: Digital innovative technologies such as social media, cloud computing and blockchain have changed both economies and societies, creating tremendous opportunities for digital enterprises. At the same time, digital changes have introduced one major challenge that digital firms need to face, namely, increased competition in the market [55]. One popular example is Google, which has been involved in both the social networking and the mobile handset markets, acquiring thousands of customers from other online businesses and leaving entrepreneurs wondering what its next move will be. With e-commerce websites, customers have access to real-time mobile data and are able to compare prices and products across multiple brands on the move; the power is thus completely in their hands. Acknowledging that rapid technological advancements as well as globalization have resulted in a highly competitive environment, entrepreneurs are intensifying their endeavors toward retaining their customers by developing new, innovative products or by shifting their focus from products to services, ultimately aiming to gain a strategic competitive advantage over their competitors. For example, Nike offers a personal customization service in a wide range of its products in an attempt to beat off competition and win the digital game. In a world where technology changes rapidly and new digital platforms and tools keep emerging, digital entrepreneurs should be aware of their market competition and seek innovative methods to retain their customers as well as gain new ones [56].

1.7 Case Studies

In this section, we discuss digital start-up success stories that have utilized digital technologies to accomplish their strategic goals and become strong and prosperous.

The first case study describes Deliveroo, a technology start-up that manages around 5,000 drivers aiming to deliver food from a wide range of restaurants to customers in a maximum time of thirty minutes. Having managed to raise $200 million from investors in its latest funding round in

2015, Deliveroo is currently available in nearly 200 cities across Europe, Asia and Australia, and aims to launch in the USA in the near future [57, 58].

Leveraging the smartphone penetration into people's lives that has radically increased in recent years [66], Deliveroo offers a customer-friendly website and application that enable customers to order online and in real time food from various premium restaurants in the nearby area; it charges a commission fee to restaurants and customers alike [67, 68]. Providing restaurants with low-cost standard Android tablets and relying on the drivers' personal smartphone devices, the majority of them being iPhones, the premium food delivery start-up offers for a small cost the exact same menu catalogs online as the restaurants offer on-site. By leveraging cheap off-the shelf mobile technology, the tech start-up, led by developer and former chief technology officer (CTO) Greg Orlowski, has developed three platforms: a restaurant app, a driver app with a highly complex algorithm and a web app for consumers. Continuously running simulations, redeveloping its software to incorporate new geographies and testing its core routing algorithm in order to select the right driver for each order, the food delivery network understands the delivery process by breaking it down into several steps from picking up food orders to interacting with customers, ultimately aiming to reach the quickest delivery times and the highest customer satisfaction levels [57, 59].

As the mobile tech revolution has significantly decreased the cost of creating an online business, Deliveroo has managed to create a new market by addressing existing but latent customer needs. Having excelled at developing a user-friendly app, providing quick delivery and a simple way of ordering food, Deliveroo has achieved a very high rate of customer retention with the average customer coming back in under twenty-one days and certain customers having spent almost $10,000 on the platform [59].

POINT OF ATTENTION: The invention of new markets has become possible due to the emergence of digital technologies; there are tremendous opportunities for digital entrepreneurs quickly to become the leader of a new market. Smartphone penetration has created new business horizons for businesses that can execute all or most of their processes online. By leveraging the power of existing technologies, these businesses can serve the needs of consumers in a novel way, thus creating new business models and making profit in markets that have not been uncovered before.

The second case study delineates the success story of Uber, a technology start-up that was founded in 2009 by serial entrepreneurs

Garrett Camp and Travis Kalanick. They developed the idea after attending a tech conference in Paris and struggling to find a cab [60]. The ride-hailing service generated revenues of around $6.5 billion in 2016 and is estimated to have a value of $50 billion; it is considered to be the fastest start-up to reach this value [61].

Aiming to fill a gap in the transportation market originating from the failure of car services to exploit modern technology, Uber introduced an application that connects passengers directly with drivers, offering the opportunity to get a cab with the simple press of a button [60, 62]. Leveraging GPS and smartphone technologies, Uber created an application that customers can use to find a ride. In more detail, the app is integrated with Google Maps, enabling the passenger to track the location of the car before it arrives and while en route as well as to rate the driver and provide feedback. Furthermore, the taxi service also facilitates cashless transactions as all payments are executed online through the customer's credit card [62]. By relying on an existing infrastructure and using it in a totally novel way, Uber has managed to disrupt the market and completely redefine the transportation and car services industry; it has transformed the whole taxi experience by offering customers mobile hailing, seamless payments, good quality as well as clean cars and a no tips policy, all of which contributes to high customer satisfaction and increases Uber's popularity through word of mouth [63]. Having demonopolized the taxi cabs market, Uber is using a very smart and efficient driver–passenger matching mobile technology to provide a novel solution to a problem that existed for a very long time, affecting thousands of people in the modern world today [64].

Initially launched in San Francisco in September 2010, Uber has achieved tremendous growth since and today has conquered almost 400 cities around the world. As depicted in Figure 1.3, Uber's exponential growth has come from several elements connected together: city-by-city launches, free rides and word of mouth. In order to fuel its growth rate, Uber has been deploying several strategic marketing methods such as organizing local events for every city launch, offering free rides to members of the community and establishing business partnerships with big organizations. As a result, it has managed to become very popular and build its growth thanks to people who enjoyed the sponsored events and free ride-hailing services then posting the news on their social media and spreading the word to friends and family [62, 63].

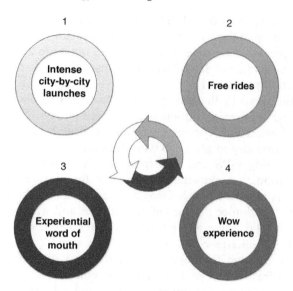

Figure 1.3 Uber's growth engine
Source: Adapted from [63].

POINT OF ATTENTION: Marketing is an integral part of running a digital firm that should not be neglected by entrepreneurs. Despite the novelty of the product or the innovative services that a new digital business is offering, developing a marketing strategy, in both digital and traditional ways, can drive up the growth of the company exponentially in the very early stages, attracting customers and gaining advantage over competitors.

Having recently hired researchers from Carnegie Mellon University's robotics center, Uber is investing into robotics research, aiming to launch in the near future self-driving cars that will perform autonomous pickups, eliminating the need for drivers, thus further reducing costs and ultimately decreasing the fares for customers [65].

1.8   Summary

The current chapter introduced the concept of digital entrepreneurship and provided the necessary theoretical foundation for potential entrepreneurs who are interested in developing and implementing a digital business to enter the digital market economy.

The chapter first presented the core characteristics of entrepreneurship, including innovation, seeking of opportunities and value creation, emphasizing the similarities between traditional and digital entrepreneurship. The chapter gave a definition of digital entrepreneurship as one that includes all the core aspects of traditional entrepreneurship but also encompasses digital technologies. In addition, the chapter analyzed the differences between traditional and digital companies, in terms of focus, activity form and business model, and showed that digital firms lie at the intersection of physical and digital economies. Then, the chapter provided an overview of digital technologies, namely digital artifacts, platforms and infrastructures, along with their particular characteristics and capabilities that make them appropriate for entrepreneurs to exploit in starting up an online business.

Furthermore, the chapter analyzed the different types of digital venture – large enterprises, SMEs, small start-ups and spin-off companies – delineating their characteristics and explaining how the sharing of ideas and resources among the different actors in the open innovation ecosystem can accrue benefits for all of them. Moreover, the chapter elaborated on the concepts of e-business and e-commerce, providing a clear understanding of their different aspects through a taxonomy of the different e-commerce models that exist today. Next, the chapter delineated the critical steps that a digital entrepreneur needs to follow in order to set up a successful online business, and investigated the risks and challenges that a new digital firm will face on its entrepreneurial journey.

Finally, the chapter concluded by presenting the success stories of two tech start-ups, showing that, by embracing digital technologies and their accruing opportunities, digital firms can climb the ladder of success to reach high growth rates and revenues.

References

1. Morvan L, Hintermann F, Vazirani M. Five Ways to Win with Digital Platform – Creating 10 Million Youth Jobs in the G20 Countries. Accenture (2016).
2. Andreessen M. Why Software Is Eating the World. (2011) www.wsj.com/art icles/SB10001424053111903480904576512250915629460 [accessed May 22, 2020].
3. Shane S, Venkataraman S. The Promise of Entrepreneurship as a Field of Research. *Academy of Management Review* (2000) 25:217–26. doi: 10.2307/259271.
4. Casson M. *The Entrepreneur: An Economic Theory*. Edward Elgar (1982).
5. Cuervo Á, Ribeiro D, Roig S. Entrepreneurship: Concepts, Theory and Perspective. Introduction. In: *Entrepreneurship*. Springer (2007) 1–20.

6. Bogdanowicz M. Digital Entrepreneurship Barriers and Drivers. Institute for Prospective Technological Studies; JRC Technical Report EUR 27679 EN (2015).

7. Knight FH. *Risk, Uncertainty and Profit*. Houghton Mifflin (1921).

8. Reynolds P, Hay M, Camp S. *Global Entrepreneurship Monitor Executive Report*. Kauffman Center for Entrepreneurial Leadership (1999).

9. Ruiz J, Soriano DR, Coduras A. Challenges in Measuring Readiness for Entrepreneurship. *Management Decision* (2016) 54:1022–46. doi: 10.1108/MD-07-2014-0493.

10. Oviatt BM, McDougall PP. Defining International Entrepreneurship and Modeling the Speed of Internationalization. *Entrepreneurship Theory and Practice* (2005) 29:537–53. doi: 10.1111/j.1540-6520.2005.00097.x.

11. Schumpeter J. *The Theory of Economic Development: An Inquiry into Profits, Capital, Credit, Interest, and the Business Cycle*. Harvard Economic Studies (1934).

12. Ngoasong MZ. Digital Entrepreneurship in Emerging Economies: The Role of ICTs and Local Context. In: *42nd AIB-UKI Conference, 16–18 April 2015, Manchester Metropolitan University, UK*. (2015) 1–27.

13. Skilton M. *Building the Digital Enterprise*. Palgrave Macmillan (2015).

14. Nambisan S. Digital Entrepreneurship: Toward a Digital Technology Perspective of Entrepreneurship. *Entrepreneurship Theory and Practice* (2016) doi: 10.1111/etap.12254.

15. Beckman C, Eisenhardt K, Kotha S, Meyer A, Rajagopalan N. Technology Entrepreneurship. *Strategic Entrepreneurship Journal* (2012) 6:89–93. doi: 10.1002/sej.

16. Quinones G, Nicholson B, Heeks R. A Literature Review of E-entrepreneurship in Emerging Economies: Positioning Research on Latin American Digital Startups. In: *Entrepreneurship in BRICS*. Springer International (2015) 179–208.

17. Tripsas M. Technology, Identity, and Inertia through the Lens of "The Digital Photography Company." *Organization Science* (2009) 20:441–60.

18. Accenture. Growing the Digital Business: Accenture Mobility Research 2015. Accenture (2015).

19. Accenture. The Promise of Digital Entrepreneurs – Creating 10 Million Youth Jobs in the G20 Countries. Accenture (2014).

20. Sørensen C. Digital Platform and Infrastructure Innovation. In: Higashikun H (ed.) *Mobile Strategy Challenges*. Nikkan Kogyo Shimbun (2013) 1–29.

21. Tilson D, Lyytinen K, Sørensen C. Digital Infrastructures: The Missing IS Research Agenda. *Information Systems Research* (2010) 21:748–59.

22. Max Marmer A, Lasse Herrmann B, Dogrultan E, Berman R. Startup Genome Report: A New Framework for Understanding Why Startups Succeed. Startup Genome (2012). www.dentonsventurebeyond.com/wp-content/uploads/2016/10/StartupGenomeReport1_Why_Startups_Succeed_v2.pdf [accessed 3 January 2021].

23. Robehmed N. What Is a Startup? – Forbes. (2013) www.forbes.com/sites/natalierobehmed/2013/12/16/what-is-a-startup/ [accessed May 22, 2020].

24. Deloitte. *DG Enterprise – Doing Business in the Digital Age: The Impact of New ICT Developments in the Global Business Landscape.* Deloitte (2012).

25. Ajuluchukwu J. A Startup or an SME? Know the Difference. (2017) www.techsuplex.com/2017/01/21/startup-sme-know-difference [accessed May 22, 2020].

26. Hull C. (2006) *Digital Entrepreneurship.* EDGE.

27. Microsoft. Microsoft Ventures. (2014) https://microsoftventures.com/ [accessed May 22, 2020].

28. Microsoft Research Microsoft Accelerator. www.microsoftaccelerator.com/ [accessed May 22, 2020].

29. Deloitte. Spin Cycle: The Rise of Technology Sector "De-mergers." (2015) www2.deloitte.com/content/dam/Deloitte/us/Documents/mergers-acqisitions/us-ma-tech-spinoff.pdf [accessed December 22, 2020].

30. Wilson G. 4 Lessons I've Learned from Spinning Off Tech Companies. (2016) www.fastcompany.com/3059390/3-lessons-ive-learned-from-spinning-off-the-%0Acompanies [accessed May 22, 2020].

31. Wilson G. Why Investors Love Spin-Off Startups. (2016) https://venturebeat.com/2016/02/21/why-investors-love-spin-off-startups/ [accessed May 22, 2020].

32. The Economist. The Art of the Spin-Off – Tips for Creating New Companies Out of Old Ones. (2013) www.economist.com/news/business/2 1577034-tips-creating-new-companies-out-old-ones-art-spin [accessed February 12, 2018].

33. Pattnaik PN, Pandey SC. University Spinoffs: What, Why, and How? *Technology Innovation Management Review* (2014) 4:44–50.

34. University of Oxford. Oxford Digital Spin-Out Completes $500m Sale. (2014) www.ox.ac.uk/news/2014-02-12-oxford-digital-spin-out-completes-500m-sale [accessed May 22, 2020].

35. eMarketer. Worldwide Retail Ecommerce Sales Will Reach $1.915 Trillion This Year. (2016) www.emarketer.com/Article/Worldwide-Retail-Ecommerce-Sales-Will-Reach-1915-Trillion-This-Year/1014369 [accessed May 22, 2020].

36. Beesley C. How to Start a Successful E-Commerce Business – 6 Tips from Seasoned Pros. (2016) www.sba.gov/blogs/how-start-successful-e-com merce-business-6-tips-seasoned-pros [accessed February 12, 2018].

37. Moon A. 7 Steps to Starting a Small Business Online. (2020) www.entrepreneur.com/article/175242 [accessed May 22, 2020].

38. Idler S. 5 Key Principles of Good Website Usability. (2019) www.crazyegg.com/blog/principles-website-usability/ [accessed May 22, 2020].

39. Reynolds J. *The Complete E-Commerce Book: Design, Build, & Maintain a Successful Web-based Business.* CMP Books (2004).

40. Hudson E. 7 Digital Marketing Strategies That Work: A Complete Guide. (2018) https://blog.hubspot.com/marketing/digital-strategy-guide [accessed February 12, 2018].

41. Byron, Lord, Green HS. *E-business And E-commerce.* Deitel & Associates (2006).

42. OECD. Unpacking E-commerce: Business Models, Trends and Policies. (2019) www.oecd.org/going-digital/unpacking-ecommerce.pdf [accessed 28 December 2020].

43. Nanehkaran YA. An Introduction to Electronic Commerce. *International Journal of Scientific & Technological Research* (2013) 2:2–5.

44. Jackson P, Harris L, Eckersley PM. e-Business Fundamentals. Taylor & Francis (2003).

45. Gupta A. E-commerce: Role of E-commerce in Today's Business. *International Journal of Computing and Corporate Research* (2014) 4:1–8.

46. Accenture. Mobile Shift: Why Retailers Need to Adopt a Mobile-First Approach Now to Meet Changing Customer Expectations. Accenture (2016).

47. Baldwin A, Shiu S, Sadler M, Horne B, Dalton C. Managing Digital Risk Trends, Issues and Implications for Business. (2010) Lloyd's 360 Risk Insight.

48. OECD. Key Issues for Digital Transformation in the G20. OECD (2017).

49. BT. Building Security into the Heart of Your Business. (2017) www .globalservices.bt.com/uk/en/point-of-view/securing-digital-enterprise [accessed February 12, 2018].

50. Hair N, Wetsch L, Hull C, Perotti V, Hung Y. Market Orientation in Digital Entrepreneurship: Advantages and Challenges in a Web 2.0 Networked World. *International Journal of Innovation and Technology Management* (2012) 9:1250045. doi: 10.1142/S0219877012500459.

51. Salamzadeh A, Kesim H. Startup Companies: Life Cycle and Challenges. In: *4th International Conference on Employment, Education and Entrepreneurship (EEE)*, Belgrade, Serbia, 2015. (2015). doi: 10.2139/ssrn.2628861.

52. Fallon N. Crowdfunding Challenges Most Startups Don't Expect. (2014) www.foxbusiness.com/features/crowdfunding-challenges-most-startups-dont-expect [accessed May 22, 2020].

53. CBInsights. The Top 20 Reasons Startups Fail. (2019) www.cbinsights.com /research/startup-failure-reasons-top/ [accessed December 22, 2020].

54. Siegfried R. Student Altitudes on Software Piracy and Related Issues of Computer Ethics. *Ethics and Information Technology* (2004) 6:215–22.

55. Finkelstein S. Internet Startups: So Why Can't They Win? *Journal of Business Strategy* (2001) 22:16–21.

56. Ernst&Young. *The Digitisation of Everything – How Organisations Must Adapt to Changing Consumer Behaviour.* Ernst Young LLP (2011).

57. Olson P. Here's How Deliveroo Built an Army of 5,000 Drivers in Just 3 Years. (2016) www.forbes.com/sites/parmyolson/2016/02/17/deliveroo-army-5000-drivers-3-years/#bfe49b520bdf [accessed May 22, 2020].

58. Deliveroo. Deliveroo. (2015) https://deliveroo.co.uk/ [accessed May 22, 2020].

59. Mignot M. Building a Local Food Delivery Network. (2014) www .indexventures.com/news-room/blog/building-a-local-food-delivery-network [accessed May 22, 2020].

60. Knight S. How Uber Conquered London – To Understand How the $60bn Company Is Taking Over the World, You Need to Stop Thinking about

Cars. (2016) www.theguardian.com/technology/2016/apr/27/how-uber-conquered-london [accessed May 22, 2020].

61. Higson C. The Value of Uber. (2015) www.forbes.com/sites/lbsbusinessstrategyreview/2015/10/09/the-value-of-uber/#7b5f02a63da8 [accessed May 22, 2020].

62. Suslo E. 6 Key Success Factors behind Uber Growth. (2016) https://taxistartup.com/blog/6-key-%0Asuccess-factors-behind-uber-growth/ [accessed February 12, 2018].

63. Brown M. Uber – What's Fueling Uber's Growth Engine. (2017) https://growthhackers.com/growth-studies/uber [accessed May 22, 2020].

64. Judd Cramer B, Krueger AB, Dowlatabadi J, Farber H, Hall J, Joskow P, Leah-Martin V, Leisy C, Spiegelman E. Disruptive Change in the Taxi Business: The Case of Uber. *American Economic Review: Papers & Proceedings* (2016) 106:177–82. doi: 10.1257/aer.p20161002.

65. Brewster S. Uber Starts Self-Driving Car Pickups in Pittsburgh. (2016) https://techcrunch.com/2016/09/14/1386711/ [accessed May 22, 2020].

66. Wigginton C, Curran M, Brodeur C. Global Mobile Consumer Trends, 2nd Edition: Mobile Continues Its Global Reach into All Aspects of Consumers' Lives. Deloitte Touche Tohmatsu Limited (2017). www2.deloitte.com/content/dam/Deloitte/us/Documents/technology-media-telecommunications/us-global-mobile-consumer-survey-second-edition.pdf [accessed January 3, 2021].

67. The Business of Tech. Deliveroo. (2016) https://thebusinessoftech.wordpress.com/2016/05/08/deliveroo/ [accessed January 3, 2021].

68. Hansen, J. Deliveroo Could Bank £11 Million per Year from New "Service Fee." (2019) https://london.eater.com/2019/2/7/18215319/deliveroo-restaurant-delivery-london-service-fee-uber-eats-just-eat [accessed January 3, 2021].

2   Digital Entrepreneurship and Innovation

2.1   Introduction

Emerging digital technologies such as mobile and social media technologies have made it compulsory for businesses to embrace the digital transformation associated with the introduction of such platforms. Start-up firms, particularly, began to transform in order to compete with well-established businesses with strong histories in their business sectors. One of the key aspects here, as discussed in Chapter 1, is innovation, which is an important factor that defines how organizations run their businesses and how they compete in nowadays highly competitive markets. Digitally focused multinational organizations [1], which were once start-ups, have seized the opportunities that have been offered by novel developments in computer science and telecommunication, among other fields, in order to offer consumers innovative products and services such as Uber and Airbnb. Similarly, big firms such as Hewlett-Packard, Intel and Apple, among others, have managed to achieve sustainable growth by continuing to innovate [2].

The intent behind innovative products or services is usually to meet and satisfy the requirements or needs expressed by consumers or to introduce novel services that can make people's lives easier and more interesting such as Instagram, Uber and Airbnb. The services provided by such firms are not a necessity for people, but now people use them extensively in their daily lives throughout the world. Such innovative ideas have created a digital disruption that has transformed the way that traditional firms conduct their businesses and made it compulsory for them to appreciate the digital transformation and embrace the opportunities offered by the Internet and the emerging technologies.

Innovation, in its simplest definition, is the process of doing something differently [3]. With this in mind, however, it is important to differentiate innovation from improvement – doing the same action or procedure in a better way – and invention – creating a new idea or procedure [4]. From

28

the firm's perspective, it is the outcome embodied in a product or service that matters, regardless of the followed theory or concept [3]. As described in Chapter 1, an innovative business is one that understands current trends and takes advantage of emerging technologies in order to seize upcoming opportunities to form innovative new products or services.

Digital entrepreneurship and innovation can take several forms. The first is where entrepreneurial start-ups – such as Metromile and Compass, which are discussed in more detail in Chapter 9 – seize the advantages offered by digital tools and social platforms to facilitate the onset of the business as well as the innovation that fuels the introduction of new products and services [5]. The second form of digital entrepreneurship and innovation is where entrepreneurial initiatives take place within already established firms such as Cisco, which leads to innovative new products and services supported by the emerging digital technologies [2, 6]. Of course, it is important to define open innovation and how it differs from innovation; I cover this in Section 2.2.

2.2   Innovation and Open Innovation

Innovation, as already described, is a process that firms utilize to introduce or adopt new approaches to producing products and designing services. In the main part, innovation happens within the business where the ideas and resources are generated and contributed internally; this is also called closed innovation [4]. Open innovation [7, 8], on the other hand, refers to the process of establishing collaboration and sharing ideas and resources among different types of organization with different cultures [4, 9]. The idea of open innovation is becoming increasingly popular among firms, as reflected in several initiatives to bring institutions together for the sake of developing innovative products and services [10]. Table 2.1 highlights six main differences between the two concepts [4].

The importance of open innovation that is based on digitally enabled collaboration is proven by the survey presented in [11], in which 97 percent of 1,000 firms and 82 percent of the same number of entrepreneurial start-ups have embraced digitally collaborative innovation as a critical factor for better future success [11] and new venture creation [12].

Figure 2.1 illustrates the answers to one of the questions in the survey: "How important will collaborating with each of the following be in driving your company's innovation and growth in the next three years?" [11]. It is clear here that, apart from collaboration with customers, both large organizations and entrepreneurial start-ups highly appreciate digital collaboration

Table 2.1 *Principles of closed and open innovation*

Closed innovation	Open innovation
"It involves smart people who all work inside our firm."	"It involves smart people from everywhere."
"To profit from R&D, we have to discover, develop and supply everything ourselves."	"External R&D can create value for our organization."
"We can get to the market first, only when we discover something first."	"Internal R&D is needed to capture the value created for our organization."
"If our organization is the first to commercialize an innovation, we will beat our rivals."	"We have to be involved in basic research to benefit from it, but the discovery does not have to be ours."
"If we create the most and best ideas in our industry, we will win."	"If we make better use of external and internal ideas and unify the knowledge created, we will win."
"As we have full control over the innovation process, our competitors will not be able to profit from our innovative ideas."	We should optimize our organization's results, combining the sale/licensing of our innovation with the purchase of external innovation processes whenever they are more efficient and economic.

Source: Adapted from [4].

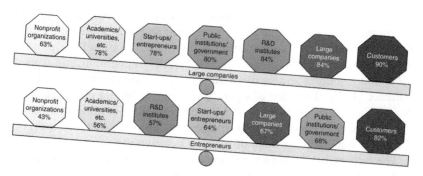

Figure 2.1 Attitudes toward working with multiple partners
Source: Adapted from [11].

with each other as one of the most important drivers for boosting innovation [11].

Although the expectations of these types of collaborator – large organizations and entrepreneurial start-ups – are different, there is a strong belief among big businesses that they can benefit from collaborating with start-

Table 2.2 *Benefits of collaboration for large companies*

What are the top benefits of collaborating on innovation with start-ups /entrepreneurs? (Ranked within the top three)

Accessing specific skills and talent	53%
Entering new markets	50%
Improving the return on in-house R&D investment	48%
Accelerating disruptive innovation in your company	42%
Designing new products and services	40%
Enhancing your company's brand/image	39%
Enhancing your company's entrepreneurial culture	17%

Source: Adapted from [11].

Table 2.3 *Benefits of collaboration for entrepreneurs*

What are the top benefits to collaborating on innovation with large companies? (Ranked within the top three)

Getting access to a large company's distribution network and customer base	49%
Being a supplier for large companies	45%
Securing investment from corporate venture funds	43%
Getting access to a large company's market knowledge	42%
Working together on joint innovation to develop new products and services	39%
Getting access to experts with specialized skills	34%
Benefiting from mentorship under accelerator/incubation programs	31%
Benefiting from brand legitimization	17%

Source: Adapted from [11].

ups. As Table 2.2 shows, large companies seek to achieve three main goals: to learn how to be more digitally oriented, to have access to digitally equipped talents and to be sufficiently innovative to keep up with current digital trends.

Likewise, entrepreneurs have their own expectations and are looking to benefit from their collaborations with large firms, for instance by achieving faster market penetration [11]. Additionally, they want to build long-term supply-chain relationships that will help them become more financially sustainable (see Table 2.3).

The potential benefits to each party of collaboration between large institutions and entrepreneurial firms suggests that such partnership is of high importance for fostering open innovation.

2.3   ICT as an Enabler of Digital Innovation and Its Ecosystem

Innovation, as the main driver for entrepreneurial firms, depends mainly on advancements in ICT. The more digitally oriented a business is, the more important the role that ICT plays in its future success; this is reflected in increased innovation as well as increased competitiveness within the market [13]. Due to its importance, the role of ICT in driving innovation has been the focus of a study prepared by the European Union [14]. This report stresses that, together, ICT and advancements in digital technologies encourage innovation that is reflected positively across the entire economy of the continent. Figure 2.2 highlights that different innovation indicators reflect the same impression about the important role of ICT for innovation. ICT share ranges from "17% in ICT R&D expenditures to 25% in high-tech goods exports, and 26% in number of patents" [14].

ICT's contribution to the economy, as presented here, is of great importance for the innovation ecosystem, which relates to value creation [15] and can be defined as a smart system that is characterized by players that form a complex adaptive structure [16, 17]. This system can be depicted as a set of interdependent layers, as shown in Figure 2.3. Each

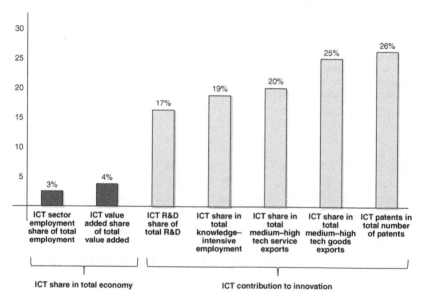

Figure 2.2 ICT share in the total economy and its contribution to innovation

Source: Adapted from [14].

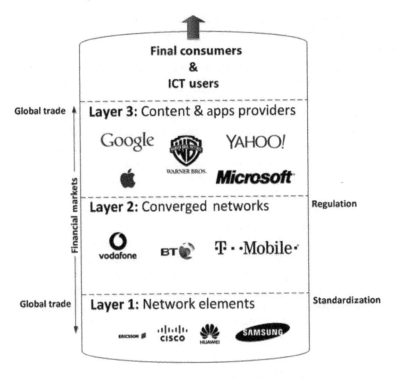

Figure 2.3 A layered view of the digital innovation ecosystem
Source: Adapted from [14].

layer represents key players in the market with different characteristics for their innovation processes [14]:

- **The first layer** is about the ICT equipment providers who need to collaborate in order to set the standards that will be followed during production. This is reflected in a slower innovation process [14]. Examples of the players in this layer include Cisco, Ericsson and Samsung.
- **The second layer** is about service providers, which include network operators who define the regulations that govern firms' operations. The players here are mainly dependent on the ICT-related innovations that emerge from the first layer [14]. Recently, however, some players in this layer have started to realize the significance of innovation and, thus, established their own innovation incubators [18]. Examples of the players here include BT, Vodafone and T-Mobile.

- **The third layer** is the layer that has witnessed most innovations and it includes firms like Google, Apple, Yahoo and Microsoft, among others [14].
- **The last layer**: is about the consumers as well as other firms from different sectors who depend immensely on ICTs and innovations from other layers to run their operations [14].

The path to an effective and fruitful open innovation ecosystem is positively related to the values and trust shared among collaborators. This path, according to Accenture [11], is set out in four phases: *corporate venture, incubators and/or accelerators, joint innovation* and *innovation ecosystem*. Depending on the firm's strategic objectives and needs, it might adopt any one of these phases. Figure 2.4 demonstrates the four phases [11] as well as the objectives and other characteristics most associated with each.

In the corporate venture category, large firms seek external innovation skills in order to neutralize the risks associated with investing in their internal R&D department. Companies in the incubators/accelerators and joint innovation categories sponsor and guide or even set up their own start-ups for the sake of finding innovative solutions to common problems. Finally, large companies as well as entrepreneurial start-ups use digital platforms to form a broader ecosystem that has shared value with the intention of finding answers for big or common issues [11].

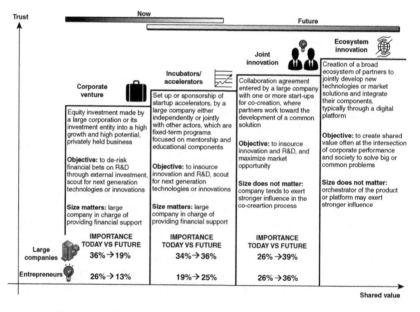

Figure 2.4 The open innovation journey
Source: Adapted from [11].

2.4   Open Innovation Hubs

Primarily, open innovation is based on sharing and collaboration of ideas and resources for the sake of establishing proper knowledge transfer channels [11]. With this objective in mind, organizations started to gather in what are called *knowledge hubs* [19] or *clusters of innovation* [2] to foster innovation and develop enterprise-related skills that increase efficiency and competitiveness. These hubs are defined as "geographic concentrations of interconnected companies, specialized suppliers, service providers, firms in related industries, and associated institutions that compete but also collaborate" [2].

Consequently, important players in the innovation ecosystem presented in Figure 2.3 – such as Cisco – have started to realize the importance of knowledge sharing and cooperation among entrepreneurs. Thus, they have seized on advancements in ICT in order to establish open and global initiatives, called I-Prize, to foster entrepreneurial collaboration that aims to propose innovative business ideas for Cisco. Such innovation hubs are facilitated by ICT tools such as Cisco Show and Share, Cisco Pulse, Cisco WebEx, and Cisco TelePresence for telecommunications, and Spigit as a management platform [2]. Innovation hubs, which form part of firms' R&D efforts, are a valuable source of knowledge for the collaborating firms. Thus, more and more firms are starting to acquire knowledge from local hubs as well as from global ones [20].

The partnership between universities and industry is one prominent example of collaboration among different players in the innovation ecosystem [21]. Universities play a crucial role in establishing innovation hubs that link industry with research [22]. For example, Stanford University fosters innovation through its Innovation Fellows Program, which encourages students from various fields throughout the USA to participate in building an entrepreneurship ecosystem based on innovation. Additionally, other universities, such as Virginia Tech's Institute for Critical Technology and Applied Science, have started to sponsor innovation challenges aimed at commercializing innovative ideas [22].

Innovation hubs enable entrepreneurs as well as companies of all sizes to partner with each other to share knowledge and resources. Big organizations can benefit from the speed and agility that entrepreneurial firms and SMEs have; in return, those firms can benefit from the resources that big firms have. Thus, innovation hubs represent win-win opportunities for both types of player in the innovation ecosystem [21]. Offering advantages like wider visioning and strategy development for businesses, access to talent and specialist expertise, mentoring and training, access to resources and finds, as well as pathways for collaborative research, innovation hubs are considered golden opportunities for organizations to come together for purposes of research.

The journey toward creating a productive innovation hub goes through several stages [23]. In a joint project by the London-based Big Innovation Centre and Lancaster University, the researchers studied several open innovation development cases and discovered that most followed a similar path of overlapping steps, as shown in Figure 2.5.

As you can see from the figure, the eight steps are categorized into four phases: opening, semi-open, open and integrated. In the opening phase, firms have to assess the available internal resources that can be used to create value and to start to manage the cultural change associated with collaboration with external organizations. Then, in the semi-open phase, companies start to explore external talents and study how to develop effective partnerships with them. Third, in the open phase, the

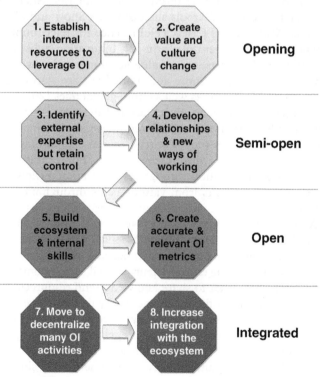

Note: "OI" stands for "open innovation."

Figure 2.5 The open innovation journey for productive hubs
Source: Adapted from [23].

collaborators work toward building an effective ecosystem with clearly defined and accurate metrics. Finally, after they have decentralized the innovation activities within the ecosystem, the big organizations and entrepreneurial start-ups find that they have an integrated working environment that has innovation as a prevailing mentality and in which their expectations on both sides can become reality [23].

2.5 Business Models for Innovative Digital Entrepreneurship

Considering innovation to be the main driver of business competitiveness, researchers have tried to analyze the essential elements for *achieving impact* from it; Herrera [24] describes "innovation that enhances corporate performance and creates significant lasting social impact." The following five points summarize these elements [24]:

- *Strategic alignment*: From the corporate social innovation (CSI) point of view, it is important to align the overall business strategy with a business context that clarifies and institutionalizes CSI [24].
- *Responsible purpose*: Innovation relies, in large part, on the clarity of the goals set for the business; thus, stakeholders need to be clear about business goals in advance [24, 25].
- *Institutional drivers*: These are divided into explicit drivers – strategy, structure and policies – and implicit drivers – values, corporate culture and leadership [24].
- *Stakeholder engagement*: This key part of the organization's social responsibility facilitates both sharing of knowledge and goals and analysis of any risks associated with opportunities [24].
- *Business model management*: Again, this is about alignment: properly aligning the business's objectives with its landscape and skills enhances its propensity to succeed [24].

Market demands change according to customers' needs; thus, business models adopted by entrepreneurs have to be agile enough to comply with these changes and to enable entrepreneurs to realign their strategic objectives to meet the new demands [26]. Innovative and flexible business models are considered powerful tools for entrepreneurs to be able to evaluate the market and potential business success and make changes accordingly [27]. Additionally, listening to customers, considering them as concerned stakeholders and involving them in the initiation of new products or services are equally important when it comes to making fast and informed decisions. This is particularly the case with technology-based entrepreneurships, which open innovation and agile development methodologies help to have faster product development streams [26].

Open innovation requires having shared vision, knowledge and resources among collaborators; this leads to what is called a "sharing economy" [27], which is an economic model where collaborators take advantage of Internet and Web 2.0 advancements to share technological assets in order to create clear and constructive innovation. A group of researchers who surveyed several companies in Europe have constructed a framework for a sharing economy that can help in building a successful and trustworthy business model (see Figure 2.6) [27].

As explained in Chapter 1, entrepreneurs are constantly exploring new opportunities for introducing innovative products and/or services [9]. The business models for these kinds of venture, however, are rather fuzzy in character, however, because there is no clarity or consistency about the conceptualizing process [28]. Thus, the elements in the framework illustrated in Figure 2.6 [27] are of great importance for achieving the intended goals. Other researchers have come up with some advice to enhance the actual implementation of digital innovation [14]. These recommendations intersect with elements and drivers illustrated in Figure 2.6 and are summarized in the following points:

- **First,** entrepreneurs need to have an open mindset regarding digital innovation and the disruption associated with it [12, 14, 27].
- **Second,** they need to understand that entrepreneurship is not only about excellence in the ICT sector; it is also about having the required skills and attitudes to boost innovation, such as managerial and financial skills, among others [14].
- **Third,** studies related to entrepreneurship can't stress enough the importance of sharing and collaboration among the various players in

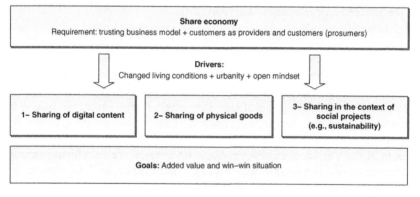

Figure 2.6 The sharing economy framework
Source: Adapted from [27].

the market, including larger firms and entrepreneurs. Sharing and collaboration help in knowledge dissemination and absorption, which in turn facilitate the innovation process. Sharing encompasses digital content, physical goods and funds, among other things [14, 27].

- **Fourth,** the heterogeneity of the innovation ecosystem explained and displayed in Figure 2.3 makes it necessary for the different players in the different layers to establish a network that embraces collaboration while still respecting intellectual property rights (IPR). The network members have to coordinate among themselves in order to establish regulations and standards [14].

Standing and Mattsson [28] have proposed a framework, based on simplicity, for conceptualizing the right business model that entrepreneurs can use at the beginning of their entrepreneurship journey (see Figure 2.7).

Business models are tools that help digital entrepreneurs to spot (digital) opportunities, but to envision the most suitable business models for

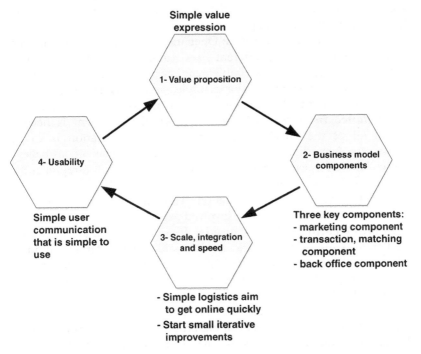

Figure 2.7 A framework, based on simplicity, for business model conceptualization
Source: Adapted from [28].

their ventures, they must take into account innovation's stepwise and gradual approach toward developing new products or services [28]. The steps in the framework displayed in Figure 2.7 are, thus, to start with a simple business idea or proposition; then to consider only the essential components of the business, that is, marketing, sales and back office operations; third, to look for the easiest and fastest way to deploy and integrate the business online; next to make small iterative improvements to gradually scale the business to the market; and, finally, as usability is an important measure of business success, to ensure that customer communication is as uncomplicated and as effective as possible [28].

2.6   Challenges for Innovation in Digital Entrepreneurship

Open innovation offers several advantages for collaborating businesses, whether large or entrepreneurial. In order for organizations to harvest these benefits, however, they have to overcome several challenges related to the practical implementation of open innovation. These challenges can be economic or cultural, among other factors, and they are summarized in the following points [11, 14]:

- *Different organization types*: Open innovation requires partnership among companies with different sizes, cultures and structures. Such collaboration is not easy to implement because of the varying ways in which companies function. For example, large firms have lengthy processes compared to the lean approach that start-ups adopt [11, 29].
- *Imbalance in perceived commitment*: Commitment is needed from all of the collaborating parties if a collaboration is to be a success. According to [11], 78 percent of large organizations believe in collaboration as a means to achieving innovation. Entrepreneurial start-ups, on the other hand, remain unconvinced that big companies really do have faith in collaboration. Thus, it is an issue of boosting mutual confidence among the involved parties [11].
- *Different cultural backgrounds*: It is expected that firms with different sizes and business models will have different cultures. When collaborating, however, these companies have to understand and manage these differences in order for the innovation to be achieved [11, 30].
- Figure 2.8 illustrates several elements pointed out by [11] that reflect the cultural differences between big firms and start-ups. For example, while start-ups embrace risk as a necessary factor for innovation, big firms consider it a crucial issue that they try to avoid. Another example is that while large organizations value centralization in their decision-making processes, small firms and start-ups have faster and

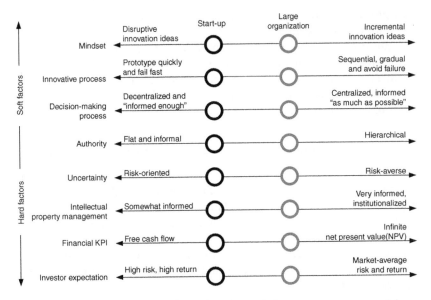

Figure 2.8 Comparative cultural trends between start-ups and large companies
Source: Adapted from [11].

decentralized decision-making processes that rely far less on pre-decision information gathering [11, 30].

- **Performance management imbalance**: Despite the benefits offered by open innovation, firms will still have their own R&D departments for internal innovation and these will naturally have different expectations. In such cases, finding the balance in resources allocation is crucial for each organization [23, 31].

- **Not enough governmental support**: Large organizations and small start-ups all agree that there is a lack of support from governmental agencies, which makes collaboration for innovation harder to attain. This agreement, however, differs from country to another. For example, large organizations in Australia, China and India believe that the governments in those countries play an important role in facilitating collaboration with entrepreneurial start-ups [11].

- **Lack of access to finance**: When the innovation process happens internally within a start-up, lack of financial support is one of the biggest issues that the firm faces. It is considered to be the bottleneck preventing access to innovation. Consequently, start-ups have to prove that their innovative ideas or concepts are worth the risk of collaboration and financing [14].

Innovation, whether it happens internally or externally through open innovation, offers many opportunities for start-ups as well as established businesses. In order to reap the promised benefits, however, firms have to plan ahead in order to manage expectations and overcome the previously mentioned challenges.

2.7   Recommended Actions to Plan and Promote Innovation

Innovation is the process that is concerned with developing new value for customers portrayed through products or services that meet existing, new or unexpected needs. As explained already, there are several challenges to innovation that must be addressed lest they impede its progress. This section will elaborate on the recommended actions that involved parties – large firms, entrepreneurs, educational institutions, governmental agencies and bridge-makers – can take to enhance (open) innovation success.

2.7.1   Recommended Actions for Large Organizations

Large organizations seek talent and agility, among other benefits, from collaborating with entrepreneurial startups. To meet these expectations, big firms have to support innovation development by considering the following factors:

- *Set a clear strategy*: Having a clear strategy based on collaboration is considered essential for ensuring the future success of any open innovation. Setting a clearly defined vision, along with goals, expectations and performance indicators, and planning steps in advance are crucial activities in order to avoid unpleasant surprises throughout the open innovation journey [11].
- *Get top management support*: This is a key factor. The firm's strategic goals must be aligned with the expected outcomes of collaborating with entrepreneurial start-ups in an innovation ecosystem [11].
- *Commit to a realistic budget*: Planning financial commitment for open innovation must consider budget needed for proofing the concept as well as for commercializing the innovative product and/or service [11].
- *Encourage a sustainable innovation ecosystem*: Big corporations need to collaborate on establishing co-investment schemes so as not to compete with each other or with the government. Such collaboration can guarantee sustainable access to resources and funds, which will be

reflected in a smart ecosystem where open innovation and knowledge transfer can thrive [11, 32].

- *Promote an entrepreneurial culture*: Constantly motivating employees to collaborate and innovate can boost a company's internal innovation and facilitate collaboration with external entities. Thus, big companies must learn to embrace the culture of entrepreneurship by adopting agile decision-making processes, a knowledge-sharing mentality, and a risk-taking attitude [11, 30, 32].
- *Create and promote the network effect*: As explained in Section 2.2, entrepreneurial start-ups seek to be suppliers for their large partners. That they should have access to their partners' extended networks is thus considered vital for broadening the ecosystem and promoting open innovation [11].

2.7.2 Recommended Actions for Entrepreneurial Start-Ups

Entrepreneurial start-ups enter the market with high expectations, hoping to have a disruptive impact on innovative products or services. They seek to collaborate with big firms in order to gain faster market penetration, among other advantages. In order for them to realize these benefits, however, they need to consider the following points as crucial to the success of their collaboration with any large organization:

- *Understand the market*: Start-up firms have their own needs and priorities. However, if they are to collaborate successfully with large companies, then they must learn about the specific needs and interests of those companies in order to foster a common understanding [11].
- *Manage cultural change*: Just as big organizations have to manage the changes associated with working with collaborators from different backgrounds, entrepreneurs need to adapt to the centralized culture that predominates within big firms [11, 30].
- *Embrace mentoring*: While entrepreneurs have the innovation mindset and like to share knowledge, when it comes to developing and commercializing their innovative products or services, they need to seek mentors from among the experts available within those big companies' environments [11].
- *Pay attention to timing*: Approaching big organizations to propose that they adopt new ideas has to be timed and well managed. This means that entrepreneurs need to have a solution that is commercially viable before they ask for support from big firms [11].

2.7.3   Recommended Actions for Educational Institutions

Universities and research institutes represent the main sources of innovative ideas. They therefore play a crucial role in driving innovation by acting as research centers and linking academia with industry by establishing collaboration with industrial firms [33]. The following few points would be helpful for universities and educational institutions to take on board:

- *Adopt policies that support entrepreneurial activity*: Universities and research centers need to adopt new legislation and policies that embrace and encourage entrepreneurial strategies. Additionally, they need to acknowledge their crucial role in the innovation ecosystem and act somehow as innovation hubs by facilitating collaboration among big organizations and innovative students [32].
- *Consider innovation as a profession*: Universities should teach their academics the skills related to innovation and co-creation, and then develop and prepare them to transfer those skills to the students [32].
- *Incentivize innovation*: New schemes should be put in place to reward innovative students, academics and scientists. These schemes should motivate knowledge transfer and collaboration among the rest of the academic environment [32].

2.7.4   Recommended Actions for Governments

Governments are important players in the innovation ecosystem, as they have the crucial role of securing sustainable financing and growth to facilitate the work of the other collaborators. These few points summarize the key recommendations for governmental agencies to motivate innovation:

- *Develop co-financing models*: Paired funding between governments and the private sector can bring sustainability, which in turn can motivate more collaborators to participate in the innovation cycle. Furthermore, securing funding resources for young firms that have a high growth rate can help them find financial stability during their crucial onset period. Additionally, backup financing schemes need to be arranged in case of emergencies [11].
- *Encourage cross-collaboration*: By creating connections among innovation hubs from different industrial sectors, governments can help nurture cross-disciplinary talents, which will be very beneficial because knowledge transfer will give involved parties wider understanding of the market [11]. This can be further supported by having relevant incentive schemes.

- **Create policies for data sharing and protection**: New and improved data policies need to be put in place in order to find the balance between sharing knowledge and protecting data [11].
- **Develop skills and talent**: Governments need to get educational institutions and businesses to co-plan training programs and structured development processes that foster learning agility and collaboration [11].

2.7.5 Recommended Actions for Bridge-Makers

As discussed in Chapter 1, bridge-makers are the players who can most easily create and sustain open innovation environments. They can be governmental agencies, R&D centers, universities or businesses from the public or private sectors. They help connect interested organizations in order to form innovation-oriented partnerships. The recommended actions for bridge-makers are as follows:

- **Enable supply chain relationships**: As explained in Section 2.2, new start-ups look for opportunities to prove themselves as trusted suppliers for big firms. Being new to the market and lacking confidence, however, can curtail their expectations. This is where bridge-makers come in, connecting newly established businesses with big firms [11].
- **Facilitate networking**: Already established and successful entrepreneurs can be very good mentors for those who are just starting out on the journey. Bridge-makers can create connections here, too, which would benefit both parties [11].
- **Bridge the physical barriers**: Having shared locations and resources for meeting can facilitate collaboration and innovation, thus, bridge-makers need to develop such infrastructure [11].

Cooperation among the different players within the innovation ecosystem can result in sustainable innovation and many benefits for all involved parties. For such collaboration to be successful, however, each stakeholder has to be aware of his or her specific responsibilities and act accordingly. Open innovation is not an easy journey and commitment is essential from all involved parties in order for any such project to achieve its intended objectives.

2.8 Case Study

In this section, we discuss a digital start-up success story that has utilized digital technologies in order to accomplish its strategic goals and become strong and prosperous.

The case study presented here is based on [34] and is about a Cambridge University spin-off named Zappar [36], established in 2011, which sets about using advancements in Augmented Reality (AR) technology to produce AR applications for handheld and wearable devices such as smartphones, tablets and smart watches [34]. As in the famous Pokemon Go game, AR technology aims to extend the reality captured by the camera using the power of the processers and graphic adaptors embedded within mobile devices. The augmented reality, thus, has additional digital contents as part of the real world [35]. The name of the company is derived from the ability of its app, available on iPhone and Android app stores, to "zap" digital contents into the real world; creating the augmented reality [34]. Applications for such technology can be found in the gaming, movie, and media industries, among others.

Due to fierce competition with other AR producers and market demands, Zappar's initial business model was based on a closed innovation process, where research and development tasks were all carried out internally. When it came time to expand the target market from the entertainment industry to other businesses, however, it was necessary for Zappar to adopt more open innovation development strategy [34]. Consequently, it started to involve new customers, representing new industries, in the innovation and development processes of the new products that suit their special needs. Also, Zappar introduced a revenue-sharing contract on new sales as part of a modified business model that the firm has started to adopt in line with its commercialization strategy. Additionally, in its attempt to become the central engine for AR development and to create an open innovation ecosystem, Zappar introduced the Zapcode Creator platform in 2014. This simplified online platform allows both technically equipped people as well as unskilled users to develop AR content that is suitable for them independently and without the help of Zappar's experts [34].

POINT OF ATTENTION: This case study shows how adopting a more open business model enabled Zappar to get into new market industries. As reflected in its wide range of partners, including Nissan, ASDA, Coca-Cola, Sony Pictures and Dunkin' Donuts, among others, the benefits of such an open business model market justify collaborating within an open innovation ecosystem.

As noted in Section 2.6, finding the right balance between internal and open innovation is crucial for a company's sustainable growth. Moreover, it is important to remember that there is no single model of innovation and that companies have to adapt to the problems they face according to the goals they set for themselves.

2.9   Summary

This chapter introduced the concept of innovation and its importance for digital entrepreneurs. It moved on to differentiate between closed and open innovation and to show how the latter can offer a wide range of benefits for both large organizations and entrepreneurial start-ups. The chapter then described the role of ICT in fostering the sustainability of the innovation ecosystem, before looking at the steps needed to create productive (open) innovation hubs.

Additionally, the chapter briefly analyzed how adopting a lean business model could be key to the success of a digital entrepreneurial start-up, especially at the beginning of its journey. Finally, it listed the main challenges to innovation in digital entrepreneurship and recommended actions for the different stakeholders – large organizations, entrepreneurial start-ups, educational institutions, governmental agencies and bridge makers – to take in order to deal with these challenges and to create stronger collaborative partnerships.

Digital innovation is not limited to the area of ICT. In fact, it has taken several forms in various industries. For example, merging the advantages brought by innovative advances in ICT with the current financial process has yielded a new area of innovation called fintech. Similarly, insurtech is the area where innovation is taking place within the insurance industry. Such examples exist in almost every industry – fashiontech, biotech and so on. Later chapters will explain in detail three of the main areas where innovations in digital technology have helped in creating innovative solutions and services for fintech (Chapter 9), manufacturing (Chapter 10) and fashion (Chapter 11).

References

1. Beckman C, Eisenhardt K, Kotha S, Meyer A, Rajagopalan N. Technology Entrepreneurship. *Strategic Entrepreneurship Journal* (2012) 6:89–93. doi: 10.1002/sej.
2. Lange A, Handler D, Vila J. *Next-Generation Clusters Creating Innovation Hubs to Boost Economic Growth*. Cisco Internet Business Solutions Group (IBSG) (2010).
3. Costello T, Prohaska B. Innovation. *IT Professional* (2013) 15:1–2. doi: 10.1109/MITP.2013.42.

4. Marques JPC. Closed versus Open Innovation: Evolution or Combination? *International Journal of Business and Management* (2014) 9: 196–203. doi: 10.5539/ijbm.v9n3p196.
5. Del Giudice M, Straub D. IT and Entrepreneurism: An On-Again, Off-Again Love Affair or a Marriage? *MIS Q* (2007) 31.
6. Henfridsson O, Yoo Y. The Liminality of Trajectory Shifts in Institutional Entrepreneurship. *Organization Science* (2014) 25:932–50. doi: 10.1287/orsc.2013.0883.
7. Chesbrough H, Bogers M. Explicating Open Innovation: Clarifying an Emerging Paradigm for Understanding Innovation. In Chesbrough H, Vanhaverbeke W, West J (eds.) *New Frontiers in Open Innovation.* Oxford University Press (2014) 3–28.
8. Chesbrough H. *Open Innovation: The New Imperative for Creating and Profiting from Technology.* Harvard Business Review Press (2003).
9. Accenture. *The Promise of Digital Entrepreneurs.* Accenture/G20 Young Entrepreneurs' Alliance (2014).
10. Gassmann O, Enkel E, Chesbrough H. The Future of Open Innovation. *R D Manag* (2010) 40:213–21. doi: 10.1111/j.1467-9310.2010.00605.x.
11. Accenture Research. *Harnessing the Power of Entrepreneurs to Open Innovation.* Accenture/G20 Young Entrepreneurs' Alliance (2015).
12. Eftekhari N, Bogers M. Open for Entrepreneurship: How Open Innovation Can Foster New Venture Creation. *Creativity and Innovation Management* (2015) 24:574–84. doi: 10.1111/caim.12136.
13. Falk M, Biagi F. Empirical Studies on the Impact of ICT Usage in Europe. JRC Working Papers on Digital Economy 2015-14. Joint Research Centre (Seville Site) (2015). https://ideas.repec.org/p/ipt/decwpa/2015-14.html [accessed December 22, 2020].
14. Nepelski D, Bogdanowicz M, Biagi F, Desruelle P, De Prato G, Gabison G et al. 7 Ways to Boost Digital Innovation and Entrepreneurship in Europe. *Publications Office of the EU* (2017) 1–24. doi: 10.2791/019397.
15. de Vasconcelos Gomes LA, Facin ALF, Salerno MS, Ikenami RK. Unpacking the Innovation Ecosystem Construct: Evolution, Gaps and Trends. *Technological Forecasting and Social Change* (2015) 136. doi: 10.1016/j.techfore.2016.11.009.
16. Jucevičius G, Grumadaitė K. Smart Development of Innovation Ecosystem. *Procedia-Social Behavioral Sciences* (2014) 156:125–9. doi: 10.1016/j.sbspro.2014.11.133.
17. Kleibrink A, Niehaves B, Palop P, Sörvik J, Thapa BEP. Regional ICT Innovation in the European Union: Prioritization and Performance (2008–2012). *Journal of the Knowledge Economy* (2015) 6:320–33. doi: 10.1007/s13132-015-0240-0.
18. Puissochet A, Bogdanowicz M. *Models of ICT Innovation: Ten Cases of Successful SMEs in France.* European Commission – Joint Research Centre – Institute for Prospective Technological Studies (2015).
19. Youtie J, Shapira P. Building an Innovation Hub: A Case Study of the Transformation of University Roles in Regional Technological and Economic Development. *Research Policy* (2008) 37:1188–1204. doi: 10.1016/j.respol.2008.04.012.

20. Gabriele R, D'Ambrosio A, Schiavone F. Open Innovation and the Role of Hubs of Knowledge in a Regional Context. *Journal of the Knowledge Economy* (2017) 8:1049–65. doi: 10.1007/s13132-015-0331-y.
21. Striukova L, Rayna T. University-Industry Knowledge Exchange: An Exploratory Study of Open Innovation in UK Universities. *European Journal of Innovation Management* (2013) 18:471–92.
22. Meador MA, Friedersdorf LE. Student-Led Companies Expand the Nanotechnology Innovation Ecosystem. *MRS Bulletin* (2017) 41:836–8. doi: 10.1557/mrs.2016.251.
23. Golightly J, Ford C, Sureka P, Reid B. *Realising the Value of Open Innovation.* Big Innovation Centre (2012) 1–69.
24. Herrera MEB. Innovation for Impact: Business Innovation for Inclusive Growth. *Journal of Business Research* (2016) 69: 1725–30. doi: 10.1016/j.jbusres.2015.10.045.
25. Herrera MEB. Creating Competitive Advantage by Institutionalizing Corporate Social Innovation. *Journal of Business Research* (2015) 68: 1468–74. doi: 10.1016/j.jbusres.2015.01.036.
26. Trimi S, Berbegal-Mirabent J. Business Model Innovation in Entrepreneurship. *International Entrepreneurship and Management Journal* (2012) 8:449–65. doi: 10.1007/s11365-012-0234-3.
27. Richter C, Kraus S, Brem A, Durst S, Giselbrecht C. Digital Entrepreneurship: Innovative Business Models for the Sharing Economy. *Creativity and Innovation Management* (2017) 26:300–10. doi: 10.1111/caim.12227.
28. Standing C, Mattsson J. "Fake It until You Make It": Business Model Conceptualization in Digital Entrepreneurship. *Journal of Strategic Marketing* (2016) 4488:1–15. doi: 10.1080/0965254X.2016.1240218.
29. Blank S. Why the Lean Start-Up Changes Everything. *Harvard Business Review* (2013) 91: 63–72.
30. Ades C, Figlioli A, Sbragia R, Porto G, Ary Plonski G, Celadon K. Implementing Open Innovation: The Case of Natura, IBM and Siemens. *Journal of Technology Management & Innovation* (2013) 8:12–25. doi: 10.4067/S0718-27242013000300057.
31. West J, Gallagher S. Challenges of Open Innovation: The Paradox of Firm Investment in Open-Source Software. *R&D Management* (2006) 36:319–31. doi: 10.1111/j.1467-9310.2006.00436.x.
32. Debackere K, Andersen B, Dvorak I, Enkel E, Krüger P, Malmqvist H et al. Boosting Open Innovation and Knowledge Transfer in the European Union: Independent Expert Group Report on Open Innovation and Knowledge Transfer. European Commission (2014). https://op.europa.eu/en/publication-detail/-/publication/5af0ec3a-f3fb-4ccb-b7ab-70369d0f4d0c [accessed January 3, 2021].
33. Hu H, Huang T, Zeng Q, Zhang S. The Role of Institutional Entrepreneurship in Building Digital Ecosystem: A Case Study of Red Collar Group (RCG). *International Journal of Information Management* (2016) 36:496–9. doi: 10.1016/j.ijinfomgt.2015.12.004.

34. Di Minin A, De Marco CE, Marullo C, Piccaluga A, Casprini E, Mahdad M et al. Case Studies on Open Innovation in ICT. JRC Science for Policy Report, EUR 27911 EN. Institute for Prospective Technological Studies, Joint Research Centre (2016). doi:10.2791/433370.
35. Koll-Schretzenmayr M, Casaulta-Meyer S. Augmented Reality. *disP – The Planning Review* (2016) 52:2–5. doi: 10.1080/02513625.2016.1235863.
36. Zappar. About: Who We Are and What We Do. (2020) www.zappar.com /about/ [accessed May 22, 2020].

3 Digital Entrepreneurship and Digital Marketing

3.1 Introduction

The digital revolution has radically transformed every aspect of modern society, including economies, businesses and consumers' behavior. The emergence of digital technologies has created new markets and radically transformed existing ones [1]. Marketing is one of the major areas that has been "shaken up" by the digital disruption.

The core aim of the marketing strategy of every business is to influence and persuade people, especially consumers, to choose the product that marketers want, visit the store of the retailer or click on the advertised website [1]. Rapid developments in digital technologies, continuously evolving and upgraded with enhanced abilities and functionality, have influenced marketing all the way through its evolution from press, radio and television to the Internet, email, social media and mobile applications of today [1].

Originally emerging in the 1990s, digital marketing transformed the existing market by promising to "deliver the right message, to the right audience at the right time" [2] (p. 1). The Digital Marketing Institute (DMI) defines digital marketing as "the use of digital technologies to create an integrated, targeted and measurable communication which helps to acquire and retain customers while building deeper relationships with them" [3, 43, 44]. Primarily aiming to develop trusting and loyal relationships with consumers, digital marketing focuses on consumers, identifying their exact needs and the most effective communication strategies [4].

Nowadays, consumers have wholeheartedly embraced digital technologies as being embedded in every aspect of their everyday lives, from video calls with friends and family to collaborative online games and SMS text updates from their favorite sports teams [1]. The penetration of mobile devices into people's daily lives, with global mobile adoption having reached 65 percent in 2016 – that is, 4.7 billion people [5] – offers an excellent opportunity for businesses and entrepreneurs to promote their products and services, to attract and engage customers and thus make profit [6]. In other words, by harnessing the power of digital media, businesses can effectively connect with their customers, earn their trust and stimulate sales [7]. It is estimated that in the USA, "CMOs [chief marketing officers] will spend nearly $150 billion on search marketing, banner and outstream advertising, instream advertising, and email marketing" [8].

The emergence of the Internet and the development of modern mobile technologies have radically transformed the field of digital marketing. In their efforts to attract customers, digital firms can leverage a wide range of digital media, embedded in marketing strategies, in order to promote their brand's products and services. These media can be grouped into paid media, owned media and earned media (Figure 3.1) [2, 9–11]:

- **Paid media:** As its name suggests, paid media includes any type of digital channel that firms have to pay to use. The most prominent examples of paid media are paid search engines such as Google AdWords and paid displays such as the advertising banners that are

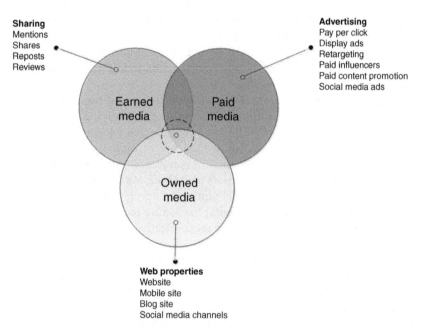

Figure 3.1 Paid, owned and earned media
Source: Adapted from [9].

visible on almost all websites across the Web. Characterized as the most suitable method for companies aiming to target specific groups of people or segmented audiences, paid media is very commonly used, especially in social media. Several social media platforms, such as Facebook, Twitter and LinkedIn, offer advertising options that companies can use in order to promote their brands. Furthermore, another very popular digital marketing method nowadays is to use paid influencers, who are (often well-known) people that companies pay to share brand website links and post brand-showcasing photographs on social media, thus gaining more exposure for the brand [2, 9, 10].

• **Owned media:** Owned media refers to any digital asset, platform or content that the firm owns, controls and manages in order to promote its products and services and engage with customers. Popular examples include the brand website, emails to subscribers and all content in the company's blogs and social media accounts. Owned media can effectively be used to extend the company's presence online, making the brand name more recognizable, and thus more reachable, to more people locally as well as internationally [2, 9, 10].

• **Earned media:** While paid and owned media constitute the most dominant types of media since the 1990s, earned media has been very recently introduced into the digital marketing world as the "new," third type of digital media for companies to use in their marketing strategies. Earned media are described as any kind of exposure that the brand or firm receives through online word of mouth (WOM) or else through "viral" communications such as online reviews, recommendations, shares, reposts and content included in articles by journalists and bloggers. WOM constitutes the most influential digital channel nowadays and is thus an invaluable asset for every business, as the generation of millennials is extremely engaged in writing online reviews about products they have purchased as well as providing feedback to other people online. Having also been characterized as "free" media, earned media can be "cultivated" by both effective search engine optimization (SEO), which leads to first page rankings, meaning that the company's website turns up on the first page of search engine results, and strong content strategy, with appealing as well as informative content so that the customer is intrigued and captivated [2, 9–11].

3.2 Understanding the Market and the Customer

Digital transformation has brought many opportunities for entrepreneurial start-ups as well as for large organizations. While seizing these opportunities can bring huge benefits for businesses, it is important to acknowledge that understanding the digital customer is crucial for the prosperity of any digital business. Thus, this section will shed light on the specifics surrounding digital markets and digital customers.

Developing and implementing an effective marketing strategy involves taking a series of steps and making well-informed strategic decisions about how the brand should be promoted, what value it will create for the customer and how it will be differentiated from its competitors [7]. Digital marketing, as an important success factor for digital entrepreneurs, differs from the traditional methods in that businesses, small or large, can reach local and global audiences [12]. Thanks to its being accessible in so many forms, far more potential customers can interact with the digital marketing contents of businesses. From the business point of view, these interactions represent a goldmine since they enable businesses to keep track of customers' communications with the digital contents. Advanced analytics, then, can help in discovering valuable insights about customers' online behavior [12, 13]. Measuring digital marketing performance will be discussed in more detail in Section 3.4.

The existence of the digital media that we use in our daily lives – smartphones, tablets, laptops, emails and social media – makes understanding customers a different mission than before. Such tools open the door for more engagement from and with existing as well as potential customers. On the hand, companies having an online presence provides more choices for today's smart shoppers [14]. Thus, considering customers from both local and global markets with different backgrounds, companies need to strive to create positive online customer experiences aimed at building longer as well as more trusting and more value-based relationships with loyal consumers [15, 16].

Understanding digital customers requires empowering and engaging them as concerned stakeholders [15]. Additional efforts from digitally oriented firms and especially from digital entrepreneurs are needed in order for them to compete in tough market conditions. These efforts could take several forms, for instance online blogs and, more importantly, verified pages on social media platforms. These online channels play a crucial role as two-way marketing streams: businesses can use them to advertise their products and services as well as to listen to their customers, and to capture and learn from their interactions, and consequently customize the customer experience [17, 18]. Thus, proper marketing strategies, discussed in Section 3.3, need to be considered in order to support customer value creation [15].

Considered as tools for communication, social media applications are the most successful digital marketing tools that small and entrepreneurial businesses can use to achieve the required market penetration [17]. Because they can have such a significant effect, however, digital businesses need to be aware that these tools can be something of a double-edged sword. Good and valuable customer experiences can benefit newly established businesses tremendously in building their reputation. On the other hand, negative feedback can cause a lot of damage to an entrepreneurial start-up that can be hard to manage. Thus, paying attention to and understanding customers' needs and engagement on social media platforms represents a challenge for businesses.

Motivated by the importance of understanding customers' engagement, Sashi [19] proposed a model that reflects the customer engagement cycle with six different stages: connection, interaction, satisfaction, retention (*loyalty*), commitment, advocacy and engagement (Figure 3.2). These elements are discussed briefly in the following points:

- **Connection**: Facilitated by social media platforms, connection is the base stone for communication between the customer and the business as well as among customers. Properly managed connection channels enhance sales prospects and customer loyalty [19].

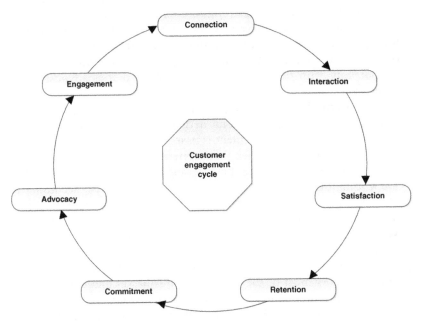

Figure 3.2 Customer engagement cycle
Source: Adapted from [19].

- **Interaction**: Thanks to advancements in ICT, connected parties are able to interact with each other using various tools such as instant messaging, email and comments. Constant interaction between the business and its customers can benefit the business by facilitating capture of its customers' changing needs and enhancing value creation [15, 19].
- **Satisfaction**: Successful connection and interaction are essential to harvesting satisfaction, which in turn is one of the essential elements for having customer engagement.
- **Retention (loyalty)**: Having positive impressions of and emotions about the company leads customers to keep coming back. Loyalty is a result of satisfaction and positive emotion [19].
- **Commitment**: This element has two types: affective commitment and calculative commitment. The first is a result of having an emotional and trust-based relationship with the seller, and it is built over time by the business providing special and customized service for the delighted customer. The latter is more rational and is a result of a customer having fewer alternatives. The ultimate aim for the organization is to achieve both affective and calculative commitment [19].
- **Advocacy**: Publicly recommending a company's products is a result of a delighted customer having strong emotions and affective commitment toward that company. Conversely, loyal customers who developed their loyalty based on calculative commitment and without emotion may not be willing to advocate the seller. Companies should seek reciprocal relationships with their customers where both parties advocate each other's best interest [19].
- **Engagement**: This phase happens as a result of the delighted and/or loyal customer participating online in their social network in favor of the company. Customer engagement is based on both affective and calcu-lative commitment, and when this happens the customer is considered a co-creator of the value and they become fans of the company [19].

Depending on the level of customer engagement, then, according to Sashi [19], customers can be categorized as *transactional*, where relational exchange as well as emotional bonds are low; *delighted*, where customers have high emotional bonds but low relational exchange; *loyal*, where customers have high relational exchange and low emotional bonds; or *fans*, where both emotional bonds and relational exchange are high [19]. The last category must be the objective of businesses and entrepreneurs who seek long-term relationships with their customers. These categories are illustrated in Figure 3.3, which reflects the customer engagement matrix.

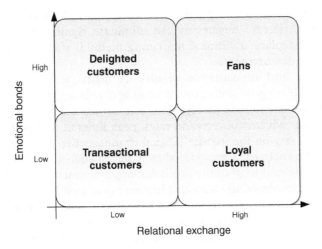

Figure 3.3 Customer engagement matrix
Source: Adapted from [19].

Having a wide variety of tools and options that a customer can use to explore products and services online provides opportunities and challenges for the entrepreneurial business. Appropriate Customer Relationship Management (CRM) needs to be planned in order to discover consumers' goals when they are online and consequently to tailor the digital marketing contents to their needs.

3.3 Digital Marketing Strategies

As mentioned in Section 3.1, the aim of a marketing strategy is to create value and benefits for the customer by promoting the brand and products or services of the firm in a way that motivates customers to buy them as well as creating loyal customer relationships [7]. Implementing an effective digital marketing strategy can offer significant benefits to both digital and traditional organizations, including lower costs along with higher revenues. The following points discuss the most significant benefits that accompany an effective marketing strategy (see [20–23]):

- **Global reach**: As digital marketing strategies leverage online channels and electronic media in order to reach consumers, companies can effectively reach larger, global audiences and thus achieve greater exposure. While traditional marketing can target only local audiences, offering limited geographical ability, digital marketing can easily access international audiences, improving the firm's outreach.

- **Lower costs**: By utilizing the power of digital technologies in their marketing strategy, businesses can eliminate significant costs and potentially replace traditional marketing methods such as TV, radio and press advertisements.
- **Real-time and measurable results**: A digital marketing strategy offers a wide range of online metric tools and web analytics that can be used in real time to produce reports as well as view the number of clicks on a specific advert, conversation rates, peak times as well as how long consumers stay on the website. Digital channels offer a wealth of data that can be analyzed to provide valuable information about the success of the online campaign or the profit deriving from each digital channel.
- **Improved conversion rates and higher revenues**: A digital marketing strategy can attract and engage customers more easily and more effectively than a traditional marketing method; instead of visiting a store or calling to make an order, consumers can click on a newsletter that was sent through email, for example, and instantly be transferred to the brand's e-store or the company's informative website. Offering a seamless and immediate customer experience, a digital marketing tactic can quickly convert customers to make purchases with only a click, thus leading to higher revenues for the company.
- **Competition with large firms**: Digital marketing enables firms to compete on a "level playing field," meaning that any small business, start-up or SME can directly compete with large corporations and gain competitive advantage over them with a strong marketing strategy.

A digital marketing strategy is vital for an organization; it dictates the strategic decisions and tactics that will be undertaken in order to drive the organization in the most beneficial direction regarding its marketing goals. Understanding how the Internet and modern technologies can be utilized, a digital marketing strategy delineates the specific tools and tactics that will be implemented in order to reach the targeted goals of the organization [7, 24]. There are several digital marketing tactics and tools that a business can implement today. In the next sections we describe the most prominent and effective ones in the current digital marketing field.

3.3.1   Email Marketing

Email marketing constitutes one of the oldest forms of advertising. Despite almost 80 percent of every person's inbox getting filled up every day with irrelevant and unwanted emails, called "junk" or "spam," email marketing is yet considered one of the most effective and powerful marketing tactics that a company can deploy in order to create value, gain new customers and retain current ones [1, 7].

Email marketing includes any email communication sent to a current or prospective customer that includes commercial messages, such as advertisements or any type of content to motivate sales, and will usually encompass a "call to action" (CTA), that is, an element that motivates the reader to interact with the brand such as by clicking on a link of the email that includes an attractive promotion or subscribing to a newsletter [1, 7, 25]. Generally, there are two types of email that a firm can deploy in its email marketing strategy:

- **Promotional emails**: Promotional emails aim to motivate the recipient to make a purchase, download some content or ask the company for additional information. The most prominent example is an email from a retail brand that includes an attractive, flashing image advertising the company's upcoming sales [7].
- **Newsletters**: Newsletters aim to create brand awareness, spread a positive attitude and enhance recognition of the brand over the targeted audience. Constituting an easy and effective tool in order to create a long-term relationship with the recipient, newsletters can be sent weekly, monthly or quarterly, encompassing different content for different segments [7, 24, 26].

Constituting a powerful strategy for both customer acquisition and retention, email marketing brings several benefits: lower costs for the organization, reaching large audiences more quickly, requiring less time for implementation and management, and increasing the speed of communication with customers [27]. An effective email marketing strategy supports the firm's endeavors to build a good reputation for its brand and products across its audience by creating a relationship of trust and loyalty with its customers. Considered an excellent cost-effective marketing strategy, email marketing can ultimately lead to increased returns on investment (ROIs) translating into higher revenues for the company [1, 7].

An effective email marketing strategy involves a series of steps and well-informed decisions [1, 7]:

- **Create a database**: A successful email campaign needs a database of recipients who have opted-in and agreed to receive marketing messages from the company. An email database constitutes the most valuable asset of an email marketing strategy so firms should be cautious when setting one up: email messages should be sent only to people who have given permission; any violation of this rule can create serious legal consequences for the firm as well as a "downfall" on the brand reputation. Furthermore, aside from email address, several other customer details can be collected – name, gender, date of birth, for example – for use in order to create more personalized email messages. However, the more personal details a company asks of individuals, the less likely they are to provide them. There are several ways that a business can populate its email database such as offering vouchers or discount codes upon customers signing up for a newsletter, collecting email addresses from completed customer transactions in the brand's e-store or even renting a list of email addresses from relevant providers.

- **Design the email and create content**: While some companies use plain text emails, most email campaigns nowadays use HTML emails facilitating complex design with enriched text, hyperlinks, flashing images and/or videos. The design of the email is very important as people will use different devices and email clients to view it. As a result, the business should make sure that the format of the email is compatible for both desktop and mobile devices. Furthermore, the content of the email should be relevant and useful to the reader; it should attempt to address their needs and be in line with their interests. The success of an email campaign depends a great deal on the email content, which should be informative and likely include promotions or even exclusive offers for subscribers.

- **Measure performance:** After deployment of the email, the business is ready to look at key measurables, to assess the effectiveness of the email campaign. By using email marketing tools, the firm can analyze several metrics such as the number of emails delivered, the number of opened emails, the number of unsubscribers, which links attracted people more and thus were clicked on more often, and what the click through rates were that resulted in conversion. As a result, the company can understand the performance of the email campaign, get valuable insights from the analyzed data and take necessary decisions to improve the efficacy of future campaigns.

3.3.2   Social Media Marketing

The penetration of mobile devices and Internet usage into people's lives has rendered social media the prevailing form of communication that people use to discuss and share content, ideas and information, that is, to socially interact. As well as socializing with each other by sharing videos, photos and web links, individuals are increasingly using social media platforms such as Facebook, LinkedIn and Instagram to write reviews and ratings based on their experiences of buying products, services and brands, and sharing them to other members of online communities. As a result, through word of the mouth (WOM), which has been characterized as the most influential digital channel today, individuals are influencing other people's opinions and "advertising" their favorite brands. This can enhance firms' digital exposure and increase awareness of their brands. In other words, social media offer a great opportunity for businesses to exploit in order to affect online consumers' attitudes [1, 7, 28].

Having recognized the power of social media in today's society, businesses have embedded them in their digital marketing strategies. There are several benefits that a business can gain from implementing a social media marketing strategy and engaging with consumers through social media channels:

- **Raise the company's profile and get valuable information**: Social media channels enable two-way communication with customers; consumers provide their feedback on the company's Facebook page or write a review about a product or even ask a question about a service. In real time, the business is able to respond to any of the above situations, engaging with the customer and building an interactive and loyal relationship with them, thus appearing caring and responsive to its audience. At the same time, the business is getting valuable information about and insight into customers' perceptions of and opinions about the offered products and services, allowing the business to make any necessary changes to increase its sales and customer acquisition [1, 7].

- **Increase brand awareness:** Social media platforms enable the creation of online communities, such as a brand's Facebook page or an online forum, which businesses can leverage in order to increase their exposure and enhance brand recognition through the positive opinions of their "fans" who act as brand evangelists [1, 7].

- **Enhance brand loyalty:** According to recent reports, businesses who use social media platforms in order to engage with their customers have noticed increased brand loyalty. In other words, customers seem to feel more connected and loyal to brands that they are already following in social media, such as Facebook and Instagram, and prefer to shop from these brands rather than their competitors [29].

- **"Go viral":** As already mentioned, social media act as a vessel for WOM communication. If a firm's social media content is popular and gets retweeted and reposted on several social media platforms, such as in a news feed or a blog article, then it is said to "go viral," spreading very quickly everywhere and getting the attention of thousands or even millions of people. This can be an excellent way to promote products and services [7].

- **Improve customer service:** Social media platforms offer a bidirectional method of communication with customers, thus creating an additional channel of customer service. As a result, businesses can instantly respond to customers' queries, comments and problems, providing much quicker customer service that increases customer satisfaction [1].

With Facebook being the most popular social media platform today and Instagram, Twitter, Pinterest and LinkedIn following, businesses have in hand a wide range of digital tools that they can deploy in order to implement a strong social media strategy and achieve robust brand exposure[30].

As will be seen further in Chapter 6, while some of the existing social media platforms offer similar functionalities, businesses should be aware of the benefits, risks and challenges that each social media solution encompasses. For example, as depicted in Figure 3.4, Facebook is generally considered to be the best platform to use in order to receive the highest ROIs, with other platforms such as Pinterest and Snapchat showing lower ROI rates [31]; nevertheless, those lower ROI rates may complement the overall ROI rate of a social media marketing strategy targeted at customers that are not necessarily active on Facebook.

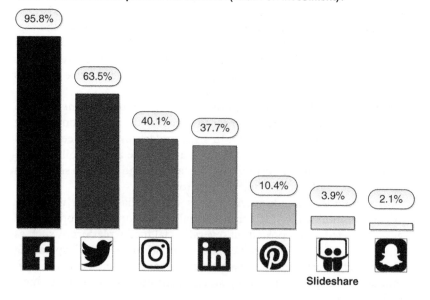

What social networks provide the best ROI (return on investment)?

Figure 3.4 Social networks' respective ROIs
Source: Adapted from [31].

3.3.3   Search Engine Marketing (SEM)

Search engine advertising involves the aggregated efforts of a marketing team to promote the products and services of the company by utilizing the underlying power of search engines. Every day, approximately five billion people around the world use the Internet and perform searches across numerous search engines such as Google, Yahoo! and Bing. Google is the winner in the market, as 73.34 percent of the desktop searches conducted in the first months of 2020 were executed through its website [25, 32]. Having recognized the dynamics of search engines and their huge potential for marketing purposes, firms are nowadays implementing search engine marketing (SEM) strategies by using search engines' results pages as a way to advertise their brands, products and services. Therefore, SEM constitutes an excellent and effective tactic for new as well as already established businesses to adopt and implement in their digital marketing efforts toward customer acquisition and retention and increased sales [7, 24]. SEM mainly involves two techniques that businesses can use either alone or in combination [7]:

- **Search engine optimization (SEO)**: SEO refers to a firm's optimization efforts in order to achieve the highest possible ranking in the page results that users get after using specific keywords or phrases in search engines. With nearly 80 percent of people accessing only the web links that appear in the first search engine results page (SERP), SEO constitutes a crucial strategy for businesses struggling to make their products and services easily "findable" through the World Wide Web [33]. Search engines use closely protected algorithms in order to determine the positions and rankings of the millions of websites that arise in the search results pages [7]. As a result, businesses cannot manipulate their SERP position in any way; however, a number of techniques can be implemented to improve a website's ranking. One of the first steps is making sure that the website content contains relevant keywords and phrases that potential customers are likely to use when searching, as search engines look to match the keywords that the user has typed in with the most relevant content destination page [24]. Furthermore, businesses should strive to gain a good number of links from highly ranked and well-established sites. Another point is that developing interesting and valuable content in the website or including useful online tools and documents makes it more likely that people will share the website's link through social media or blogs [7, 24, 25]. Moreover, on-page optimization efforts can considerably improve the ranking of a website by using relevant title and metatags in the site's HTML code [7, 24]. Overall, SEO is an excellent marketing technique that can effectively drive traffic to a firm's website and thus increase the possibilities of its acquiring new customers and gaining advantage over its competitors. However, it should be highlighted that SEO becomes effective in long-term prospects, meaning that results are obtained only after a period of six to twelve months [7, 24, 25].

- **Pay-per-click (PPC)**: PPC is an advertisement tactic, similar to traditional advertising, where the advert of a business appears in SERPs, after a search has been performed with specific keywords of phrases. However, the business does not pay when its advert appears on search results, only when clicks are performed on the ad redirecting the user to the firm's website. One of the most popular PPC platforms is Google AdWords (now Google Ads), which enables users to use the currency of their choice, targets specific audiences around the globe in specific geographical areas and utilizes extensive analytics tools. Offering a wide range of benefits, such as measurable results, quick entry into the competitive market and a wealth of data to analyze for valuable insight, PPC advertising constitutes one of the most powerful tactics that can have a great impact on a business's strategic goals by increasing traffic to the website and ultimately sales and revenues [7, 24, 34].

3.3.4   Affiliate Marketing

Affiliate marketing describes the strategic partnership established between a digital firm and a third party, where the latter gets paid to place adverts and links on its site to direct visitors to the former's e-store or website. As depicted in Figure 3.5, in affiliate marketing, a third party advertises the products and services of a company, on an agreed commission basis, drives traffic to the partner's website and is rewarded for every customer referred. Affiliate marketing is mostly used to gain more customers, increase the number of visitors landing on the company website and enhance brand awareness and exposure over the targeted audience.

Although affiliate marketing offers several advantages – it is easy to implement, creates high-volume traffic to the business's website, quickly reaches new customers and global audiences and has a low barrier to entry – it also includes important challenges for the implementing organization. For instance, at first, affiliates might perform "false" advertising just to receive the agreed commission. Also, the absence of contracts between merchant and affiliates and the absence of industry regulations are factors that businesses should be aware of before embedding affiliate marketing into their digital marketing strategy.

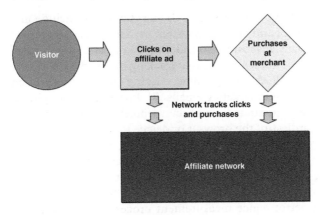

Figure 3.5 How affiliate marketing works
Source: Adapted from [7], p. 324.

3.4 Measuring Digital Marketing Performance

Customers of digitally focused businesses provide valuable interactions with the digital contents of these companies. Within the digital marketing area, data analytics focuses on capturing consumer generated media (CGM), which are the data produced by customers in online forums, blogs, comments and surveys [35], as well as measuring the performance of marketing campaigns [7]. By capturing and analyzing consumers' interactions with the (1) *digital contents of companies' websites*, (2) *marketing advertisements* and (3) *links embedded within marketing emails* as well as (4) *comments on verified social media pages* that represent opinions on new products or services, insights about customers' behavior and preferences can be discovered. Consequently, tailored products and services can be offered, resulting in digital marketing content that is more appropriate to customer needs.

CGM data can be very big, very quickly generated, and in any form: structured or unstructured. While structured data represent statistical and demographic information, unstructured data could be in the form of comments or tweets. The volume, variety and velocity that characterize the data generated online constitute what is called "big data" [36, 37]. Measuring the performance of digital marketing campaigns, thus, involves big data analytics in order to discover aggregate, segmented or individual insights. That encompasses measuring trends, discovering patterns and investigating anomalies in the collected data using cookie- and server-based tracking [7].

Data gathered by cookies for web analytics (WA) include information about the device and operating system used as well as customer behavior on the company's website. Considering that cookies are not available on some mobile devices, server-based tracking can be the solution to logging users' clicks while shopping online, clicking on advertisement banners or opening links from marketing emails [7]. Powered by Google, "Universal Analytics" is a solution for tracking people's behavior and interactions online, regardless of the browser or device they used [7].

Offering companies metrics for measuring digital marketing performance, web analytics can be of great significance for the profitability of marketing campaigns. To demonstrate how crucial its role is, we provide, as an example, a framework proposed by [38] that outlines the digital marketing performance measurement process and tools in use (Figure 3.6). The process starts with performing the digital marketing activities using marketing campaigns, email and social media. The second step is about automated data collection using tools such as Google Analytics and online surveys, among others. Then, analysts perform in-depth data analysis in order to discover valuable insights into customers' behavior

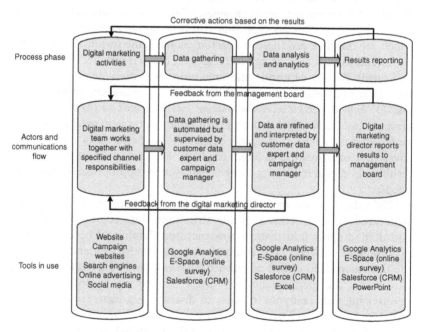

Figure 3.6 Digital marketing performance measurement process and tools in use

Source: Adapted from [38], p. 124.

and preferences. The last phase is about interpreting and presenting the results, which are then used as input to repeat the process [38].

Being able to integrate different types of measure, web analytics provides many advantages for the digital marketing team. It is useful, however, to know in advance what types of data need to be considered for analytics because it makes it easier to choose and plan the correct marketing strategies [24].

The data in Figure 3.7, adapted from [24], are partitioned into three layers. The operational data, located in the first layer, represent the information collected from various tools. The tactical data, located in the middle layer, are for evaluating profitability as well as level of engagement of online users. Finally, the strategic data provide the big picture for executives and senior managers using scorecards and dashboards, and representing trends and performance comparisons with competitors [24]. Overall, it can be concluded that successful measurement of marketing performance needs proper planning of the marketing metrics that depends on the characteristics of the organization [38].

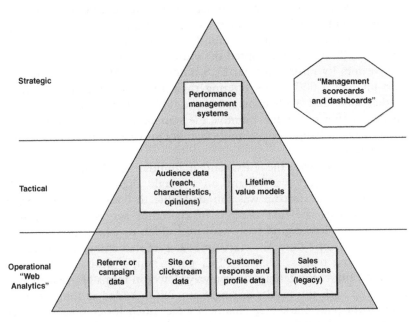

Figure 3.7 Different data types within a performance management system for internet marketing
Source: Adapted from [24], p. 427.

3.5   Case Study

In this section, we discuss a start-up in the educational sector that introduced an innovative idea into the market but found its future cut short due to its inability to take well-informed decisions regarding its digital strategy.

Founded in 2010, Tutorspree was a digital start-up aiming to offer web-based tuition services to students in need. Having graduated from the famous Y Combinator in 2011 [39, 40], Tutorspree introduced an innovative idea into the education industry by offering an online marketplace where students could find tutors to help them with their courses. Introduced as the "Airbnb" of tutoring [39, 40], the application enabled prospective interested parents to type in their location and search for available tutors. The application then showed a list of tutors along with their details, price and availability for the parents to choose from. Tutorspree made sure to follow a very strict, carefully controlled screening process that allowed only tutors with the right qualifications and enough classroom experience to sign up to the platform [39–41].

Offering its services at an affordable price, the student–tutor matching start-up was holding a strong competitive advantage. Entering a market where a "monopoly" was in place, with the main competitors offering similar services either large established agencies or the controversial Craigslist, Tutorspree disrupted the industry and grabbed the attention of investors by raising in total $1.8 million. By 2013, the educational start-up had 7,000 tutors offering their services through the online marketplace and had managed to double its revenues [39, 40]. However, after only a few months, the start-up fell apart. According to its founders, it happened due to its inability to scale up. But why did this really happen?

As Aaron Harris, the CEO and a founder of Tutorspree, stated later, the start-up was reliant on a single digital marketing tool, SEO. When the start-up was founded, due to limited funding, SEO was chosen as the first method of customer acquisition as it was a completely free digital tool, with no hidden or exponentially rising costs. After some time, the start-up began implementing a wide range of marketing tactics, such as PPC, partnerships, deals and targeted mailings, but the outcomes were always lower in terms of performance compared with the results arising from SEO. Added to that, conversions from paid marketing channels were much lower than the conversion rates from SEO. As a result, the founders of Tutorspree were strongly convinced that SEO was a very valuable tactic for achieving high traffic as well as high revenues [41, 42].

> **POINT OF ATTENTION:** Implementing a strong digital marketing strategy is crucial for achieving strategic business goals and ultimately for the success of the start-up. Adopting a combination of marketing tools and tactics such as SEO, PPC, affiliate and search advertising provides diversification; relying too much on only one digital tool or channel can prove disastrous for the viability of the company.

As reported by the founders, the effectiveness of SEO blinded them so that they favored it over other existing marketing tools [41]. As a result, in March 2013 when Google changed its underlying algorithm, Tutorspree saw a sharp 80 percent decline in its traffic [41]. After this, the start-up turned to alternative marketing tactics but, as they were already weak and achieving low results, the situation could not be saved. After three years of operation, the New York-based start-up that had expanded into more than five cities in the USA announced that it was shutting down [41].

The major lesson to be learned from this start-up story is that every business, entrepreneur and investor should be extremely careful when deciding on their marketing strategy. Investing in multiple tactics, in order to spread the risk, and being aware of the benefits as well as the challenges of each tool, in this case the fact that a business has no control over SEO, constitutes the best *and safest* method for achieving steady growth and desired goals [41, 42].

3.6   Summary

The present chapter discussed the importance of digital marketing for today's organizations and analyzed the profound impact of the digital marketing strategy on the firm's goals and overall success.

First, the chapter introduced the concept of digital marketing and defined it, per the DMI, as "the use of digital technologies to create an integrated, targeted and measurable communication which helps to acquire and retain customers while building deeper relationships with them" [3, 43, 44]. It explained that digital marketing aims to promote the products and services of a business by focusing on the customers and creating a relationship of trust and loyalty with them. The different types of media that businesses can utilize today – paid, owned and earned – were presented and discussed.

Next, the chapter described how understanding and engaging with customers is a significant success factor for businesses in general and for entrepreneurial start-ups in particular. Social media platforms are tools that businesses can use to listen to and communicate with their existing as well as their potential customers. Additionally, the chapter explained the seven stages for successful customer engagement: connection, interaction, satisfaction, retention, commitment, advocacy and engagement. These stages can yield four different types of customer depending on their levels of emotional bond, relational exchange and engagement on different social media platforms.

Furthermore, the chapter discussed the importance of a digital marketing strategy for driving the company in the right direction. It thoroughly presented the benefits of a digital strategy – reaching global audiences, low implementation costs, achieving high revenues and high conversion rates. Moreover, it introduced the four most prominent and effective digital tactics, namely email marketing, social media marketing, search advertising and affiliate marketing, that companies embed in their marketing strategies in order to attract and retain customers, gain exposure, enhance brand awareness and increase sales. The chapter described each tactic in detail, explaining how each can be applied in practice as well as its accompanying benefits and possible challenges for the organization.

Moreover, the chapter explored how businesses can use web analytics to analyze the data collected from their online customers, using cookies and server data to measure and track the efficiency of digital marketing campaigns and uncover interesting patterns. Additionally, it gave a taxonomy of the different types of analytical data, explaining how top management and executives can use strategic data to get valuable insights into the performance of each adopted marketing tactic and the market competition.

Finally, the chapter presented a case study of a start-up that entered the educational sector with an innovative idea and disrupted the existing market but, despite attracting attention from investors and raising almost $1.8 million in funding, announced its shutdown just three years after it was founded. The lesson learned was not to depend on only one digital tool, which is a valuable lesson for start-ups, entrepreneurs and investors alike.

References

1. Ryan D, Jones C. *Understanding Digital Marketing*. Kogan Page (2009).
2. Hemann C, Burbary K. *Digital Marketing Analytics: Making Sense of Consumer Data in a Digital World*. Que Publishing (2013).
3. Royle J, Laing A. The Digital Marketing Skills Gap: Developing a Digital Marketer Model for the Communication. *International Journal of Information Management* (2014) 34:65–73. doi: 10.1177/0266242610391936.

4. Baltes LP. Content Marketing – The Fundamental tool of Digital Marketing. *Bulletin of Transilvania University of Braşov. Series V: Economic Sciences* (2015) 111–18.
5. George D, Hatt T. Global Mobile Trends, GSMA Intelligence (2016).
6. Virgin Media Business. Your Guide to Digital Marketing – Unleash the Power of Digital Marketing. www.virginmediabusiness.co.uk/insights/your-guide-to-digital-marketing/ [accessed March 19, 2018].
7. Stokes R, The Minds of Quirk. *eMarketing: The Essential Guide to Marketing in a Digital World*, 5th ed. Quirk eMarketing (Pty) Ltd. (2013).
8. VanBoskirk S, Verblow B, Johnston K, Majewski B, Sobchuk A, Birrell R. The US Digital Marketing Forecast, 2018 to 2023: Diverse Budget Priorities Will Boost Spend to Nearly $150 Billion. Forrester (2019).
9. Machin E. What Is Earned, Owned & Paid Media? The Difference Explained. (2017) www.titan-seo.com/newsarticles/trifecta.html [accessed May 23, 2020].
10. Meyer K. The Difference between Earned, Owned & Paid Media. (2017) https://blog.hubspot.com/marketing/earned-owned-paid-media-lead-generation [accessed May 23, 2020].
11. Smith KT. Longitudinal Study of Digital Marketing Strategies Targeting Millennials. *Journal of Consumer Marketing* (2012) 29:86–92. doi: 10.1108/07363761211206339.
12. Cave J. Digital Marketing vs. Traditional Marketing: Which One Is Better? (2016) www.digitaldoughnut.com/articles/2016/july/digital-marketing-vs-traditional-marketing [accessed March 19, 2018].
13. SAS. Digital Marketing – What It Is and Why It Matters. (2017) www.sas.com/en_us/insights/marketing/digital-marketing.html# [accessed May 23, 2020].
14. Microsoft Dynamics. *Connected Customer Centricity: Customer Relationship Management in the Digital Age*. Microsoft (2010).
15. Rowley J. Understanding Digital Content Marketing. *Journal of Marketing Management* (2008) 24:517–40. doi: 10.1362/026725708X325977.
16. Saunders M. Understanding Your Digital Customer, Tomorrow Today (2010).
17. Shabbir MS, Ghazi MS, Mehmood AR. Impact of Social Media Applications on Small Business Entrepreneurs. *Arabian Journal of Business and Management Review* (2016) 6:1–3. doi: 10.4172/2223-5833.1000203.
18. Zohra G. The Digital in Store and the Re-enchantment of the Customer Experience: What Impact on the Immersion in the Experience of Consumption? *Journal of Knowledge Management, Economics and Information Technology* (2014) IV:1–12.
19. Sashi CM. Customer Engagement, Buyer-Seller Relationships, and Social Media. *Management Decision* (2012) 50:253–72. doi: 10.1108/00251741211203551.
20. Faulkner R. 10 Benefits of Digital Marketing vs Traditional Marketing. (2013) www.businesszone.co.uk/community-voice/blogs/robbo75/10-benefits-of-digital-marketing-v-traditional-marketing [accessed May 23, 2020].

21. Victor. Digital Marketing and Its 13 Benefits to Drive Your Business Growth [Infographic]. (2020) https://mytasker.com/blog/benefits-of-digital-marketing/ [accessed May 23, 2020].

22. MacDougall A. Top 6 Benefits of Digital Marketing. (2018) www.simplycast.com/blog/top-6-benefits-of-digital-marketing/ [accessed May 23, 2020

23. Nibusinessinfo.co.uk. Develop a Digital Marketing Plan – The Benefits of Digital Marketing. (2017) www.nibusinessinfo.co.uk/content/benefits-digital-marketing [accessed May 23, 2020].

24. Chaffey D, Ellis-Chadwick F, Mayer R, Johnston K. *Internet Marketing: Strategy, Implementation and Practice*, 3rd ed. Pearson Prentice Hall (2006).

25. Netmark.com. The 6 Fundamentals of Digital Marketing. (2015) www.netmark.com/the-6-fundamentals-for-digital-marketing-success/ [accessed May 23, 2020].

26. TutorialsPoint. Digital Marketing. (2018) www.tutorialspoint.com/digital_marketing/index.htm [accessed May 23, 2020].

27. Zhang XA, Kumar V, Cosguner K. Dynamically Managing a Profitable Email Marketing Program. *Journal of Marketing Research* (2017) 54 (6):851–66.

28. Nakara WA, Benmoussa FZ, Jaouen A. (2012) Entrepreneurship and Social Media Marketing: Evidence from French Small Business. *International Journal of Entrepreneurship and Small Business* 16:386–404. doi: 10.1504/IJESB.2012.047608.

29. DeMers J. The Top 10 Benefits of Social Media Marketing. (2014) www.forbes.com/sites/jaysondemers/2014/08/11/the-top-10-benefits-of-social-media-marketing/#41adae3a1f80 [accessed May 23, 2020].

30. Chaffey D. Global Social Media Research Summary 2017. (2020) www.smartinsights.com/social-media-marketing/social-media-strategy/new-global-social-media-research/ [accessed May 23, 2020].

31. Keath J. 5 Unpublished Stats on the Future of Social Media Marketing. (2016) www.socialfresh.com/the-future-of-social-media-marketing-stats/ [accessed May 23, 2020].

32. Smart Insights. Search Engine Statistics 2020 – Smart Insights Digital Marketing Advice. (2020) www.smartinsights.com/search-engine-marketing/search-engine-statistics/ [accessed May 23, 2020].

33. Patrutiu-Baltes L. Inbound Marketing – The Most Important Digital Marketing Strategy. *Bulletin of Transilvania University Brasov. Series V: Economic Sciences* (2016) 9:61–8.

34. Morris C. 7 Incredible Benefits of PPC Advertising. (2019) www.searchenginejournal.com/ppc-guide/ppc-advertising-benefits/#close [accessed May 23, 2020].

35. Ahuja V. Market Influence Analytics in a Digital Ecosystem. *International Journal of Online Marketing* (2012) 2:42–53. doi: 10.4018/ijom.2012100103.

36. Chen H, Chiang RHL, Storey VC. Business Intelligence and Analytics: From Big Data to Big Impact. *MIS Q* (2012) 36:1165–88.

37. Morabito V. *Big Data and Analytics*. Springer International (2015).

38. Järvinen J, Karjaluoto H. The Use of Web Analytics for Digital Marketing Performance Measurement. *Industrial Marketing Management* (2015) 50:117–27. doi: 10.1016/j.indmarman.2015.04.009.
39. Tsotsis A. YC-Backed Tutorspree Is an Airbnb for Tutoring. (2011) https://techcrunch.com/2011/01/26/tutorspree/ [accessed May 23, 2020].
40. Taylor C. Tutorspree, the Tutor-Matching Startup Backed by Sequoia and YC, Shuts Down. (2013) https://techcrunch.com/2013/09/08/tutorspree-shut-down [accessed May 23, 2020].
41. Harris A. When SEO Fails: Single Channel Dependency and the End of Tutorspree. (2014) www.aaronkharris.com/when-seo-fails-single-channel-dependency-and-the-end-of-tutorspree [accessed May 23, 2020].
42. Chan J. What These 4 Startup Case Studies Can Teach You about Failure. (2018) https://foundrmag.com/4-startup-case-studies-failure/ [accessed March 19, 2018].
43. Wymbs C. Digital Marketing: The Time for a New "Academic Major" Has Arrived. *Journal of Marketing Education* (2011) 33:93–106. doi: 10.1177/0273475310392544.
44. Smith KL. What Is Digital Marketing? (2007) http://digitalmarketing101.blogspot.ch/2007/10/what-is-digital-marketing.html [accessed May 23, 2020].

4 Digital Entrepreneurship Education and Skills

4.1 Introduction

Digitally oriented firms utilize advancements in information and communications technologies (ICTs) to provide customers with innovative digital products, services or both. As explained in previous chapters, start-up companies are characterized by their digital marketing activities, digital selling channels and generally digitized business processes. Similar to other businesses, however, there are certain skills that any entrepreneur needs, including leadership skills, proper goal orientation, the ability and willingness to take risks, management skills, as well as creativity and innovation. Mixing the entrepreneurial mindset with digital skills can help digitally oriented entrepreneurial start-ups to achieve their intended marketing penetration.

Mastering digital skills is fundamental for the sustainability of the digital business. These skills include effective communication and networking, good finance management, analytical abilities, proper branding strategies, and the ability to learn from mistakes in order to adapt business models [1]. Additionally, open innovation is expected to be at the core of the firm's strategy, to help the company succeed long term and become an effective member of the open innovation ecosystem [2]. The following points summarize some of the most important skills an entrepreneur needs to have for setting up and managing successful digital entrepreneurship:

- **Presentation and communication**: Pitching new ideas to investors requires excellent presentation and communication skills, thus, they are amongst the most important skills for an entrepreneur to develop. An investor is more likely to pursue the opportunity presented if the entrepreneur displays excellent communication skills and delivers a well-structured and clear presentation [1, 3, 4]. Additionally, good communicators can motivate team members to get better outcomes and reflect confidence and respect [1].

- **Finance management**: Learning how to manage the business capital is essential for any business owner, to avoid wasting valuable resources especially during the important early stages [1, 5].
- **Big data analysis**: As presented in Chapter 3, there are many resources available for collecting data about the customers of a digital business, but the successful entrepreneur must understand the nature of these resources and know how to use the analytics data that they generate [1].
- **Creativity**: Creativity is defined as the process of forming an original idea. Within business contexts, however, that idea must also be appropriate, useful and possible to implement [6]. Creativity as a skill is usually considered an enabler for innovation; as such, it is an important skill that needs more attention from entrepreneurial course providers [5, 7].
- **Ability to respond to changes**: Market fluctuations happen frequently, so the entrepreneur must be flexible enough to cope with changing customer and market demands [4].
- **Digital marketing**: One of the main marketing streams, digital marketing, whether on the firm's website or through social media, offers a variety of marketing channels that entrepreneurs need to cultivate in order to understand customers and gain better market penetration [1, 5].

Considered as a tool for economic development, entrepreneurship helps to energize and stimulate economic growth [8]. Its importance stems from its ability to form new businesses that lead to additional national income, employment for young graduates and motivation for innovation [9].

4.2 The Entrepreneur

As detailed in Chapter 1, entrepreneurship can be defined as the practice of spotting and defining problems and exploring opportunities for the sake of creating innovative products or services that can address them [10–12]. Consequently, entrepreneurship is a practical activity; it is not a "gene" or habit that an entrepreneur possesses, although behavioral traits may enable entrepreneurship [9]. Based on that, an entrepreneur is a person who uses innovation skills to create value, reflected in a new product or service, to address emerging opportunities. Figure 4.1 illustrates the process that entrepreneurs go through until achieving their intended financial and social goals, as proposed by Bolton and Thompson [13]. In this diagram, note that the urge to "make a difference" is thought to be one of the main motivators for an entrepreneur embarking on the entrepreneurial process [13]. More

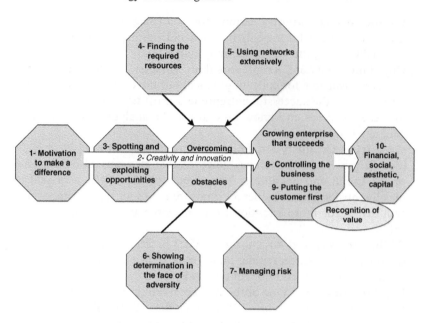

Figure 4.1 The entrepreneurial process
Source: Adapted from [13], p. 33.

importantly, recognize that the entrepreneur's ability to "create and innovate" is at the heart of the process.

The actual process starts when the entrepreneur spots an opportunity that attracts their attention, followed by attempts to exploit it by finding relevant resources from the entrepreneur's network. Pitching the opportunity to potential investors requires determination and persistence as well as knowledge of risk management. After establishing the project, the entrepreneur needs to be able to manage and control the business effectively and to have a well-planned strategy that makes customers the central focus by engaging and listening to them [13, 14]. As illustrated, the successful initiation of the start-up is followed by recognition of the value and capital creation [13, 15].

Acting as opportunity spotter, the entrepreneur might exploit prospects of making money, creating social entrepreneurship, or producing something of artistic value that the inventor of the idea might not be aware of [13]. It is important, however, for entrepreneurs to realize that gap in the market based on the environment they exist and function within and the talent they have. Figure 4.2 shows how entrepreneurs spot and exploit an opportunity by acting as the champion of the project they embark upon.

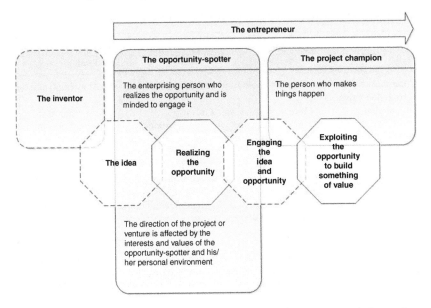

Figure 4.2 The entrepreneur, the opportunity-spotter and the project champion
Source: Adapted from [13], p. 34.

After spotting the opportunity and embarking on the project, entrepreneurs need implementation abilities to make things happen, to allocate the relevant resources while acting as the project champion. Successful entrepreneurs need both skills – to be able to come up with innovative ideas but also to be able to make them take shape.

4.3   The Entrepreneurial Education Process

Considering its role as a major driver for economic growth, job creation and stability for uncertain economies, the exponential growth of entrepreneurial education is justified in the higher education sector [16]. Table 4.1 summarizes the areas that are affected by entrepreneurial education and explains its importance for the individual, organizational and societal levels. Note how teaching an entrepreneur-relative curriculum has different impacts on higher education institutions compared to secondary schools. The former perceive entrepreneurial curricula and education as an engine for job creation, economic stability and success in ever-changing markets and societies, while the latter see it as a source of joy, engagement and creativity [16].

Table 4.1 *Why entrepreneurial education is important*

	Individual level	Organizational level	Societal level
Commonly stated reasons for entrepreneurial education, but less effective in schools and for embedded approaches			
Job creation	More individuals are needed that are willing and able to create job growth	Growing organizations create more jobs	Entrepreneurship and innovation are primary paths to growth and job creation
Economic success	Entrepreneurship can give individuals economic success	Organizational renewal is fundamental to every firm's long-term success	Renewal processes are fundamental to the vitality of economies
Globalization, innovation and renewal	People need entrepreneurial skills and abilities to thrive in an ever-changing world	Entrepreneurial firms play a crucial role in changing market structures	A deregulated and flexible market requires people with higher-level general skills
Rarely stated reasons for entrepreneurial education, but promising for schools and embedded approaches			
Joy, engagement, creativity	Creation/value creation/creativity is a main source of joy and pride for people	Employee creativity and joy are essential for the performance of new and existing organizations	The economic wealth of nations correlates with the happiness of their citizens
Societal challenges	People can make a difference to society, and marginalized people can achieve economic success	Corporations can collaborate with small social entrepreneurship initiatives to create social value	Social entrepreneurship addresses problems in society that the market economy has failed to address

Source: Adapted from [16].

Additionally, regardless of the level receiving the entrepreneurial education, value creation must be at the core and the main goal of the education process within entrepreneurial programs [16]. Students can develop entrepreneurial competencies by creating value for sponsors or stakeholders from outside the institution, thus "learning by creating

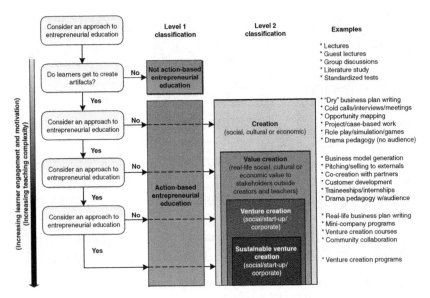

Figure 4.3 Classification of action-based entrepreneurial education
Source: Adapted from [16], p. 24.

value" is very important for students. Value creation tends to happen depending on the level of action-based entrepreneurial education (Figure 4.3). In Figure 4.3, the assumption is that the highest level of value creation can be achieved at a higher level of education that requires more complex teaching practices. Consequently, factors such as purpose, ability, resources, interest as well as relevance can be controlled by the education provider. However, educational institutions need to be careful about the deliverables in order to make sure that they represent value or venture for the potential investors, and not only a business plan [17].

In order for educators to get students involved in the value creation process and thus develop entrepreneurial competencies, they have to give innovation-based assignments that motivate learners to create value or venture [16]. Figure 4.4 illustrates how educational assignments can play a part in triggering different kinds of entrepreneurial competencies such as emotional events, situations and activities. As displayed in Figure 4.4, educational assignments involve recurring interactions with communities outside the institution boundaries. This can trigger motivation to work as a team to face the uncertainty, ambiguity and confusion associated with dealing with outside

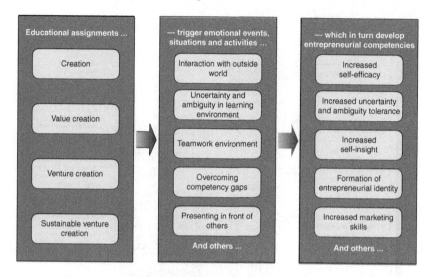

Figure 4.4 A model of entrepreneurial education and outcomes
Source: Adapted from [16], p. 27.

problems in order to identify opportunities and innovative solutions to them. Successful handling of problems as a team can help students to have increased self-efficacy and self-insight as well as to develop better marketing skills, tolerance for uncertainty and ambiguity, and clearer entrepreneurial identity. Additionally, examples of the methods and tools that can be used in each level of the creation process are provided in what follows to further explain the process of value creation.

The significance of value creation as an outcome of entrepreneurial activities has motivated many researchers to propose various models and frameworks to help entrepreneurs achieve successful value creation. On the basis of the discussion provided by [16], the following points list six tools or approaches that help in delivering entrepreneurial education in an effective manner:

• **Effectuation**: Considered as a powerful tool for the educator, value creation through effectuation is achieved by iterating through a decision-making process and active commitment. Usually, the iterations start with questions about the identity, knowledge, past experiences and network of the learner that help in identifying their current status and resources and assessing what is needed to address the problem under study [20].

- **Business model canvas**: This canvas proposed by [18] can be seen as a nine-item checklist that reflects the building blocks of value creation, namely categorizing customers into segments, specifying value proposition and marketing channels, planning customer relationship strategies, defining revenue streams, identifying key resources, sketching key activities and partnerships, and planning cost structures [18]. These steps are especially useful when carried out in a group because group members can discuss and share ideas [16].
- **Customer development / Lean start-up**: These two concepts share many ideas, methods and tools that put emphasis on testing the viability of the product to create value for the customers in the real world. Similarly, educators can use the tools offered by these two concepts to teach students how to approach the real business world and get people involved in the testing process [16].
- **Appreciative inquiry**: This theoretical framework focuses on opportunities and generating new ideas instead of being hindered by problems. It uses positive energy and joy to motivate team members. By using this theory, team members can learn from past experiences to make a better future by adapting to changes [16].
- **Service learning**: Following [16], this term is defined as "an organized educational experience that both meets needs of the community and fulfills learning objectives" [19]. This tool tries to achieve learning goals by providing services to the community. The challenge here, however, is the ability of educators to design activities that can fulfill both the community's needs and learning goals [16].
- **Design thinking**: The word "design" can have various meanings depending on the context it is used in. When talking about entrepreneurial education, "design" can be defined as "a process of actions and decisions aimed at producing products, services, environments, and systems that addresses a problem and improves people's lives" [20] (p. 409). Design thinking goes beyond the "necessity" to the "possibility" of creating value through an iterative process of spotting opportunities, conceptualizing possible ideas and testing them with potential users [16].

4.4   Innovation and Successful Entrepreneurial Education

Innovation, as already described, is a process that firms utilize to introduce or adopt new approaches to producing products and designing services [21]. Both the significance of and the increasing demand for successful entrepreneurship knowledge that is based on innovation have motivated some educational institutions to set up entrepreneurial programs that help young people in building sustainable start-ups [22]. Despite entrepreneurship's importance for the economy and the innovation ecosystem, however, it seems that innovation-based entrepreneurship as a mindset is still not well embedded within the educational system in Europe; the level of entrepreneurial attitude is less than desired [23]. As an example, Figure 4.5, adapted from [23], provides an interesting comparison of how students in the USA and Europe in 2013 perceived the entrepreneurial education courses available. As can be seen, entrepreneurial education is somehow responsible for promoting an entrepreneurial attitude in Europe; it allows students to develop a sense of initiative and to better understand the role of entrepreneurs in society [23].

Additionally, 41 percent of the students in Europe agreed that entrepreneurship degrees trained them in skills that are relevant for establishing and running a business, compared to 54 percent in the United States. However, overall, Europe seemed to lag behind in the intention to create new ventures as only 28 percent of the students in Europe showed an interest in pursuing entrepreneurship as a targeted profession after graduation, compared to 39 percent in the United States [23]. These figures

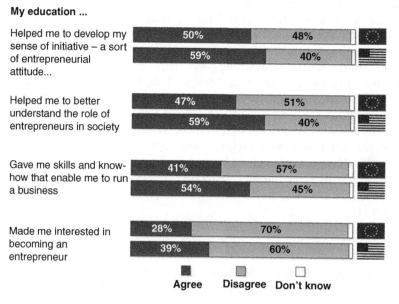

Figure 4.5 Entrepreneurship and the educational system: the EU versus the USA
Source: Adapted from [23].

make it necessary to analyze the situation further. Taking these issues into account, according, for example, to [22], the success of these entrepreneurial programs depends on factors such as the focus of the program, the design of the curriculum and how these are aligned to market needs:

- **The focus of the program**: Innovation can be a driver for start-up firms and established corporations. Developing an entrepreneurial mentality means that students need to learn how to think and to conceptualize innovative ideas by conducting relevant research and development (R&D) activities as well as measuring the value generated in order to optimize the new product or service. According to [22], such skills need to be tailored according to the focus of the program: start-up entrepreneurs in general or digitally focused entrepreneurs. For example, media professionals, communication/journalism educators, media entrepreneurs and entrepreneurship educators agree that entrepreneurship courses that are suitable for the media industry need to focus on team building, revenue streams and content development [24].

- **The curriculum**: Usually, universities and colleges design their degrees by having cross-listed courses among the programs. For example, a management curriculum could be taught in both management and entrepreneurship degrees [22]. Such practice could affect the focus of the entrepreneurship program since the contents of the module would not address the specific needs of students studying entrepreneurship; the viewpoints of the two programs are different. As in the previous point, the focus of the degree plays an important role in designing and shaping the curricula of the modules taught [22].

- **Alignment of the focus and curriculum with market needs**: Market needs and geographical locations dictate how entrepreneurship programs are designed. For example, if the institution is located in an area where opportunities for fresh graduates are limited, then both the focus and the curriculum should be aligned accordingly and should focus on skills that will help graduates to build their own start-up businesses [22].

Table 4.2 summarizes the previously mentioned characteristics and provides a comparison between start-up innovation and corporate innovation as targeted employment arenas after graduation. Note how the focus of the entrepreneurial program can affect how the curriculum is designed and how well it aligns with the market and skills needed to succeed.

4.5 Skills for Open Innovation

As explained in Chapter 2, open innovation refers to the process of establishing collaboration and sharing ideas and resources among different

Table 4.2 *Characteristics of entrepreneurship programs*

Characteristics	Start-up innovation	Corporate innovation
Focus	Value creation by designing and creating new products and services	Value creation by improving processes, revamping products and services, or conducting R&D
Curriculum	Technology versus design orientation coursework	Functional versus cross-functional coursework
Experiential learning	New venture competitions	Internships
Alignment with market needs	Digital versus traditional businesses	Small and medium enterprises versus large organizations
Skills	Systems thinking, problem solving, critical thinking and communication	Functional knowledge of business, teamwork and communication

Source: Adapted from [22].

types of organization with different cultures [21]. Collaboration, being central to open innovation, is thus an essential learning-by-doing skill that needs to be addressed in entrepreneurial programs offered in educational settings [25]. It is important for entrepreneurial course providers to offer multiple collaboration opportunities for students that allow them to exchange knowledge and experience [25]. Moreover, students can get additional benefits from intergenerational collaborating with experts from outside the university's environment. Table 4.3 lists possible collaboration channels and their characteristics among the different parties involved in the entrepreneurial-educational process, as proposed by [25].

Achieving the full potential of collaboration within entrepreneurial programs requires working in teams. Forming these teams, however, can require educators to overcome some limitations. Overfamiliarity among team members before the course starts, for example, is a limitation because it might affect the desired outcome; students might have a hidden agenda of how to work and what to achieve [26]. Nevertheless, the collaborative nature of open innovation cannot be successful without other factors such as diversity of team members' skills [27], willingness and readiness to exchange resources and information, acceptance of others' opinions, encouraging other team members, and trust, which is the basis for collaborative work and the co-creation of innovative value [25]. Additionally, trust is considered to be the enabler of knowledge flow among team members and partners within an open

Table 4.3 *Collaboration channels*

Collaboration channel	The character of collaboration
1 Intra-group collaboration	Within each group students divided responsibilities for product solution, finances, society or market research, exchanging findings and discussing further activities with their group-mates
2 Students–teachers collaboration	Teachers were open to discuss, consult and facilitate students' learning both at individual and at group level
3 Inter-group collaboration	At the end of each intermediate phase, groups presented their work and discussed the challenges faced with the other groups of students and the teachers who had to be their critical friends and potential partners
4 Students–entrepreneurs–teachers collaboration inside the university	Entrepreneurs were invited to share their experience and to answer students' questions, helping them to understand practical aspects of entrepreneurship as well as elaborate joint projects
5 Intergenerational collaboration with specialists from outside the university	Each group could recruit one member from outside the university when they realized that they needed specific experience and knowledge they didn't have

Source: Adapted from [25].

innovation ecosystem [25]. Trust among partners can facilitate risk-taking because of the increased connectivity and frequent successful interaction to which it leads. The significance of trust means that entrepreneurship educators must enable interaction as well as effective communication among the players at different levels within the institution – the students, tutors, entrepreneurs and investors [25]. Moreover, the university has the responsibility to clarify the benefits of such interaction for all parties.

4.6   E-leadership as an Enabler for Innovation

E-leadership is considered a necessary skill that needs to be further supported by policymakers in European countries, among others. It enables the use of innovative digital technologies that facilitate strategic digital transformation. E-leadership as a skill is in high demand as of 2020 as Europe currently requires 40,000 new e-leaders every year [28].

Successful e-leaders need to have certain skills and abilities and these include strategic leadership as well as being digital and business savvy. Strategic leadership is important because it helps entrepreneurs in managing interdisciplinary and multicultural teams and external stakeholders. Additionally, having the skills to run innovative businesses and seize the opportunities offered by new digital innovations and trends helps entrepreneurs to be successful e-leaders [28, 29].

E-leadership skills can be classified into *strategic*, *practitioner* and *user* skills. As proposed by [29], these can be visualized as an "atomium" – see Figure 4.6 – that reflects the connections among the three skill categories [29]. Within the "atomium," strategic skills are relevant for chief executive officers (CEOs), entrepreneurs, managers and visionaries who need to think and act in a strategic manner in order to make use of emerging digital technologies and allow innovative products and service to reach the market. Practitioner-related skills are relevant to those who have to use these skills to deal with current as well as future ICTs. More particularly, the skills here enable chief information officers (CIOs) to be vital

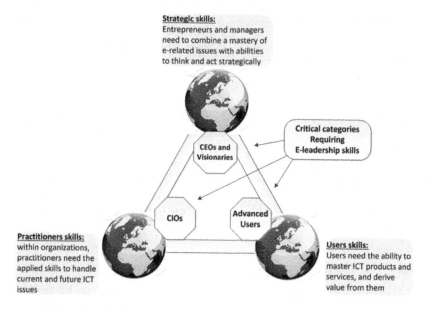

Figure 4.6 The e-leadership skills "atomium"
Source: Adapted from [29].

parts of the business strategy by fully aligning the firm's IT capacity with its innovation objectives.

Finally, the skills that are important for advanced users are those that enable them to get value from ICT products and services. It is crucial to realize that early engagement of these users in the planning and implementation process when creating innovative technologies helps to achieve the intended innovative goals such as accelerated adoption and increased innovation productivity. Having e-leadership skills means that the entrepreneur can spot business opportunities and develop business plans based on them, and, at the same time, knows how to use relevant technologies to transform these opportunities into real business ventures [29]. Thus, innovation, as an objective for entrepreneurs, requires several skills to enable it within start-ups and other businesses. Skills for innovation cover a wide range of competencies that need to be addressed by the entrepreneurial education system. The following points cover the most essential set of skills needed to promote and achieve innovation [29]:

- *starting point skills*, which cover the basic abilities for working in "knowledge-based" environments [29];
- *technical skills* such as managing engineering projects, implementing ICT-related projects, analyzing data and getting meaningful results, designing innovative products and services, exploring marketing channels and dealing with financial and legal issues [29];
- "*soft skills*," which include the ability to work in a team and collaborate efficiently and respectfully with team members [29];
- *cognitive skills*, such as creativity and critical thinking, which allow individuals to process and understand situations and make sense of data in order to transform them into meaningful information [29];
- *management skills* that enable the entrepreneur to handle management responsibilities such as risk-taking and dealing with failures [29];
- *leadership skills* that give the entrepreneur the ability to lead and influence the team [29].

Having these skills is essential; it can make a big difference in terms of ensuring successful initiation of the start-up venture and achievement of the intended innovation goals. However, it is also vital to recognize that the final goals of the start-up affect the skills set that is required for innovation, because the two are highly correlated. Thus, defining the required set of skills for innovation is considered a challenge because of the difficulty associated with exactly characterizing innovation as a process. Consequently, measuring how innovation changes over time and knowing what skills are needed at each stage is a difficult task [29].

4.7   Challenges of Entrepreneurial Education

Entrepreneurship, as a key competency for a sustainable innovation ecosystem, requires well-planned curricula in universities in particular and the school system in general. To develop successful entrepreneurial skills, however, program planners have to tackle several challenges that hinder effective entrepreneurship education [30, 31]. This section will cover most of the challenges covered in the literature and introduce a model that can be used by educators to achieve better entrepreneurial education.

4.7.1   Key Issues

The following points list the main obstacles and issues discovered in research into entrepreneurial education in various countries that need to be addressed in order to have fruitful implementation of entrepreneurial education [16, 30–34]:

- **Lack of mutually constructive relationships with industry**: Educators and schools must find a way to facilitate relationships that benefit both parties. Institutions need to discover and maintain research channels with organizations, and companies need to approach educational establishments when they require innovative solutions to problems [33].
- **Lack of sufficient practical content in courses**: Programs need to be designed in a way that allows interactions between students and business experts from various fields. Such interactions will allow students to view success stories as good experience as well as motivation [30, 32].
- **Higher financial needs than other courses**: Successful implementation of entrepreneurship courses requires institutions to invest in necessary infrastructure [16, 30]. It also requires program managers to arrange field visits that allow students to get in touch with and see real-life entrepreneurs and businesses in action. All of this requires additional funding compared to other courses [16, 32].
- **Teachers lacking specialized / up-to-date training**: Teachers within entrepreneurship programs need to have proper and specialized entrepreneurship-related training that covers relevant topics. Additionally, refresher courses need to be offered in order for educators to keep up to date and be able to deliver valuable materials and contents to students [32].
- **Ill-planned curricula**: Many researchers have identified this issue as a main failing factor for entrepreneurship programs. Adequate planning

is a must to ensure proper phasing and integration of the modules within the program [30]. Additionally, curricula need to pay attention to "problem-based learning activities" instead of focusing only on developing theoretical business plans that don't provide practical problem-solving experience [30].

- **Lack of common expectations among involved parties**: Well-planned entrepreneurial programs require the involvement of many stakeholders with different expectations and goals. Failing to level out these expectations can cause problems in the running of successful entrepreneurship courses [16, 31].

4.7.2 Best Practices for Entrepreneurship Educators

A course in entrepreneurial education should be mainly a practical one that aims to engage students with real-world problem-solving experiences by facilitating their getting in contact with entrepreneurs and experts from the business world. Having this in mind, the various stakeholders need to address the challenges outlined in Section 4.7.1 to achieve uniformity in course content and to meet all parties' expectations and goals. Table 4.4 lists recommendations and best practices for entrepreneurship educators based on [34].

Real-world experience gained by experiential learning [30, 34] and problem-based learning [25] can help students to deal with realistic

Table 4.4 *Best practices and strategies that entrepreneurship educators should promote*

1 Experiential learning, rather than transmission of knowledge
2 Diversity of educational experiences
3 Learners' active participation and student-approved systems to enhance student motivation in the learning process
4 Multidisciplinary approaches
5 Direct participation of experienced entrepreneurs in training programs
6 Experience of failure in the learning process
7 Risk, responsibility and opportunity identification training
8 Individual meta-competences
9 Contingency and constructivist approaches
10 Use of the Internet/online social media
11 A portfolio of techniques to practice entrepreneurship
12 Adaptation of programs to cultural contexts
13 Entrepreneurial environment, mindsets and attitudes

Source: Adapted from [34].

business mistakes and understand organizations' strategies. Thus, it is important for educational institutions to build mutually beneficial connections with industries, which could enable students to learn from their experiences and strategies [30, 34]. In addition, diversity and cultural contexts need to be considered while designing and implementing entrepreneurial programs [34]. Furthermore, governments can play an important role in entrepreneurial venture by building bridges between universities and businesses and by providing support for viable business ideas [34]. Problem-based solving is another aspect that needs to be given special attention by entrepreneurial education providers. Its importance motivated the researchers in [25] to propose a seven-step opportunity-oriented problem-based model (see Figure 4.7) that can be used by institutions to enhance and develop students' entrepreneurship. According to [25], this model has been tested in European and Asian universities, where groups of three to six students started by creating a database of problems. Then they discussed and decided on which problem to solve. Later, after a few iterations of presenting prototypes

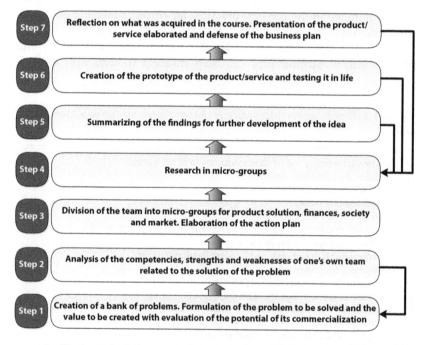

Figure 4.7 An opportunity-oriented, problem-based learning model
Source: Adapted from [25], p. 4.

to potential investors, refining the product through extra research, and presenting again, the model proved to be effective in guiding the students through the entrepreneurial process [25].

4.8   Case Study

In this section, we discuss a digital entrepreneurial education provider that has utilized digital technologies, enabling it to accomplish its strategic goals and provide a unique educational system.

The case study relates to a school in Liverpool called "The Studio." Established in 2013, it delivers specialized gaming and digital media education in addition to the traditional high school curricula [35–36]. However, what makes this school unique is that it is located within the Baltic Triangle area in the city of Liverpool, which is famous for having multiple digital start-ups led by digital-savvy entrepreneurs [35–36]. Consequently, the school's proximity to and connections with the digitally focused industrial firms are very beneficial for the enrolled students, providing them with direct support from creative experts and learning from entrepreneurs' real-life experiences [35–36].

Among the three pathways that the school offers, those focused on entrepreneurship and creativity are considered to be very attractive for students with a creative and innovation-oriented mindset [36]. As the school principal describes it: "The Studio is a thriving learning hub providing innovative, partner-led applied education for the next generation of creative and digital entrepreneurs. The Studio blurs the divide between school and employment by providing a professional environment and ethos in which future digital leaders can thrive" [35].

The framework adopted at The Studio is CREATE, which is based on various skills typologies, including communication and emotional intelligence [35], that aim to equip students for entrepreneurship as well as employment [35–36]. Students' experience at The Studio is integrated with strong partnership with main players in the digital market such as Doris, Ripstone and Catalyst, all prominent producers of digital contents and solutions [37]. The success achieved by The Studio has prompted the UK Office for Standards in Education, Children's Services and Skills (Ofsted) to give it a good evaluation [38]. More particularly, the students have the education they receive at the school and regard their teachers as partners and collaborators [35].

POINT OF ATTENTION: This case study shows how successful entrepreneurial education cannot be achieved without strong connection and collaboration with industry specialists. Building such mutually successful relationships, however, requires dedication and patience from the involved stakeholders: educational institutions, industrial firms as well as policymakers.

Achieving successful entrepreneurial education requires thoughtful planning and collaboration with industry partners. Additionally, as can be seen from this case study, the focus of the curriculum is another success factor; finding collaborators with similar specialties is better than having a broad program. Finally, considering aspects like location can be of additional benefit for all parties involved, educational institutions, businesses and students.

4.9   Summary

This chapter has discussed digital and leadership skills that are essential for entrepreneurs seeking successful start-up initiation and long-run management. The skills range from soft skills such as effective communication and collaboration with others to technical skills that enable the entrepreneur to transform an opportunity into a viable business idea. Making sure that upcoming generations have the right set of skills, however, is the responsibility of the education system, which must offer well-planned and high-quality entrepreneurial education. The curricula have to equip students with the required knowledge by facilitating their interacting and working closely with other entrepreneurs and industry partners.

The discussion presented here covered the essential elements of planning and running entrepreneurship education. Understanding the context in which education is delivered can help in designing more-relevant curricula. Furthermore, students need to learn how to use digital innovation so that they can "pitch" their business ideas to potential investors and be able to exploit the available resources and networks in order to overcome obstacles and set up and run their business.

Having productive entrepreneurial education contributes to economic growth and provides job opportunities for young graduates. Additionally, open innovation, as an important enabler for successful digital entrepreneurship, requires productive collaboration among the involved parties. Consequently, curricula need to focus on specialized respect-based collaborative skills that will prepare students to work in the real world's open innovation hubs. E-leadership skills for different groups of users also need to be integrated within teaching materials and practical exercises.

There are several main challenges to successful planning and delivery of entrepreneurial education that need to be overcome across the board. However, as the case study showed, it can be done and well-planned entrepreneurial education alongside close working relationships with industrial partners can produce successful entrepreneurs.

References

1. Laurinavicius T. Ten Digital Skills You Need to Master to Become an Entrepreneur. (2016) http://observer.com/2016/10/ten-digital-skills-you-need-to-master-to-become-an-entrepreneur/ [accessed May 25, 2020].
2. Accenture. *The Promise of Digital Entrepreneurs*. Accenture/G20 Young Entrepreneurs' Alliance (2014).
3. Clark C. The Impact of Entrepreneurs' Oral "Pitch" Presentation Skills on Business Angels' Initial Screening Investment Decisions. *Ventur Cap* (2008) 10:257–79. doi: 10.1080/13691060802151945.
4. Braun P. Chapter 3: A Skilling Framework for Women Entrepreneurs in the Knowledge Economy. In: *Innovating Women: Contributions to Technological Advancement*. Published online March 8 (2015): 35–53. https://doi.org/10.1108/S2040-7246(2010)0000001008.
5. Jusoh R, Ziyae B, Asimiran S. Entrepreneur Training Needs Analysis: Implications on the Entrepreneurial Skills Needed for Successful Entrepreneurs. *International Business & Economics Research Journal* (2011) 10:143–8.
6. Amabile T. *How to Kill Creativity*. Harvard Business Review (1998).
7. Babu RR, Krishna MM, Swathi A. Role of Creativity and Innovation in Entrepreneurship. *Innovative Journal of Business and Management* (2013) 2:112–15.
8. Baijal R. 4 Reasons Why Entrepreneurship Is Important. (2016) www.entrepreneur.com/article/269796 [accessed May 25, 2020].
9. Anonymous. What Is an Entrepreneur? Understanding Who They Are and How They Can Benefit. *Strategic Direction* (2011) 27(6):22–5. doi: 10.1108/02580541111135571.
10. Shane S, Venkataraman S. The Promise of Entrepreneurship as a Field of Research. *Academy of Management Review* (2000) 25:217–26. doi: 10.2307/259271.
11. Álvaro Cuervo, Domingo Ribeiro SR. Entrepreneurship: Concepts, Theory and Perspective. *Entrepreneur* (2005) 21:11–21. doi: 10.1007/978-3-540-48543-8.
12. Ruiz J, Soriano DR, Coduras A. Challenges in Measuring Readiness for Entrepreneurship. *Management Decision* (2016) 54:1022–46. doi: 10.1108/MD-07-2014-0493.

13. Bolton B, Thompson J. *Entrepreneurs – Talent, Temperament, Technique*. 2nd ed. Oxford (2004).

14. Sashi CM. Customer Engagement, Buyer-Seller Relationships, and Social Media. *Management Decision* (2012) 50:253–72. doi: 10.1108/00251741211203551.

15. Rowley J. Understanding Digital Content Marketing. *Journal of Marketing Management* (2008) 24:517–40. doi: 10.1362/026725708X325977.

16. Lackéus M. Entrepreneurship in Education: What, Why, When, How. Background Paper OECD-LEED 1–45. (2015) doi: 10.1515/kbo-2016-0075.

17. Lackéus M, Williams Middleton K. Venture Creation Programs: Bridging Entrepreneurship Education and Technology Transfer. *Education + Training* (2015) 57:48–73. doi: 10.1108/ET-02-2013-0013.

18. Pigneur Y, Osterwalder A. *Business Model Generation: A Handbook for Visionaries, Game Changers, and Challengers*. John Wiley & Sons (2010).

19. Steinke P, Fitch P. Assessing Service-Learning. *Research & Practice in Assessment* (2007) 2:24–9.

20. Boni A, Weingart L, Evenson S. Innovation in an Academic Setting: Designing and Leading a Business through Market-Focused, Interdisciplinary Teams. *Academy of Management Learning and Education* (2009) 8:407–17. doi: 10.5465/AMLE.2009.44287939.

21. Marques JPC. Closed versus Open Innovation: Evolution or Combination? *International Journal of Business and Management* (2014) 9:196–203. doi: 10.5539/ijbm.v9n3p196.

22. Berry RI, Kumar A, Scott JP. Is Innovation Being Addressed in Entrepreneurship Undergraduate Programs? An Exploratory Study. Educ Res Int (2014) 2014.

23. Fosty V, Eleftheriadou D, Combes C, Willemsens B, Wauters P, Vezbergiene A. *Doing Business in the Digital Age: The Impact of New ICT Developments in the Global Business Landscape – Europe's Vision and Action Plan to Foster Digital Entrepreneurship*. Deloitte for the European Commission DG Enterprise and Industry (2013) 1–71.

24. Ferrier MB, Batts B. Educators and Professionals Agree on Outcomes for Entrepreneurship Courses. *Newspaper Research Journal* (2016) 37:322–38. doi: 10.1177/0739532916677054.

25. Oganisjana K. Promotion of University Students' Collaborative Skills in Open Innovation Environment. *Journal of Open Innovation: Technology, Market, and Complexity* (2015) 1(18). doi: 10.1186/s40852-015-0021-9.

26. Warhuus JP, Tanggaard L, Robinson S, Ernø SM. From I to We: Collaboration in Entrepreneurship Education and Learning? *Education and Training* (2017) 59:234–49.

27. Giuri P, Ploner M, Rullani F, Torrisi S. Skills, Division of Labor and Performance in Collective Inventions: Evidence from Open Source Software. *International Journal of Industrial Organization* (2010) 28:54–68. doi: 10.1016/j.ijindorg.2009.07.004.

28. Hüsing T, Dashja E, Gareis K, Korte WB, Stabenow T, Markus, P. e-Leadership Skills for Small and Medium Sized Enterprises – Final Report. EUR 2014.2859 EN. European Union (2015).
29. van Welsum D, Lanvin B. e-Leadership Skills Vision Report. Prepared for the European Commission, DG Enterprise and Industry, October (2012).
30. Agbonlahor AA. Challenges of Entrepreneurial Education in Nigerian Universities: Towards a Repositioning for Impact. *Journal of Educational and Social Research* (2016) 6:208–14. doi: 10.5901/jesr.2016.v6n1p208.
31. Ruskovaara E, Ikävalko M. *"You Get What You Measure" – Challenges of Entrepreneurship Education in Schools.* Pap Present NCSB (2008).
32. Nkirina SP. The Challenges of Integrating Entrepreneurship Education in the Vocational Training System: An Insight from Tanzania's Vocational Education Training Authority. *Journal of European Industrial Training* (2009) 34:153–66. doi: 10.1108/MBE-09-2016-0047.
33. Wardale D, Lord L. Bridging the Gap: The Challenges of Employing Entrepreneurial Processes within University Settings. *Higher Education Research & Development* (2016) 35:1068–82. doi: 10.1080/07294360.2016.1139549.
34. Naia A, Baptista R, Januário C, Trigo V. A Systematization of the Literature on Entrepreneurship Education: Challenges and Emerging Solutions in the Entrepreneurial Classroom. *Industry and Higher Education* (2014) 28:79–96. doi: 10.5367/ihe.2014.0196.
35. Tech North. Northern Schools Trust – The Studio Liverpool. In: Tech North Talent Ski Case Study. (2018) http://technorth.dontpanicprojects.com/casestudies [accessed May 25, 2020].
36. The Studio. What We Do. (2020) https://thestudioliverpool.uk/what-we-do/ Accessed May 25, 2020].
37. The Studio. Partners & Supporters. (2020) https://thestudioliverpool.uk/who-we-are/sponsors-and-partners/ [accessed May 25, 2020].
38. Ofsted. The Studio School Liverpool. (2019) https://reports.ofsted.gov.uk/provider/23/139589/ [accessed May 25, 2020].

Part II

Digital Business Systems

5 Digital ICT Challenges for Digital Entrepreneurship

5.1 Introduction

The digital age is changing the processes for many things, in government, in business, in the home, in the financial, health, retail, insurance and biotechnology sectors and so on. Financial technology service companies, also known as "fintechs," focus on driving the financial service sector through innovative ways of making payments, carrying out transactions and navigating the entire banking system. Fintech has been experiencing rapid growth internationally since 2015 when analysts marked a record high in this sector, with overall global investment exceeding US$19 billion and global funding to venture capitalist (VC) supported fintech companies rising by 106 percent from the previous year [1].

The insurance sector is also having its share of technology-driven innovations with tech-related businesses known as "insurtech" companies. The traditional model of insurance companies is the covering and underwriting of risks incurred by their clients. An individual who subscribes to insurance services has to be exposed to an accidental risk or loss of valuables to be entitled access to a premium paid on that particular insurance. Insurtech entrepreneurs are modifying such conventional techniques whereby they can foresee risks that their clients will encounter before they happen [2]. This type of predictive analysis is possible only through accumulated data, and such actionable insights aid in the development of relevant tech products and services. Achieving this feat requires strategic partnership among insurers, tech giants (who have access to big data) and insurtech entrepreneurs.

Digital entrepreneurs are also cashing in on tech-related changes in retail-based businesses. The retail sector is arguably the largest in any nation. It drives global trends, globalization and international trade. It links consumers with other areas of the economy while also connecting manufacturers and producers. Globally, in 2019, retail revenue augmented by 4.1 percent (with 5 percent five-year revenue growth), resulting in US$4.74 trillion aggregate revenue for the world's top 250 retailers

[3]. The sector has experienced growth through digital technology advancements such as e-commerce-driven applications that enhance the sale of consumer goods and services. Digital products such as music MP3s can now be downloaded and played online unlike in days when CDs had to be physically distributed. Practically every consumer good is now sold online, including food. These developments have led to the evolution of digital entrepreneurs, but not without challenges, as discussed in later sections of this chapter.

Biotechnology, commonly referred to as biotech, is an area that involves the use of scientific tools that comprise cells, molecules and biological materials for the production of bioproducts meant for various industries. As they are based on an emerging tech-based business model, biotechs have demands that exceed those of regular ICT start-ups. They are faced with issues involving research and development (R&D), working capital, getting together efficient scientific teams, patents and intellectual property and, of course, management [4–5].

Furthermore, the area of health has mostly become connected through online networks rather than being disconnected and scattered. Healthcare is quickly becoming digitalized, and entrepreneurs are moving toward a time when patients may not even need doctors to make a simple diagnosis of cases such as fever or flu. Individuals will soon be able to do it themselves with machines that provide real-time information that was once privy only to health practitioners [6].

Turning now to the fashion industry, another colossal industry worldwide, it is almost incredible to consider the reach of the disruption that technological innovation has produced on it. In fact, when we think of a futuristic world, we think of the amalgamation of fashion and technology: holographic computers that users can wear on their sleeves, sunglasses that double as smartphones. Digital entrepreneurs are beginning to perceive the enormous potential of the technology and fashion culture in our current world. Creativity, imagination and innovation are qualities that those in both fashion and technology have in common, thus facilitating the blending of everything from e-commerce to fashion blogging to smart watches, all under the broad umbrella term "fashiontech," one of the newest tech-innovation fields throughout the globe [7].

Overall, the digital economy has come to stay and will continue to grow until perhaps innovation starts experiencing undesirable growth or diminishing returns. However, the journey to more breakthroughs and development is fraught with various challenges and risks. Each sector driven by ICT-related change has limitations that affect those creating the solutions – the tech founders, innovators and venture capitalists – as well as the end-consumers. Section 5.2 discusses the key challenges encountered by digital entrepreneurs and start-ups in the fintech, insurtech, retailtech, biotech, healthtech and fashiontech industries.

5.2 Fintech Challenges

The fintech revolution is growing fast; over the past few years, it has garnered a plethora of positive attention from consumers that has led to investors taking keen interest in this prospect. Notwithstanding the growth and popularity of fintech, the digital entrepreneurs must address a number of obstacles if they are to access the maximum potential of fintech and ultimately achieve optimum success in the field. The challenges include integration with legacy IT systems, big data analytics, stringent regulations and inadequate customer understanding.

5.2.1 Integration with Legacy IT Systems

The first problem to tackle is the difficulty inherent in trying to integrate incompatible old/legacy IT systems with newer technology. Before the advent of fintech companies, other systems were in place in the financial sector, such as the manual input of financial data, automated generation of financial transactions, use of paper forms to carry out operations and physical movement of cash. This involved use of various technology systems that financial professionals and customers were relatively comfortable with. However, having adapted over decades to such traditional tech systems, those same professionals and customers are now finding complete migration to or incorporation of fintech painstaking [8].

Changing a tech culture from old to new is a major challenge that fintech entrepreneurs often encounter. It involves infrastructural costs as well as customer education and enlightenment, all of which increases the overall operational cost of fintechs. Efforts to move from the old systems will alter the known business models of organizations and financial institutions. Some entrepreneurs prefer maintaining the status quo rather than embracing change, particularly as some changes imply that existing processes will become automated, meaning that certain jobs could be threatened, although it would also mean that individuals with new relevant skills would become sought after.

Considering the burden of change required for fintech implementation, many financial institutions and organizations seem likely to continue with old/legacy systems. It would thus take a good level of convincing to get them to accept new changes. Many organizations are already operating with legacy systems that have now become outdated and need to be substituted or assisted by new technologies. However, this process is not as easy as it seems. The older systems resist the change, meaning that a balance has to be created between the two systems in order to create a suitable work environment. It is thus a difficult obstacle that must be overcome.

5.2.2   Big Data Analytics

The financial sector is known for the management of sensitive data ranging from customer purchase information, credit card and bank details as well as other transactions. For a fintech business to offer better products and services for customers, it must understand their purchasing behavior. Gathering such information is often carried out using website cookies and other web-monitoring tools, for example Uptrends, Site24x7, AppBeat, StatusCake, Jetpack, Pingdom and so on. There is also the challenge of managing confidential data that must not be disclosed to a third party. For a sector that deals with finances, there are many risks associated with the industry. Being able to gather and analyze the huge volume of data generated by the financial sector is a daunting task, but businesses must achieve it if they are to stay afloat and be profitable [8].

Most fintechs are adopting big data analytics to make sense of significantly massive amounts of seemingly unintelligible data and to identify patterns that can help predict future human behavior. Such predictions can help fintechs in satisfying the demands of their customers. Through big data analysis, archaic analog systems and operations can be replaced by efficient software solutions that yield better results. However, all internal and external company data must be made machine-readable for data analysis to be performed on it, which can be a key challenge considering the often unstructured nature of some key data. And while resolving these issues, fintech entrepreneurs must also ensure that they comply fully with regulatory policies.

5.2.3   Stringent Regulations

The financial sector is characterized by overwhelming regulations to check entrants into the industry and largely for the security of customer funds. Such abundance of regulations demonstrates the interest of government agencies in the financial sector. For some countries like Indonesia, India, Nigeria and Australia, the central bank is responsible for regulating the activities of fintech companies with other counterpart government agencies. For instance, in Indonesia, Bank of Indonesia takes care of monitoring the payment system while the Financial Services

Authority (Otoritas Jasa Keuangan – OJK) does almost the same thing but focuses more on the banking and nonbanking financial institutions [9]. In a situation where these regulations come with stringent rules, most entrepreneurs find it daunting to cope. This can add to their running costs, infrastructure and setup costs, especially in situations where they have to pay charges and rates to the government.

Be that as it may, regulation and compliance policies are arguably the toughest uncertainties that entrepreneurs in the field of fintech encounter. In addition, the financial services market presents numerous regulatory policies that usually become obstacles to the innovative ideas of fintech start-ups. Many institutes and newly starting firms are not aware of this maze of regulatory policies and see themselves getting tangled up in heavy fines and license delays as they fail to comply.

5.2.4 Inadequate Customer Understanding

With fintechs, there are tendencies for numerous risks to occur, such as fiscal irresponsibility, fraud issues, hacking of personal data, cloning of credit/debit card details, multiple payments, password compromise using email addresses, the risk of losing a device that might expose confidential data like login passwords and so on. Many individuals prefer to deal with their money issues traditionally, primarily due to the fear of challenges associated with fintechs. Most customers have no understanding about how fintechs can remove bottlenecks and carry out transactions safely with few cost implications [10]. Fintech entrepreneurs have largely considered the media, publishing and music industries. Intellectual property creators and artists can sell their products seamlessly by harnessing the direction in which technology is headed, as with the digital download of books, videos and audio podcasts. Mobile devices can also be used to purchase songs, download e-books and subscribe to various platforms like magazines and newspapers.

In general, fintechs are negatively affected when customers get the wrong perspective by focusing more on risks than on benefits. Lack of customer awareness associated with the fintech industry leads to much misunderstanding and confusion regarding what can and cannot be done in this field. This lack of understanding has led individuals to believe that the fintech industry is not secure, whereas the truth lies opposite of this notion. Fintech has the potential to completely disrupt the financial services market and to open up opportunities for ordinary individuals. Fintech is different and unconventional compared with the average tech start-up. For this reason, it isn't a simple matter for just anyone to venture into this area and make a success of it. Nevertheless, by maintaining a flexible approach, entrepreneurs can readily modify and improve with each technological innovation and, consequently, enjoy its potential and well-established benefits.

5.3   Insurtech Challenges

In retrospect, innovation has become an essential element for the survival and thriving of digital entrepreneurs in any field. The insurance sector is no different. More big names in the tech industry are considering investing heavily in the insurance sector due to the disruption that technology is creating across the board. Hence, it poses a significant opportunity for insurers as they are compelled to reinvent themselves as better prospects for customers due to this disruption. Practically, the 2020 report of Accenture's Technology Vision for Insurance shows that more than 81 percent of the interviewed executives believed that technology has become an "inextricable part of the human experience" (p. 9), while 83 percent believed that there is a need to advance relationships with customers toward co-creation "to compete in a post-digital world" (p. 19) [27].

Although many individuals in the industry and those considering getting into it have realized its enormous possibilities, entrepreneurs continue to battle with several challenges. These include (i) limited customer insights on the basis of which to develop new products and services, (ii) the need for sophisticated underwriting and risk reduction using machine learning and cloud computing, (iii) reaching operational excellence through innovative technology and (iv) the need for guaranteeing high standards of data protection.

5.3.1   Limited Customer Insights on the Basis of Which to Develop New Products and Services

Any business organization committed to affecting the lives and well-being of people designs and develops products and services to satisfy customers' needs. If customers do not perceive the newly developed products to be useful and cash-worthy, then the organization goes out of business. Therefore, it is imperative to "know your customers," understanding their lifestyles and activities. For insurtechs, the challenge of understanding the risks against which potential clients need to be insured is a significant part of their business model [11]. Entrepreneurs need to be aware that a customer might be in danger of losing their car, life, house or job. The abundance of such information would allow the creation of relevant and timely products and services. For example, a product like the Apple Watch is designed to diagnose changes in the body of the user, which can help with health insurance and provide relevant data for insurtechs.

Some mobile devices like Samsung's S8 have the capability to check the blood pressure and temperature of users. This customer information can be acquired in various ways, but the insurtech may not have the needed infrastructure for rich data extraction. Therefore, strategic partnership with tech giants like Google and Amazon, which have extensive data banks, poses an enormous opportunity for insurtechs. However, insurtech entrepreneurs require huge financial lump sums to acquire such data and get third-party consent, and adequate infrastructure for efficient management of the information might not be available. Additionally, it may take a long time to analyze and understand the living patterns of potential users of their products and services [12].

In an insurtech environment, a customer-centric methodology can be adopted to ensure that the product that customers receive is personalized to their taste and appeals to their liking. An omnichannel model is adopted to encourage cross-selling and allow customers to engage with the insurance company in many different ways and through multiple media.

5.3.2 Sophisticated Underwriting and Risk Reduction Using Machine Learning and Cloud Computing

The insurance sector evaluates risk for clients and customers. Such a task involves understanding how much they should pay and what the amount paid will be sufficient to cover in terms of costs when unexpected incidences occur. Insurtechs are expected to foresee these incidents using available customer data, but understanding the data requires precision. When such risk is evaluated and taken care of, there is then a need to understand what the customer premium should cover since the risk was foreseen and reduced from causing further damage [13].

New technologies such as cloud computing, predictive analysis and machine learning allow organizations to perform a level of data analysis which is more thorough than any other technique. They assist in uncovering more patterns and information that is helpful in formulating the future actions of the organization in the market. Integrated data can also be used to substantially reduce risk and increase the efficiency of operations for insurtech entrepreneurs.

5.3.3 Operational Excellence through Innovative Technology

The first major milestone of insurtech entrepreneurs is developing a business model that works. The delivery system of the products and services needs to ensure minimal costs, seamless customer acquisition and, of course, that customers will be interested enough to return for more products and services. Insurtechs need to be sufficiently creative and innovative to meet the challenges of running such a company. Handling and analyzing big data is a big deal that requires use of giant tech companies' customer databases. Amazon, for instance, could be useful to ascertain different users' exposure to risk, their demographics, geographical locations and whatever risks can be determined by their purchasing behavior [13].

Being able to put all these together seamlessly and achieve excellence in the delivery of service is a challenge that insurtechs must overcome to stand out. Innovation must be adopted as the common denominator across the operations of the organizations otherwise survival in the insurtech industry becomes very difficult. Entrepreneurs must be willing to demonstrate flexibility and adjust to accommodate new, innovative models that appeal to potential customers [14].

5.3.4 Data Protection Challenges

The work carried out by insurtechs, and most tech companies, in fact, involves the use of data. Such data include customers' personal records, activities, histories, daily lives, behavio, and the status of everything that happens around them. Much of this information is highly confidential and so needs to be safeguarded. Though insurtechs get these data from big tech companies that have a more advanced infrastructure to manage them, they (insurtechs) are unlikely to have the capacity to manage such big data. A breach of customer confidentiality could potentially terminate the business lifecycle. An insurtech needs to build credibility in data management before getting data from tech giants or through other mediums. Data breaches and loss can lead to criminal charges, and many other consequences can arise from exposing customers to this risk and making them feel insecure [15].

Furthermore, while using new technology such as cloud computing, big data analytics and machine learning provides an efficient work environment, it also opens up a new host of problems related to the security of sensitive data. However, these data-centric clouds can be used to detect potential cyber-threats and ultimately to protect confidential information. Since the evolution of technology is disrupting the insurance sector, it is also creating a plethora of opportunities. Thus, being able to adapt swiftly to changing conditions is key if insurtechs want to execute their operations efficiently.

5.4 Retailtech Challenges

Undeniably, digital technologies have changed the world and how regular consumer markets operate. Individuals have become incredibly centered on devices such as smartphones and laptops with internet connections to access almost anything in the world. Online stores and online shopping are as big a thing today as any other trend in the world, all because of the utter convenience and accessibility that this consumer-based retail practice provides to customers. Retailtech has made inconsequential the size of your property or its physical boundaries – what matters is the availability of the online network to markets globally. ICT has disrupted existing consumer practices, and it has undoubtedly affected the retail industry a great deal. Consumers now expect retail stores to offer global connectivity across multiple platforms and e-commerce solutions that are efficient and convenient. The perception of digital entrepreneurs that retailtech is a booming industry has been solidified. As customers are inclined to automatically expect the stores they visit to have certain technological capabilities, keeping up with these expectations suggests new challenges for entrepreneurs. The challenges include changes introduced by big data and finding suitable digital transformers.

5.4.1 Changes Introduced by Big Data

Retailtech has become competitive for both big and small players in the global economy. Data analysis is the new wave of business advantage for most sectors, including the retail economy; it allows businesses to understand the market demand from existing and potential customers. Analysis of data requires a lot of expertise, especially if it is with the aim of matching retailtech decisions with those of prospective buyers. A company like Google is a leader in big data; through IP addresses, locations and search targeting it can understand what users want. Such data can be monetized and sold to big players like Walmart and other tech-driven retail organizations that can afford it [3]. There are many benefits of using insights from competitive data analytics;

- *Customer knowledge*: When retailtech entrepreneurs understand the needs of customers and their target market, it significantly influences their choice of tech tools such as website templates, layouts, cart systems and overall digital marketing approaches.
- *Targeted advertising*: This determines users' choice and the specific platform of the advertisement. A digital entrepreneur needs to understand which advertising channels are most likely to bring bestselling leads, for example Facebook ads, Twitter ads or Instagram. Also, using

specific keywords could produce magnificent results. For example, when targeting potential antivirus software buyers using Facebook ads, instead of using generic keywords such as "computer security" or "cybersecurity," digital entrepreneurs should target users who have shown interest in specific security books, conferences and so on.

- **Pricing**: With useful insights into customer demand, knowledge of competitors and shareholder value, retailtech companies can determine the best pricing strategies and dynamics.

- **Personalized shopping experience**: Data analytics can offer retailtechs the competitive advantage of providing customers with a personal and predictive shopping experience. For instance, blogs and websites using "Google AdSense" ensure that Google ads based on the past and recent activities on the web are displayed to their web visitors. For example, users who have searched for items such as shoes and bags could be served product ads that complement their searches.

Being able to give structure to disorganized irrelevant data and to extract the relevant information can help retailtechs to predict current and future patterns and trends in the market and can completely change the operations of a retail store or the entire industry altogether, as we have seen happening for insurtechs [16]. The advent and popularity of online shopping have also encouraged the system of online reviews, which are readable by anyone who has an electronic device and an Internet connection. This makes retailtechs much more attentive to the criticism that they receive from their customers online, leading to a more consumer-centric approach. However, as we have seen above for insurtechs, current tools do not always provide retailers with the analyses they need. Furthermore, applying big data to the operations of a retail business can be an incredibly complicated process and a costly one, which drives people to be wary of going through with the idea of actually applying that new sort of technology.

5.4.2   Finding Digital Transformers

Another challenge for start-ups in this industry is finding and keeping people who can digitally transform a company. It's hard to compile a team of individuals who are skilled enough to take the business to the desired level through technological innovation, especially at affordable wages. For example, an entrepreneur aiming to design and manufacture products, market them efficiently, and analyze the data gathered from potential leads would require highly skilled individuals in product design, manufacturing, and data science. Privacy is also a big concern in the retailtech industry as the consumers become more worried about their private information stored across various database servers. Consumers need assurances that their location, transaction and login details are in safe hands and will remain as private as they should be. For example, if customers sign up to an e-commerce site, they do so on the understanding that their details are remotely secure and will not be found in the wrong hands. A lack of capable and technically skilled personnel to manage this task often results in lawsuits for violation of clients' privacy. Hence, having the right team matters: do it right while hiring.

5.5   Biotech Challenges

Biotechnology – the technology used to create products from living organisms that are beneficial for the welfare of human beings – is arguably one of the most important fields of our generation. Through biotechnology, we are able to conjure up remedies to so many different diseases, predict trends in biological beings, and extract some of the staples of our diet and daily use. Biotechnology goes beyond making cheese with bacteria or alcohol with yeast. We can now edit the genomes of living organisms to engineer their qualities and features and make exact copies or clones of organisms with desirable characteristics. To sum it up, the importance of biotech in our world is undeniable and has been for a long time. However, that does not mean that entrepreneurs entering this popular and well-researched field face no challenges. The challenges of biotech include data collection and analysis, lack of automated validation, regulatory compliance, data security, and storage capacity.

5.5.1   Data Collection and Analysis

To get the needed data for scientific and bio-based research takes time, effort, money and verification, as data from some years ago might be irrelevant today. Biotechnology is one area that requires precision, for instance, in producing medicines and ways to prevent people from getting sick. One mistake in combining minerals, for instance, could degenerate the end-product into a bio-weapon that could cause great harm. Data for biotechs, therefore, need to be verified through consistent tests and analysis [4].

Performing research and collecting relevant data in the field of biotechnology can be one of the toughest jobs primarily because it is much more complex and thorough as compared to other similar branches such as pharmaceuticals. The research must be performed by a team of experienced and qualified individuals who can also use technology to do the relevant analysis. The real challenge is creating the perfect balance between the fair use of new technology for data collection and the commercialization of the research.

5.5.2 Automated Validation

For a biotech to be registered with the Food and Drug Administration (FDA) requires it to get clearance in a systems validation process. The process is a rather extensive one, taking up days, weeks or even months at a time; it can thus delay operations until confirmation is received by the biotech organization that the state of its working environment is acceptable. The solution to this problem of wasting time waiting for FDA validation is to have automated validation within compliance software [17].

This involves validation of healthcare products using automated systems to ensure that they comply with regulations in the industry. Programs could be in hardware or software and are designed to provide documented evidence. One such system that tech start-ups can install is based on the Supervisory Control and Data Acquisition (SCADA) concept. The challenge of this new qualification and validation system is security, however, as it is paperless. Biotechs must therefore ensure that any validation plan is based on national and international standards and practices for the development of automated systems and software.

5.5.3 Regulatory Compliance Issues

The biotech industry is always under extreme scrutiny from all directions and has imposed upon itself thousands of compliance policies and regulations. Automated compliance software, as mentioned in Section 5.5.2, is a solution to this problem provided the current regulations are maintained. Such rules, their compliance and enforcement require both hardware and software standards. The national and international standard of infrastructure is a requirement to build certain products or manage various kinds of data. These will require an enormous amount of start-up cost and capital for small biotech organizations. This is a major challenge, as confirmed in a report from the Kellogg's School of Management: "a lack of understanding of the industry by the regulatory bodies adds another challenge to startups" [4] (p. 19). There being continual changes at policy level is a risk for various biotech groups, for example R&D teams, clinical trial groups and so on, as biotechs must pay a significant amount of money and effort to revalidate each time in order to comply with the policy updates [4].

5.5.4   Data Security

The issue of data security is another obstacle that can infringe on the efficiency of an organization in the biotech industry. With most of the data being stored in the cloud, it becomes necessary for companies to invest in foolproof methods of detecting potential leaks of private information and identifying cybersecurity threats in time. Biotechnology development of products for humans and health-related issues requires information on users, customers and patients. Research that involves surveys requires information from respondents, and such information must be kept confidential. Biotech start-ups need to ensure that confidential customer data never get into the hands of unauthorized third parties.

5.5.5   Storage Capacity

For a sector that requires information from previous years to aid in future research and inventions, a huge storage capacity is needed. Most biotechs do not have the required storage for significant research discoveries of the past and the recent future. Add to that the challenge of not having enough storage capacity to safeguard all of the collected data and research on-site, and it is easy to see how companies end up having too much on their plate. Shifting to cloud solutions can help solve the storage problem, but the organization must then focus on ensuring that the necessary layers of cybersecurity are implemented.

5.6   Healthtech Challenges

ICT plays a huge role in creating better solutions within the health sector. From online drug stores to websites for consulting with a doctor, to devices that detect and diagnose changes in our bodies and much more, healthtech is a major breakthrough in solving human health challenges; however, problems such as difficulty in harnessing data, data inaccuracy, costs of maintaining security and compliance, as well as interoperability issues often reduce the potential benefits of this sector.

5.6.1   Harnessing Data

One of the biggest challenges facing healthtech is harnessing interesting data from patients not previously researched on. With all the data available on the Internet, patients can quickly search for symptoms and potentially self-diagnose an illness. As such, learning this information from a medical practitioner may not impress them or build on their knowledge, thus redefining the relationship between a physician and a patient at a healthcare center. The motivation for healthtech start-ups is for better health, prevention, and early detection, pre-treatment or precision medicine that detects disease and treats before it becomes full-blown [6]. Gathering those kinds of data and patients' biometrics entails a great deal of creative innovation and development of smart gadgets. An obvious example is the Apple Watch that can run diagnostic tests just by skin contact. If a healthtech develops any product or service that has advanced capabilities beyond present-day medicine, data and information are key. While patients' information, health history and other details are needed [18], such data are relatively expensive and difficult for a start-up to generate.

5.6.2   Data Accuracy

An essential aspect of running a healthtech organization is earning the trust of the potential patients [6]. The authenticity of the data provided to patients by healthtech organizations must be duly verified to ensure the avoidance of inaccurate data, which could potentially break the relationship between a healthcare provider and a patient irreparably. It is important that data and information that will be used for health-related matters are without error. Any mistake of any kind can cost patients their lives or bring other consequences that might be dire. The accuracy and verification of such data will need collaboration with health professionals and institutions, thus requiring a good technical team and financial resources that most healthtech start-ups are unable to afford [6].

5.6.3   Security and Compliance

Health records need to be secured from unauthorized access especially when the patients have not consented to the divulgence of their records to third parties. The scaling up of healthtechs is dependent on their having the needed and approved infrastructure to keep health-related data. Compliance in an area like health cannot be compromised, and this covers capacity and systems used for managing it. Vast numbers of patents and regulations that demand compliance for the survival of an organization can deter start-ups from venturing into healthtech. The healthtech industry has hundreds of regulatory compliance policies attached to it. To successfully comply with these policies, entrepreneurs need to be knowledgeable about the processes as they can otherwise be a discouraging factor.

5.6.4   Interoperability

While the collision of the digital world and the world of healthcare is creating tremendous disruption across the board, it is also paving the way for some incredible multiple opportunities. The convergence will ultimately create a culture that is much more complicated than today's and that focuses a lot more on self-treatment and self-diagnosis through the help of technology, making healthcare accessible to a larger population of users. So, while it may seem like the healthcare industry is undergoing a drastic makeover, it is definitely for the better. With the increasing adoption of healthtech comes the major impediment of inability to facilitate cross-functional use, sharing and transfer of data. A healthtech start-up may not have access to certain medical data and records, meaning that it will need to cooperate with health institutions to get this information. However, compiling data and setting parameters for usage of products can be difficult when working with others, especially when people are competing with one another and seeking originality.

5.7   Fashiontech Challenges

Fashion technology (fashiontech) is gaining traction on an enormous scale. As demand for fashion products increases due to the unlimited possibilities of design and manufacturing, strategies for sales have also developed with the aid of e-commerce and m-commerce. Nevertheless, digital entrepreneurs need to circumvent a number of challenges in this sector, including user experience issues, mobile experience issues, and integrating health and fitness factors into wearable tech.

5.7.1   User Experience Issues

As discussed, user acceptance and appreciation are important aspects going forward in digital entrepreneurship, and they apply to fashiontechs as much as to other entrepreneurial endeavors. If the user experience with the product is not satisfactory, then the product will not succeed in the market. The product needs to work efficiently and also appear good enough to compel users to leave a positive review, which will then lead to further traction for the product. Without achieving such user acceptance through great graphics, cool-looking integrated tech and stylish merchandise, a brand cannot move forward in this field [7]. E-commerce and the sale of fashion products come with challenges that only a few big players have been able to handle [7–19]. Also, the limitations of the Internet and errors in loading websites may create a less responsive user experience. Sometimes chosen items don't appear the way they did on the screen when delivered physically. Delivery hiccups and payment issues are further challenges that affect this industry [7].

5.7.2   Mobile Experience Issues

As ICT takes a whole new turn and gravitates toward mobile use, consumers' desire to have a seamless experience has also increased. The ability to shop with a mobile is a convenience like no other. Fashiontech start-ups need to surmount the challenge of making their websites user-friendly across various mobile platforms. Making their website able to adapt to different Internet signal strengths and locations needs to be considered as well.

While online shopping has become more of a routine than a simple trend nowadays, it is still a complicated enough process to perform on a smartphone, which impedes purchase motivation. Due to the steady shift from personal computers to mobile devices such as smartphones, consumers are more inclined to access fashiontech products through mobile devices. However, purchasing fashion or wearable tech through a smartphone is still not as comfortable an experience as it could be in the twenty-first century.

5.7.3   Wearable Tech

Another immense challenge that fashiontech entrepreneurs encounter is attempting to figure out new ways of integrating health and fitness factors into wearable tech [20]. Fitness tracking through wearable tech has become relatively common across the globe today, and brands now need to find new and innovative means through which the two can be integrated into irresistible pieces of innovative wearable tech. The bigger challenge would be finding ways to communicate the purpose and the message of the integration along with the apparel that is being sold. Fashion may be the fourth largest market worldwide, but it is by no means an easygoing field [7–21]. As an entrepreneur, dealing with the constant scrutiny and criticism of customers and complying with their demands can be a tough challenge; it requires proper knowledge of the field.

5.8   Security Challenges of Digital Entrepreneurs

The digital world is not a secure sphere; it has become quite susceptible to cyber-attacks that have been suspiciously prevalent in the past couple of years. An entrepreneur thinking about building a new start-up in any of the abovementioned tech-focused sectors should be aware of the potential security challenges. By preparing properly, they may avoid becoming extremely vulnerable to cyber-attacks that may result in the loss of very private, critical and sensitive information. An entrepreneur should be aware of the security challenges that plague the digital world and be ready to counter them with proven and efficient strategies to protect the roots of their business and ensure future success. The following security challenges are a few of the most prevalent for digital entrepreneurs.

5.8.1 Identity Management

A standard feature of any digital business, online business or solution is the collection of user information through the various access requirements – username, email address, password and other details – depending on the platform. Every digital start-up that involves users, sign-ups and even guest customers has to collect data transferred over the World Wide Web. Such information, whether personal or business, must also be verified to ensure the safety of any digital platform or business. Digital entrepreneurs should be able to keep user information safe and to verify that users are humans and not software applications ("bots") programmed with bizarre motives. Actually, most identity management is done by bots driven by artificial intelligence. Authentication should be user-friendly, however; it can be done remotely without customers getting frustrated when using a particular platform. The challenge in this is that every tech start-up needs to get their business model right before going public. Identity management processes should be test-run thoroughly before requesting the personal and business details of real users. Any initial mismanagement of user identity can mean a loss of confidence in the business.

5.8.2 Malware Threats

Malware threats seem to be the most daunting challenge that faces entrepreneurs in this digital age. They affect everyone, including users and private citizens who use technology solutions, products and services. With criminal activities progressing from hacking to cybercrime and terrorism, security precautions have never been more crucial [22]. A single malware attack can alter the entire infrastructure of a system. Handling malware threats requires constant monitoring because the ones developing such threats are working daily to find ways to compromise various solutions. At the forefront of building a great digital start-up is the security network to keep the business safe.

Also, threats such as ransomware are becoming more prevalent as time passes and many organizations are unable to formulate a proper strategy against them. Malware mainly compromises systems through an infected vector, which could be a simple email, social media post or flash drive. Ransomware exploits weaknesses in operating systems or applications and then encrypts files, requiring victims to pay a certain amount before it decrypts them. Ransoms demanded by malware attackers are mostly in the form of digital currencies, as these are much more difficult to trace. Digital entrepreneurs can enhance their protection from malware attacks by updating their applications and operating systems and conducting regular penetration tests to detect vulnerabilities swiftly.

5.8.3   Data Breach and Recovery

As previously mentioned, data remain the defining asset and competitive advantage for most start-ups. A breach in data security damages the start-up's integrity as users become the targets of the attackers. Allowing details of debit and credit cards to fall into the hands of third parties puts customers at risk. The cloud has opened up a world of possibilities and convenience, and data breaches have become prevalent. Data breaches can be fatal to the efforts put into developing trust between digital entrepreneurs, stakeholders and clients [6]. Creating effective data recovery strategies should be a top priority for organizations, so that action can be taken quickly in the event of a data breach [23]. Such recovery measures may involve informing all employees about possible breaches and collecting evidence with the help of a specialized agency to identify the source of the breach.

5.9   Case Studies

In this section, we discuss two case studies that illustrate how digital entrepreneurs move through existing challenges to execute their business agendas. The cases are from the biotech and fashiontech industries, respectively.

To introduce the first case study: as highlighted before, start-ups in the biotech industry face challenges that include there being lengthy regulatory compliance policies, a shortage of resources, and complex and slow approval and validation processes. The significance of these difficulties can be observed in the case of a client of Pisano & Associates LLC, a global biopharmaceutical company involved in the research, discovery, development and commercialization of various pharmaceutical and therapeutic products [24]. In the effort to keep up with demand for its products, Pisano's client fell behind in their Environment, Health and Safety (EHS) compliance. Consequently, Pisano stepped in to assist its client in complying with the EHS regulations as well as keeping up with the demand for products through efficient production and operation. Pisano made it possible through an extensive and comprehensive EHS compliance audit that highlighted all the compliance requirements to ensure that the processes and the facility were "compliance-ready" [24]. It constructed a detailed written plan, which it communicated to all employees through an online shared platform.

POINT OF ATTENTION: Regulatory and compliance issues can be resolved by asking for help from an external source. Such sources must have the necessary expertise to help the company develop a suitable compliance plan that will also make it easier to maintain standards, thereby avoiding hefty fines or bans.

In this case, proper communication of the Pisano audit and compliance plan led to its successful implementation – and the company was able to meet all of its manufacturing deadlines. The main challenge faced by Pisano's client was its inability to comply with the regulations and patents set out by the FDA and EHS. It put its focus into manufacturing enough drugs to fulfill the production quota without taking valuable time to develop plans to deal with regulations and compliance requirements.

Moving now to the second case study, it demonstrates the importance of user acceptance in the fashiontech industry, with organizations keen to reach out to their customers using suitable media. If brands are prepared to go above and beyond simply meeting their customers' demands and expectations, they will tend to succeed at tremendous scale.

LazyLazy.com is a Danish online shopping center [25]. On the website, various brands have their own sections like virtual shops in a virtual shopping mall and customers can interact with the brands, view their products and ultimately purchase them. LazyLazy.com attempts to satisfy customers' needs by offering virtual "try rooms" where users can virtually try on clothing to get an idea of what it would look like on them. Customers can also share product images with their social media friends, which demonstrates the network-based approach adopted by many e-commerce platforms in the past few years. LazyLazy.com also offers customers tools for creating fashion blogs and allows them to follow various fashion experts who provide them with guidelines on writing articles on the website as well [25].

> **POINT OF ATTENTION:** Executing an effective marketing campaign that will appeal to potential customers and create a modern brand image is a new challenge that demands that organizations use technologies such as big data analytics in order to identify trends in the market and the likes and dislikes of their customer base, as well as machine learning and predictive analysis.

This case study highlights the current trend of taking a more customer-oriented approach and integrating different social networking sites in the e-commerce experience. Adopting a customer-centric approach is not easy, however, as it requires the development of complex programs and technologies.

5.10   Summary

Digitalization has significantly impacted all sectors, producing waves of disruption in almost every field or industry including healthcare, fashion, biology, financial services and insurance. While these areas have great potential to attract big investors, there are still some challenges that arise for start-ups within them. These challenges primarily revolve around regulatory and compliance issues, problems associated with the use of big data and predictive analysis, challenges regarding the security and privacy of data, as well as matters related to cloud computing and storage. Also, there is still a lack of understanding in the people utilizing digital applications, which limits their adoption.

One of the recurring challenges relates to big data and its harnessing to produce tangible results. In this regard, digital entrepreneurs need to be strategic in using data to understand the market demand that will shape their product and service solutions. Insightful data help in marketing and advertising to potential customers. With data, start-ups can understand market trends and adjust their programs and business models to accommodate likely "futuristic" paradigm shifts. Considering the healthcare domain, for example, data on patients' health and lifestyles can be used to design health products that cater to different people with various kinds of illness. Moreover, data in fintech are used to understand users' buying patterns. Also, e-commerce start-ups are changing rapidly thanks to evolving data realities and expectations. Likewise, data influence the design and production of fashionwear. However, governments and other regulatory bodies still shape the extent of innovation and can eventually stunt growth, limiting the potential of organizations that are unable to scale up to the necessary standards. Also, it requires massive infrastructure to manage start-ups like the biotech ones. Security must be a priority to avoid any compromise of user information. Data analysis is also necessary to understand trends and occurrence frequencies; this involves systems that adopt cloud computing *and* management.

Furthermore, the team of "digital transformers" must have the right skills, capacity, competencies and motivation. A working business model must be developed to ensure efficiency in the delivery of services. Digital entrepreneurs need to understand the specialty aspect and how important it is to build relationships with key business players. As start-ups often lack the necessary confidence and experience to handle elaborate projects, strategic collaborations with tech giants like Amazon, Alibaba and Google, who have access to data, funds, infrastructure and public confidence, could be the difference between failure and success.

References

1. KPMG. Fintech Funding Hits All-Time High in 2015: China Accounts for Almost One-Fifth, KPMG Analysis Finds. (2016) https://home.kpmg/cn/en/home/news-media/press-releases/2016/03/fintech-funding-hits-all-time-high-in-2015.html [accessed May 25, 2020].

2. Behrens J-E, Freiling A, Nadkarni P, Sachdev R . Operational Excellence for Insurers Focusing on Emerging Consumers. EY (2014).

3. Deloitte. (2015) Global Powers of Retailing 2020. Deloitte Touche Tohmatsu Limited.

4. Durai A, Li B, Metkar S, Pelayo M, Phillips N . *Challenges in a Biotech Startup. Healthcare Nuts.* Kellogg School of Management (2006).

5. Pisano GP . *Science Business: The Promise, the Reality, and the Future of Biotech.* Harvard Business School Press (2006).

6. Labrien D . The 3 Key Challenges Health Tech Startups Face Today. (2016) https://tech.co/key-challenges-health-tech-startups-2016–10 [accessed May 25, 2020].

7. McDowell M. The Future of Fashion Tech in 2020. (2020) www.voguebusiness.com/technology/future-fashion-tech-predictions-2020 [accessed May 25, 2020].

8. Drummer D, Jerenz A, Siebelt P, Thaten M . FinTech – Challenges and Opportunities How Digitization Is Transforming the Financial Sector. McKinsey Co (2016) 1–7.

9. Rohman I, Diannegara A . Fintech: Understanding Risks and Challenges. (2016) www.thejakartapost.com/academia/2016/10/31/fintech-understanding-risks-and-challenges.html [accessed May 25, 2018].

10. Pollari I . The Rise of Fintech: Opportunities and Challenges. *The Finsia Journal of Applied Finance* (2016) 15–21.
11. Volosovich S. InsurTech: Challeges and Development Perspectives. *International Journal of Innovative Technologies in Economy* (2016) 3: 39–42.
12. Abril B, Gutierrez A, Acevedo A, Garcia D, Urien A, De Rueda H, Monleon G, Rebull R. Insurtech Outlook, Executive Summary September 2016. Everis (2016).
13. PwC. Opportunities Await: How InsurTech Is Reshaping Insurance. PwC (2016).
14. KPMG. Key Regulatory Challenges Facing the Insurance Industry in 2017. Americas FS Regulatory Center of Excellence. KPMG (2017).
15. Altus Consulting. The InsurTech Journey ... Are We There Yet? Altus Consulting (2017).
16. Quigley R. Summer of Insurtech. InsurancePOST (2017) 21–6. www .postonline.co.uk/technology/3252386/technology-summer-of-insurtech [accessed December 29, 2019].
17. ETQ. Top 3 Challenges Facing Biotech Today (and How to Tackle Them). (2015) https://blog.etq.com/top-3-challenges-facing-biotech-today-and-how-to-tackle-them [current version accessed May 26, 2020].
18. Groves P, Kayyali B, Knott D, Van Kuiken S . The "Big Data" Revolution in Healthcare: Accelerating Value and Innovation. *McKinsey Global Institute* (2013) 1–22. doi: 10.1145/2537052.2537073.
19. Segran E . This Startup May Have Just Solved the Biggest Problem in Plus-Size Fashion | The Future of Business. (2017) www.fastcompany.com/404 35531/this-startup-may-have-just-solved-the-biggest-problem-in-plus-size-fashion [accessed May 26, 2020].
20. Gerber S. 9 Ways Wearables Could Change Health and Fitness. (2015) h ttps://thenextweb.com/entrepreneur/2015/08/11/9-ways-wearables-chang e-health-fitness-startups/ [accessed May 26, 2020].
21. Nagtegaal F, Verzijl D, Dervojeda K. Internet of Things: Wearable Technology. Case Study *Business Innovation Observatory European Union* (2015) 44.
22. Grossman J. Cross-Site Scripting Worms & Viruses – The Impending Threat & the Best Defense. White Hat Security (2007) 1–18.
23. Oltsik, J. Advanced Malware Trends, Opinions, and Strategies. Enterprise Strategy Group (2013).
24. Pisano. Case Study: Compliance Ready – Biotech Start-Up Challenges. Pisano Associates (2017) 1–2.
25. Batista L. New Business Models Enabled by Digital Technologies: A Perspective from the Fashion Sector. Study Rep EPSRC RCUK Res Proj NEMODE (New Economic Models in the Digital Economy) (2013).
26. Crunchbase. LazyLazy.com. (2015) www.crunchbase.com/organization/la zylazy-com#section-overview [accessed May 26, 2020].
27. Rangwala A, Starrs A, Viale A, Presutti D, Bramblet J, Saldanha K, Shibata N. Technology Vision for Insurance 2020 | We, the Post-Digital People – Can Your Enterprise Survive the "Tech-Clash?" Accenture (2020).

6   Digital Entrepreneurship and Social Media

6.1   Introduction

Entrepreneurship is the capacity and willingness to undertake the conception, organization and management of a productive venture with all attendant risks, while seeking profit as a reward [1]. As seen in Chapter 1, in economics, entrepreneurship is regarded as a factor of production together with land, labor, natural resources and capital. Entrepreneurial spirit is characterized by innovations and risk-taking, and it is often considered an essential component of a nation's ability to succeed in an ever-changing and ever more competitive global marketplace [1]. Moreover, digital entrepreneurship can be generally described as the means or methods of creating fresh and innovative businesses, products or commodities as well as services that are enabled, permitted and provided via the Internet. These means or methods of creating fresh and innovative businesses, products or commodities as well as services consist of start-ups (new businesses that deliver new products and services) as well as existing businesses. Digital entrepreneurship can be generally defined as the creation of new businesses as well as the transformation of existing businesses through technological innovations (through the development of digital technologies and the innovative practice of these innovative technologies) [2, 3].

Digital entrepreneurship has brought about the innovations of various digital technologies and these digital technologies have been spreading rapidly. The speedy spread and increase of digital technologies coupled with new innovations and functional abilities have overwhelmingly brought about changes in the modern world's highly competitive and spirited environments, restructuring the strategies and processes that accompany traditional businesses [4]. Thus, it is worth emphasizing that digital entrepreneurship is powered by the innovation of digital technologies.

Nowadays, digital entrepreneurship is seen as a vital tool for the growth of the economy. It is also seen as a powerful tool for the creation of jobs and for the eradication of unemployment in many countries. Notably, the capacity of digital entrepreneurship in any country is highly dependent on entrepreneurial behavior, traditions, customs, sophistication, strategies and the support of the ecosystem in which all parties involved (governments, private sectors, industries, educational institutions, businesses as well as nongovernmental organizations (NGOs)) cooperate.

However, digital entrepreneurship is not possible without new innovative technologies such as social media, big data and a host of other innovative technological platforms. These last create new avenues for partnership (collaboration), leveraging resources, product design, service design, development and deployment. This chapter focuses on social media.

> **POINT OF ATTENTION:** Although digital technologies such as social media have created immense opportunities, they also bring certain challenges, as shown, for example, by reports questioning the future of workforces such as that published in 2015 by the Committee for Economic Development of Australia [5].

As discussed in Chapter 3, social media simply refers to the mode by which people interact online, exchanging ideas and information and creating and sharing files in virtual networks. However, using social media platforms for entrepreneurship can also bring about a level playing field in various sectors in which opportunities such as working remotely at any time and on the go are created. Also, the use of social media platforms for entrepreneurship means that many organizations are smaller with regards to manpower; the number of one-person companies and partnerships is increasing [3]. Consequently, the effects of social media on digital entrepreneurship cannot be overemphasized.

6.2   Insights into Social Media

As well as a mode via which people interact and share ideas, social media can also be defined as a collection of applications that are based on the Internet and built on the framework and technological foundations of Web 2.0, which permits the conception and sharing of user-generated content [6]. Furthermore, social media can be defined as a means of getting messages and pieces of information across to as many people as possible, in as few words as possible and within the shortest possible time

[7]. The purpose of social media in digital entrepreneurship is to serve as a means of marketing products and services and engaging with targeted audiences in a bid to make profit. Probably, anyone marketing products and services through social media intends to do so in a cost- and time-effective manner. This is one of the major ways in which a social media strategy is different from a traditional media strategy. In addition, there are lots of social media platforms (categories) in existence today, including Facebook, Twitter, YouTube, Blogger, Instagram, WhatsApp, Bing, Flickr, LinkedIn, Slideshare and a host of others. The next sections discuss a sample of the various social media platforms (categories).

6.2.1 YouTube

Since its creation in 2005, YouTube has cemented itself as the most widely accepted and most used video sharing website. On the YouTube platform, every intending user is required to register an account. When this is done, the registered user can then begin to upload, share and view videos without any limit to their access. YouTube as a company used to deploy Adobe Flash video technology to display video content generated by its users [8], but it moved to HTML5 in 2015 and streaming video through Dynamic Adaptive Streaming over HTTP (MPEG-DASH). A vast majority of the content on the YouTube website is uploaded by the users (individuals and companies). Companies such as the BBC offer some of their materials through this website as part of the YouTube partnership program [9]. A lot of start-up entrepreneurs as well as young entrepreneurs have discovered the immense power of YouTube. With regards to digital entrepreneurship, YouTube is an extremely useful social media platform for getting messages across to target audiences as well as building strong brand awareness at minimal cost. For example, a musician without a manager or any publicity personnel now has access to being discovered on YouTube just by uploading a clip of their music to YouTube. Take Joe Penna (nickname MysteryGuitarMan) as an example: he started uploading videos to YouTube in 2006 and, by 2010, he had become the eighth most subscribed-to channel on YouTube [10]. This is immense bearing in mind that there was no involvement of any manager or publicity personnel. This to a large extent shows the huge part that YouTube plays in digital entrepreneurship.

6.2.2 Instagram

Instagram is a photo-sharing application that permits the private or public sharing of pictures and videos. Instagram was created in 2010 with the main aim of allowing its users to experience different moments in the lives of their friends through pictures as they happen, because the world becomes more connected through photos [11]. Furthermore, Instagram can be said to be a free mobile or desktop application and it's available for download in the Google Play Store and the App Store. It can also be used on computers by visiting the website. However, it would be challenging to a degree for businesses to employ Instagram through the website rather than on the mobile platform as the website does not generally permit the upload of pictures.

When using Instagram for business purposes, entrepreneurs can benefit immensely, as it is a principal and prevailing social media platform for sharing pictures and videos. It is worth noting that there are no barriers to the creation and sharing of pictures and videos as a result of the widespread use of tablets and mobile phones. For entrepreneurs to go digital by deploying Instagram as a social media platform, they need to create high-quality content as this facilitates their reaching out to more people (target audiences). Furthermore, there is a high probability that the entrepreneur's Instagram account will be discovered by people who were not following it due to the fact that some posts become visible on the News or Explore tab, where people see the posts that other users they follow have liked. Instagram users have a higher likelihood of purchasing the products or employing the services of a particular brand if there is a picture or video of the presentation or review of the product or service. Therefore, Instagram is a vital social media platform for digital entrepreneurship.

6.2.3   WhatsApp

WhatsApp is a social media platform as well as a cross-platform mobile messaging application that permits the free sending and receiving of messages (exchange of messages) from one person to another or from one person to a group of people. These messages are encrypted from one end to another. WhatsApp also facilitates the making of voice and video calls and the sending of unlimited images, documents, videos and audio files. WhatsApp was created in 2009 and is one of the most widely used instant messenger (social media) platforms across the globe. In February 2014, Facebook acquired WhatsApp, at which point it became WhatsApp Messenger, and it is available for download on Windows, Nokia, BlackBerry, iPhone, Mac/PC and Android devices [12].

WhatsApp has numerous advantages for entrepreneurs (businesses), which explains their widespread interest in using this platform. It is worth noting that the founders of WhatsApp had the main aim of making the platform serve as a means of providing services to people rather than being a business-friendly platform [13]. In spite of the initial purpose behind the creation of WhatsApp, however, various entrepreneurs deploy it as their social media platform as a means of communication. WhatsApp allows entrepreneurs and other businesses to offer products and services including real-time support and online purchase. It also serves as a medium for customers to air their views and give feedback on products and services. Therefore, it is a vital social media platform for digital entrepreneurship.

6.2.4 LinkedIn

LinkedIn is the largest social media networking site for businesses and professionals across the globe. Through LinkedIn, these businesses and professionals are able to connect and promote their skills, proficiency, knowledge, products, services and brands. LinkedIn can also be defined as a social media platform that is business-oriented and employment-oriented; it operates through its website and mobile applications and is free to download and use. It was founded in 2002 and launched in 2003. It is a social media platform that is of high benefit to entrepreneurs and business owners as it serves as a medium through which they can achieve an online presence. Moreover, LinkedIn helps entrepreneurs and businesses stay in touch with and stand out in the highly competitive market. Entrepreneurs and businesses can give information not only about themselves but also about their products, services and available employment opportunities on their LinkedIn pages.

Furthermore, LinkedIn pages can facilitate the sharing of professional views in a particular field. It is worth noting that LinkedIn pages can be followed by any user of LinkedIn, which increases the entrepreneurs' likelihood of engaging their customers. LinkedIn provides numerous benefits for entrepreneurs, allowing them to get their message across to a larger audience that could turn out to be potential customers, to receive endorsements and recommendations from present and previous customers about the products and services they offer and to link up with experts and professionals and possibly partner with them.

As a final point, entrepreneurs and business owners can employ the LinkedIn platform for recruitment as it is a faster and easier means of communication than email. Therefore, for success in digital entrepreneurship, LinkedIn is a vital social media platform.

6.2.5   *Periscope*

Periscope is a social media platform that permits people to stream or broadcast live video across the globe. It notifies all followers as soon as there is a live broadcast by other users and the followers are then able to post comments and give video likes in real time. The higher the number of video likes (the hearts users receive), the higher the live video broadcast pulsates on the screen [14]. On Periscope, live video broadcasts can no longer be viewed after twenty-four hours. Periscope is owned by Twitter and it is analogous to Snapchat in some ways. The length of the live broadcast is limited. A good number of entrepreneurs and companies actively deploy Periscope as it serves as an excellent way of getting their business visible. In the initial stages of a business, the audience on Periscope might be fairly small, but with consistent promotion of their Periscope channel, the entrepreneur or company stands an immense chance of attracting a higher number of people and thus gaining engagement.

Furthermore, Periscope serves as a medium for entrepreneurs and companies to engage their target audiences in real time by live streaming tutorials and big events, showcasing product launches and running Q&A (question and answer) sessions. As much as Periscope offers great benefits and is vital to digital entrepreneurship, however, entrepreneurs and companies should take adequate care in deciding how they make use of this platform due to its lack of privacy; Periscope hackers are out there, putting their skills to use. Therefore, it is advisable for entrepreneurs and companies to evaluate whether Periscope is the right social media platform for them.

6.2.6   *Snapchat*

Snapchat is a social media platform that is simple to use and allows users to share temporary messages, videos and pictures, referred to as "*Snaps.*" It has features such as captions, drawings and filters which users can enhance their videos and pictures with. The videos and pictures are visible for one to ten seconds before disappearing permanently as soon as other users have viewed them. Of course, some users might be fast enough to take a screenshot of the material first; in this case, the person who shared the video or picture is notified with regards to the user that took the screenshot. Snapchat had 398 million active users on a monthly basis as of April 2020 [15].

Since Snapchat permits users to follow and delve into the everyday lives of celebrities and the developments in any brand, especially the big brands, entrepreneurs and businesses can't fail to benefit by putting their products and services out there. Snapchat can serve as a means of delivering effective customer service and sharing Snaps with a URL caption, with the possibility that some followers will take a screenshot of the URL. These followers could possibly visit the website to learn more about the offered products and services.

However, one disadvantage of using Snapchat is that it lacks any kind of public analytics or key performance indicator (KPI) tool, meaning that it is not possible to measure the level of progress, activity or business performance in the social media. That said, entrepreneurs and companies can produce KPI tools for themselves by considering the average number of daily views of their Snaps, which can help them to measure their level of progress and performance relative to their set goals on a daily, monthly, quarterly or yearly basis, as the case may be.

6.2.7 Tumblr

Tumblr is a social media platform that is characterized by short bursts of content. These contents could be text, photos, videos, audio or a host of other types of content. Tumblr can be defined as a flexible platform for storytelling that gives room for numerous types of content to be pulled in. Tumblr is a type of blogging community, implying that it could be referred to as a "blog." Tumblr provides an avenue for its users to share anything (text, quotes, links, photos, music, videos) from their browsers, mobile phones, desktops or wherever [16]. It also provides an avenue for users to customize everything from colors to the HTML theme [16]. Within the Tumblr community, hashtags on posts are used for the purpose of search. Tumblr was created in 2007 and is one of the most attractive social media platforms with regards to the time consumed through the engagement of users in the community. It allows users to follow other users within the platform. However, it is worth noting that about half of the overall content on Tumblr is photos.

Tumblr is a useful tool in entrepreneurship and business as it can be integrated into websites, allowing entrepreneurs and businesses to engage their customers (audiences). One other benefit of Tumblr for entrepreneurs and businesses is its ability to be used for search engine optimization (SEO). For entrepreneurs and businesses to get maximum benefit from using Tumblr, they need to plan the content of their blogs ahead of posting. However, Tumblr is still a vital social media platform for successful digital entrepreneurship.

Table 6.1 *Differences between traditional media and social media*

Traditional media	Social media
• It is not and does not operate in real time	• It is and operates in real time
• Its media mix is very limited	• Its media mix is unlimited as different media (videos, photos and a host of other media) can be mixed
• This does not give rise to or foster the sharing of information	• This gives rise to and fosters the sharing of information
• It is fixed and cannot be changed	• It is not fixed and can be changed instantly
• It cannot be updated instantly	• It can be updated instantly
• It is rigid and this implies that it is not flexible	• It is not rigid and this implies that it is flexible
• It gives rise to limited comments, observations and reviews	• It gives rise to unlimited comments, observations and reviews

6.3   Social Media versus Traditional Media

It is hard, if not impossible, for anyone to reject the claim that the world has experienced immense transformation in the media sector since the days when television, newspapers and radios brought about the trend of mass marketing. This transformation has moved from deployment of traditional media to deployment of social media for the strategic purpose of raising brand awareness.

Nevertheless, there are some differences between traditional media and social media (Table 6.1). Section 6.4 looks at the advantages of social media for digital entrepreneurship.

6.4   Advantages of Social Media for Digital Entrepreneurship

Social media is a technological innovation that helps entrepreneurs and businesses to create a platform for connecting with individuals (target audiences) as well as other entrepreneurs and businesses, to increase customer engagement. As we have seen, social media consists of a variety of platforms that contribute to entrepreneurial capacity through extension of the entrepreneur's asset base of human, financial, technical, marketing and social capabilities. Thus, when entrepreneurs use social media platforms, they are increasing the likelihood that their business ventures will be successful. Moreover, social media platforms can serve as inspiration for starting up a business when an intending entrepreneur discovers *a need* of others through their own online interaction. In the same vein, social media platforms can serve as means of starting up a business when an intending entrepreneur discovers *resources* that others possess as a result of their own online interactions. Furthermore, social media platforms can serve as means for entrepreneurs to begin *investing in social capital*. The benefits to entrepreneurs of using social media platforms can be categorized into two types: *general benefits* and *innovative benefits*.

The *general benefits* that entrepreneurs can obtain from using social media platforms include *extension of contacts*; *support, motivation* and *encouragement* for their business ventures; and *information sharing*. Some of the *innovative benefits* that entrepreneurs can gain from the use of social media platforms include *business quality improvement*; *reduced costs* (social media platforms help to save costs), *production process improvements*; and *improvements in the marketing of products and services*. Therefore, it is of the utmost importance for entrepreneurs to look into the use of social media platforms as a tool to help their business ventures succeed.

6.5 Challenges and Potential Future of Social Media for Digital Entrepreneurship

Before discussing what the future potentially holds for social media and digital entrepreneurship, this section will first look at the challenges and risks associated with using social media for digital entrepreneurship, as overcoming these would help in creating a platform that social media companies could build on in order to strengthen their association with entrepreneurship. Some of these challenges are:

- Conflicts may arise between the preexisting traditional media and the social media due to differences in behavior and degree of accountability.
- Conflicts may arise with regards to organizational structure when social media platforms are used in formal organizations (e.g., since they are often structured in hierarchy).
- Issues may arise as a result of the deployment of social media platforms in businesses if such businesses don't make decisions about who is permitted to take part in such deployment.
- Issues may arise as a result of the deployment of social media platforms in businesses if such businesses don't put rules of usage of such social media platforms in place.
- Issues may arise as a result of the deployment of social media platforms in businesses if such businesses don't develop policies and governing rules that aid the successful use of such social media platforms.

- Businesses that decide to deploy social media platforms may be concerned about their staff getting distracted at work. This could lead to decreased productivity of both staff and the business overall.
- A couple of entrepreneurs or businesses may decide to deploy a particular or the latest social media platform because it's in vogue. This could lead to a down trend of productivity and engagement in such business ventures.
- Entrepreneurs and business owners may be concerned about their staff posting unsuitable, hateful or highly sensitive content on social media platforms.
- Entrepreneurs and business owners may be concerned about the issue of privacy (especially with regard to passwords) associated with social media platforms.
- A good number of entrepreneurs and business owners pay a lot of money for paid adverts without bearing in mind that such adverts can be blocked.
- A good number of entrepreneurs and business owners don't critically analyze which social media platform/s is/are highly beneficial to their business.

Notwithstanding these challenges and risks, the future of social media use in digital entrepreneurship is still bright. Therefore, measures should be put in place in order to make this bright future a reality. Some of these measures include:

- Businesses should improve password security to help prevent hackers from gaining access to business ventures through either accounts or databases.
- Social media companies should encourage users to always choose very strong passwords for their accounts, as this helps to prevent hacking.
- Social media companies should encourage users to change their passwords on a quarterly or monthly basis as this helps to make accounts secure.
- Business owners and entrepreneurs should decide specifically who is involved in the deployment and maintenance of social media platforms.
- Business owners and entrepreneurs should put in place policies and governing rules to aid the successful use of social media platforms.
- Entrepreneurs and business owners could use monitoring tools to prevent staff from getting distracted at work (especially during working hours) and should take measures for any staff member found wanting in this regard.
- Not all social media platforms are beneficial to all businesses. Therefore, entrepreneurs and business owners should ensure that

they critically analyze the available social media platforms in order to decide which of them is/are highly beneficial to their businesses.

- Entrepreneurs and business owners should ensure that their employees don't post unsuitable, hateful or highly sensitive content or material on social media platforms. They could offer training to facilitate this.

6.6   Case Studies

In this section, we focus on two well-known social media companies: Facebook and Twitter.

The first case study is Facebook, which is predominantly for social networking and currently the largest social media platform in the world [15–17]. Have you ever wondered how it all began? The first Facebook website was limited to Harvard students. Within a short period of time, it grew, as more colleges in the Boston axis then virtually all the universities across North America had access to it. At the time of its launch, it was called Facemash (Facemash.com) because its focus was on posting pictures of two students side by side and inviting classmates to decide who was "hot" and who was "not hot" [17].

In 2004, Mark Zuckerberg launched Facebook and the hype surrounding the site intensified and soon reached the ears of Sean Parker, a former co-founder of Napster, who began to offer his advice, informally. Later in that same year (2004), Peter Theil, the founder of PayPal, made a private investment of $500,000 in exchange for 10.2 percent of the Facebook company [17]. Facebook had more than a million people registered in that first year (2004), more than half a billion active users as at July 2010, and by 2013, it was one out of every seven people in the world [17]. Presently, a lot more people are on Facebook, which has nearly three billion monthly active users as of April 2020 [15–18]. The Facebook model allows users to create personal profiles; send friend requests to other users; share messages, videos and pictures; receive automatic notifications of posts and updates; and create their own Facebook pages.

Facebook users can join like-minded groups, organizations and even brands, too. For instance, Coca-Cola has its own Facebook page, with the company information and logo clearly visible, which updates customers on latest news and offers and enables the company to communicate with existing and intending customers. Coca-Cola was selected as an example because it has always been the most highly ranked Facebook page, as a result of Coca-Cola's state-of-the-art promotions as well as its ability to create good-quality interaction. One of the most remarkable Coca-Cola promotions was the "Summer Snapshot Contest" in 2010 where fans were encouraged to take photos with their summer Coca-Cola cans.

Thus, entrepreneurs wanting to make the best use of Facebook as a social media platform should take their cue from Coca-Cola and create sessions to engage past, present and potential customers, to help promote and grow their businesses.

Furthermore, Facebook is equipped with efficient analytic features that are useful in assessing the progress made via Facebook pages. Entrepreneurs and businesses should use these analytic features to discover which area(s) to improve on and what strategies to employ on their Facebook pages.

The second case study is Twitter, which started in 2006 from an idea of Jack Dorsey, one of its founders [19]. Dorsey initially thought that Twitter would be an SMS-based communication platform where groups of friends would all keep a close watch on each other through status updates [19]. He proposed the idea to Evan Williams, a co-founder of podcasting company Odeo, during a brainstorming session [19]. Williams advised Dorsey to spend more time developing the project further so, alongside himself and Williams, Dorsey also brought in Noah Glass (a co-founder of Odeo) and Biz Stone (then a former Google employee involved in Odeo) as early key players [19–21]. Dorsey was the first to send a message on Twitter on March 21, 2006 at 9:50 p.m.; the message read "just setting up my twttr" [19]. Afterwards, the name Twitter was adopted and it started growing rapidly. At the event tagged South By Southwest (@sxsw) interactive conference in 2007, a massive increase in the use of Twitter was witnessed in which more than sixty thousand Tweets were sent per day (during this event) [19]. This demonstrates Twitter's popularity as a social media platform that allows users to post, communicate and network through messages. These messages are referred to as "*Tweets*" and used to be limited to 140 characters; they were expanded to 280 characters on November 7, 2017 [22]. With regards to business, Twitter can be defined as a means by which businesses can interact with their customers, monitor such conversations and engage their customers. Twitter offers a platform that creates marketing opportunities for brands as users of Twitter have the tendency to patronize brands they follow. Accordingly, Twitter can also be used as a platform for customer service.

6.7   Summary

This chapter looked at digital entrepreneurship and social media, first defining entrepreneurship and the entrepreneurial spirit and then discussing how social media platforms, including Facebook, Twitter, YouTube, Instagram and WhatsApp, can offer a level playing field to various sectors and create opportunities such as working remotely at any time and on the go.

The chapter explored in more detail Facebook, Twitter, YouTube, Instagram, WhatsApp, LinkedIn, Periscope, Snapchat and Tumblr as examples of social media platforms (categories) in existence today and looked at the differences between social media and traditional media as well as the advantages of social media for digital entrepreneurship, such as contributing to entrepreneurial capacity through extension of the entrepreneur's asset base of human, financial, technical, market and social capabilities.

Moreover, it was mentioned that when entrepreneurs use social media platforms for their businesses, it helps them to gain access to more benefits including extension of contacts; support, motivation and encouragement; information sharing; improved business quality; reduced costs; production process improvements; and improvements in the marketing of products and services.

The chapter also looked at the potential future of social media in digital entrepreneurship. In particular, it discussed the challenges and risks associated with using social media for digital entrepreneurship and highlighted measures to be put in place to mitigate those risks and challenges. Finally, the chapter presented case studies of two popular social media companies, Facebook and Twitter.

In conclusion, it is paramount to note that for digital entrepreneurship to work successfully hand-in-hand with social media platforms, entrepreneurs should research carefully which platforms to use and how best to promote their brands on them.

References

1. BusinessDictionary. Entrepreneurship. (2018) www.businessdictionary.com/definition/entrepreneurship.html [accessed May 27, 2020].
2. European Commission. Digital Transformation of European Industry and Enterprises; A Report of the Strategic Policy Forum on Digital Entrepreneurship. (2015) http://ec.europa.eu/DocsRoom/documents/9462/attachments/1/translations/en/renditions/native [accessed May 27, 2020].
3. Zhao F, Collier A. Digital Entrepreneurship: Research and Practice. In: *9th Annual Conference of the EuroMed Academy of Business, Warsaw, Poland* (2016) 2173–82.
4. Bharadwaj A, El Sawy O, Pavlou P, Venkatraman N. Digital Business Strategy: Toward a Next Generation of Insights. *MIS Q* (2013) 37:471–82.
5. CEDA. Australia's Future Workforce? (2015) www.ceda.com.au/Research-and-policy/All-CEDA-research/Research-catalogue/Australia-s-future-workforce [accessed May 27, 2020].
6. Kaplan AM, Haenlein M. Users of the World, Unite! The Challenges and Opportunities of Social Media. *Business Horizons* (2010) 53:59–68. doi: 10.1016/j.bushor.2009.09.003.

7. Lake C. What Is Social Media? Here Are 34 Definitions ... (2009) https://econsultancy.com/blog/3527-what-is-social-media-here-are-34-definitions [accessed May 27, 2020].

8. Gill P, Arlitt M, Li Z, Mahanti A. YouTube Traffic Characterization: A View from the Edge. In: *Proceedings of the 7th ACM SIGCOMM Conference on Internet Measurement, New York, USA* (2007) 15–28.

9. Weber T. BBC Strikes Google-YouTube Deal. (2007) http://news.bbc.co.uk/2/hi/business/6411017.stm [accessed May 27, 2020].

10. Nicholas T. Top 25 Young Entrepreneur Success Stories. (2010) https://entrepreneurthearts.com/25-young-entrepreneur-success-stories/ [accessed May 27, 2020].

11. Instagram. About Us. (2013) https://about.instagram.com/about-us [accessed May 27, 2020].

12. WhatsApp Inc. WhatsApp Inc. (2017) https://www.whatsapp.com [accessed May 27, 2020].

13. Kerrigan S. 9 Ways Your Business Can Use WhatsApp as an Effective Communication Tool. (2015) www.linkedin.com/pulse/9-ways-your-business-can-use-whatsapp-effective-tool-sarah-kerrigan [accessed May 27, 2020].

14. Twitter Inc. Periscope – Live Video Streaming around the World. (2020) https://itunes.apple.com/app/id972909677 [accessed May 27, 2020].

15. Statista. Most Popular Social Networks Worldwide as of April 2020, Ranked by Number of Active Users (in Millions). (2020) www.statista.com/statistics/272014/global-social-networks-ranked-by-number-of-users/ [accessed May 27, 2020].

16. Tumblr. Tumblr. (2018) www.tumblr.com/ [accessed May 27, 2020].

17. Zeevi D. The Ultimate History of Facebook [INFOGRAPHIC]. (2013) www.socialmediatoday.com/content/ultimate-history-facebook-infographic [accessed May 27, 2020].

18. Facebook. Company Info. (2020) https://about.fb.com/company-info/ [accessed May 27, 2020].

19. MacArthur A. The Real History of Twitter, In Brief – How the Micro-messaging Wars Were Won. (2017) www.lifewire.com/history-of-twitter-3288854 [accessed May 27, 2020].

20. Henry Z. Twitter Co-founder Biz Stone on How to Know It's Time to Make a Big Move. (2017) www.inc.com/magazine/201703/zoe-henry/founders-forum-biz-stone.html [accessed May 27, 2020].

21. Wolan C. The Real Story of Twitter. (2011) www.forbes.com/sites/christianwolan/2011/04/14/the-real-story-of-twitter/#1817a87466af [accessed May 27, 2020].

22. Perez S. Twitter Officially Expands Its Character Count to 280 Starting Today. (2017) https://techcrunch.com/2017/11/07/twitter-officially-expands-its-character-count-to-280-starting-today/ [accessed May 27, 2020].

7   Digital Entrepreneurship and the Internet of Things (IoT)

7.1   Introduction

Entrepreneurs and business owners serve as the main forces for the creation of great innovations as the Internet of Things (IoT) is bringing about change in the existing ecosystem. Before we go further, let us briefly recall the definition of entrepreneurship provided in Chapter 6: the capacity and willingness to undertake the conception, organization and management of a productive venture with all attendant risks, while seeking profit as a reward [1]. Moreover, the entrepreneurial spirit is characterized by innovations and risk-taking and is an essential component of a nation's ability to succeed in an ever-changing and ever more competitive global marketplace [2]. Also, digital entrepreneurship can be generally defined as the means or methods of creating fresh and innovative businesses, products or commodities as well as services that are enabled, permitted and provided via the Internet. These means or methods include start-ups (new businesses that deliver new products and services) as well as existing businesses. Accordingly, digital entrepreneurship can be further outlined as the creation of new businesses as well as the rapid transformation of existing businesses through technological innovations (through the development of digital technologies and the innovative practice of these innovative technologies) [3, 4]. The speedy spread and increase of digital technologies coupled with innovations and functional abilities have overwhelmingly brought about changes in highly competitive environments, restructuring the strategies and processes that accompany traditional businesses [3]. So, it is worth noting that digital entrepreneurship is powered by the innovation of digital technologies and it is not possible without new innovative technologies such as social media, big data and a host of other innovative technological platforms. New innovative technologies create new avenues for partnership (collaboration), leveraging resources, product design, service design, development and deployment. From among those technologies, this chapter focuses on the IoT.

So, what is IoT? It refers to the interconnection of smart devices, physical devices, buildings and other objects and devices that have inherent software, electronics, actuators, network connectivity and sensors that make it possible for them to exchange and collect data. IoT can also be defined as the application of physical objects that are made up of embedded technology in order to communicate with their internal states and/or their external environment [5]. IoT technology is widely used across the globe, particularly as it replaces the traditional way of doing business. Nowadays, various business ventures have implemented and are in the process of implementing the latest technological innovations to boost their businesses.

7.2   Insight into the IoT

Building on the definition of IoT from Section 7.1, it can also be defined as data streams to and from connected physical devices, that is, physical devices delivering data from and to centralized repositories to create further interactions [6]. The physical devices that deliver the data may or may not create the data themselves and they may or may not process the information before delivering it [6]. These devices can be intelligent or not intelligent, ranging from an item tagged with a radio frequency identification (RFID) chip coded with a unique identifier to a complex heavy industrial machine that has sensors that monitor and control every phase of operation and output [6].

In addition, data communication can be carried out through various combinations of wired and wireless networks, which can be either open or private [6]. Furthermore, we can also define IoT as the developmental stage in the complete value chain of both organization and management. The IoT environment consists of smart mobility, smart buildings, smart homes, social web, business web, smart logistics, smart grid, cyber-physical production systems (CPPSs) and the smart factory (entrepreneurial and other business ventures) [7]. IoT has brought about what has been called the Fourth Revolution, or *Industry 4.0*, based on revolution numbers that are characterized by degree of complexity, the Fourth Revolution being more complex than the First, Second and Third Revolutions [7]. Table 7.1 describes the different revolutions and the increasing complexity of changes associated with each.

Prevalent use of IoT by start-ups, entrepreneurs and other business ventures as well as ICT industries is closing the gap between the virtual world and the real one. The systematized online networks of the various social machines – CPPSs [7] – may be considered analogous to the social networks [7]. It is worth noting that start-ups, entrepreneurs and small and medium enterprises (SMEs) are the forces behind these various technological innovations. IoT has modified the existing IT ecosystem

Table 7.1 *The different revolutions: descriptions and complexity*

Revolution	Description	Complexity
First Revolution	Water and steam power are used for mechanical production facilities	Slightly complex
Second Revolution	Electrical energy is introduced to increase production levels	More complex than the First Revolution
Third Revolution	IT and electronics are introduced to automate production at all levels	More complex than the Second Revolution
Fourth Revolution	CPPSs are introduced, merging the virtual and the real worlds	More complex than the Third Revolution

Source: Adapted from [7].

by giving room for various devices to be used and for data to be obtained from such devices on a large scale, especially when combined with other technologies such as big data and cloud. IoT has brought about and is still expected to bring about more innovative developments as well as opportunities for entrepreneurs (especially web entrepreneurs) and other business owners. IoT is based mainly on the end-to-end digitalization of every physical asset and the integration of these into the digital ecosystem with value chain partners; this creates a network of innovative new technologies in order to generate value [8].

However, with regard to the characteristics of Industry 4.0 where IoT plays a key role, as pointed out by [7] there are basically four main characteristics: *vertical networking of smart production systems, horizontal integration of the global value chain networks of the new generation, engineering throughout the whole value chain* and *exponential technologies*. In what follows, we briefly discuss each of these characteristics, based on the arguments provided by [7].

The *vertical networking of smart production systems* applies the use of CPPSs in order to allow quick reaction to variations in demand and faults. Entrepreneurial ventures as well as other business ventures and industries coordinate and structure their businesses so as to produce goods and offer services that are in accordance with customers' specifications. This calls for data to be integrated to a great extent. CPPSs allow for better management of production and maintenance, including networking and easier location of available resources and materials. Processes are recorded and discrepancies are automatically listed, which facilitates making changes to orders, undertaking rapid repair of machines and other equipment in the event of breakdown and monitoring to detect any form of wear and tear in any material or item.

The *horizontal integration of the global value chain networks of the new generation* allows the real-time optimization of networks to give room for transparent integration and high-level flexibility in the rapid response to any fault. It also improves global optimization [7]. Networking is facilitated by CPPSs from logistics that are inbound – warehousing, production, marketing and sales – to logistics that are outbound [7]. The history of any product or service is recorded and can be retrieved at any time, which guarantees traceability. Moreover, there is flexibility and transparency in the whole process chain (from supplier to entrepreneurial or business venture or industry to customer). It also allows customers' specifications to be altered at any point, from the planning and development stage, to the production stage, even up to the distribution stage, thus building dynamism into the quality, price, timing, risk and other factors at any of the value process chain stages in real time. Furthermore, as a result of this characteristic of IoT, entirely new models for entrepreneurial ventures and businesses can be created through horizontal integration of customers as well as partners in business.

Engineering throughout the whole value chain also cuts across the full life cycle of the products/services and customers [7]. The engineering takes place in the design development and manufacturing stages, as new products and services require either an entirely new or an improved (revised) system of production. In addition, data are made available at every stage of the life cycle of the product or service, thereby increasing flexibility.

Finally, *exponential technologies* act as a catalyst by enabling individualized solutions, high-level flexibility and cost-saving in the processes involved in the value chain with respect to entrepreneurial ventures and businesses [7]. Sensor technology, robotics as well as artificial intelligence (AI) can further speed up individualized solutions as well as increasing flexibility and autonomy. AI can aid in the planning of flexible routes for driverless vehicles, saving both time and costs, and it can help increase the level of reliability in production and create new solutions in design, service delivery, and construction. Moreover, AI is useful in the analysis of big data and can enhance delivery of services by improving the collaboration between humans and machines. Further, using functional nano-materials and nano-sensors in production control functions can increase both quality and efficiency. These functional nano-materials and nano-sensors can be used to create robots that work safely with humans. An example of exponential technology is 3D printing [7], which enables production of new solutions with higher levels of complexity, functionality, flexibility – albeit still with challenges related to costs – while also facilitating new supply chain solutions with respect to reduction in inventory and faster delivery times [20, 21]. Exponential technologies commonly used include 3D printing, biotechnology, neurotechnology, nanotechnology, new energy and sustainability, ICT and mobile technology, sensoring, AI, drones and robotics [7]. These technologies have brought about drastic changes in business processes thereby accelerating businesses and making them more flexible.

7.3 The IoT State of the Service Market

The state of the service market of IoT includes the following areas, elements and requirements (see also [6]):

- **IoT is developing in two distinct strains:** Industrial production IoT has a very strong, durable, mature and interoperable services culture that is rooted in the workflow logic of IT. However, for entrepreneurial ventures and other businesses that are focused mainly on services, IoT is rapidly transforming and advancing for the future, making it difficult to come up with repeatable processes within their teams [6, 8].

- **IoT is a broader digital innovation:** A large number of the activities that presently go on in entrepreneurial ventures, businesses and other industries are focused on the innovation and planning stages rather than the execution stage. The ability to generate, collect and record data on a transforming and advancing set of physical assets and interactions will bring forth results when actionable insights bring about strong and well-defined business value.

- **The opportunities in IoT call for the collaboration of competitors:** Organizations look for various digital platforms to help integrate data from different sources in order to obtain the best and most comprehensive values. IoT solutions are of little or no use if they will not solve a particular business issue or bring forth the required results as well as strong and well-defined business value [8].

- **End-to-end security is of the utmost importance across IoT:** It is highly relevant to the collaboration of different service providers, as well as being an entry point for hackers.

- **Data are easily accessible through plug-and-play digital services:** A good number of entrepreneurs across various industries are applying IoT to drive their businesses.

- **Various skills are required to work together for sound IoT solutions and services:** IoT connects the various skills that are accommodated within the practice lines of service providers: telecommunications, cloud, engineering, business strategy, security, digital strategy, analytics, user experience as well as mobility are put together in dexterous teams or groups for different customers after defining the calculated or preplanned aims and objectives as well as the targeted goals [6]. For entrepreneurial and other business ventures to be successful, the parties involved must all recognize and realize the actual business values.

Finally, IoT services can be divided into the following five main categories [6]:

- **IoT connectivity**, encompassing governance strategy, security strategy, data transmission, cost of telecommunications consulting, a roadmap of IoT technology and strategic planning.
- **IoT consulting**, encompassing governance strategy, security strategy, data transmission, cost of telecommunications consulting, a roadmap of IoT technology and strategic planning.
- **IoT management**, encompassing data security, devices management, network management and cloud hosting.
- **IoT enablement**, encompassing development of sensors, devices security, product engineering, software engineering and the development of custom apps.
- **IoT integration**, encompassing the deployment of analytics, security, system integration, the design and deployment of databases and the renovation of applications.

7.4   Advantages of IoT for Digital Entrepreneurship

The advantages of IoT for entrepreneurial as well as business ventures are numerous. Some of these advantages are: increased *competition*, accelerated *transformation*, improved *IT and other skills and IT resources*, *development of segments*, and creation of *more opportunities*. Here is a brief discussion of each:

- **Increased competition:** For most entrepreneurial ventures as well as other businesses, IoT is having an immense impact on local and global value chains and providing an all-round platform for improved competition since there is increased competition in the market [9]. These businesses are thus offering better and improved products and services.
- **Accelerated transformation:** A huge number of entrepreneurial and business ventures are beginning to embrace IoT implementation in their developmental and production processes as well as other business processes [10].
- **Improved IT and other skills:** Most entrepreneurial and business ventures are short of highly skilled professionals in the area of IoT, thus they tend to improve the skills of their existing staff by engaging them in various forms of training [10]. For successful IoT transformation, it is of utmost importance for entrepreneurial and business ventures to invest in highly suitable skills.

- **Improved IT resources:** Many entrepreneurial and business ventures have improved IT infrastructure to cater for IoT, which is essential for a successful IoT transformation [7]. Moreover, it is fast becoming harder to separate products and services rendered by entrepreneurial and business ventures from their IT infrastructures [3, 10].
- **Development of segments:** Presently, production, procurement, sales, warehousing, research and development (R&D), logistics and sales are the core of the transformation to IoT by various entrepreneurial and business ventures. Developing business segments creates vast space for customization [7].
- **Creation of more opportunities:** IoT creates more opportunities for entrepreneurial and business ventures as it opens up new methodologies through which such businesses can integrate the needs and choices of their customers into their innovative, developmental as well as their production processes as well as facilitating direct sharing of data with their machines and systems [11]. This makes analysis of machine data much easier and helps to improve the quality of and prevent the development of faults in production processes.

As much as IoT brings advantages to digital entrepreneurship, however, it also creates technical and knowledge challenges, as follows:

- **Technical challenge:** The fast development of IoT embeds not just one but numerous technologies. For entrepreneurs to make the best use of IoT and deliver great value to their ventures, they must clearly understand these options [3, 12]. There must thus be easy access to knowledge with regard to the "digital" options provided by IoT. In addition, there should be set standards in order to create trust [3]. For ideas to move to concept and proof-of-concept stages, then to market, requires key strategic steps to be taken to ensure the continuous functioning of the system beyond the proof-of-concept test environment [9].
- **Knowledge challenge:** The difficulty here is in entrepreneurs and business owners knowing which knowledge to access. The accessible knowledge may not be adequate due to the lack of highly skilled professionals in the fields of big data analysis and real-time data analysis. Such skills must be taught and developed in schools (for discussion of adding these skills to school curricula, see Chapter 4) [3].

7.5   Potential Future of IoT for Digital Entrepreneurship

As a result of its numerous advantages, IoT's future is bright with regard to entrepreneurship. However, certain things have to be put in place if we are to enjoy all that IoT has to offer. This section discusses IoT's future within Industry 4.0 (vertical networking of smart production systems, horizontal integration of the global value chain networks of the new generation, engineering throughout the whole value chain, and exponential technologies). With regard to the vertical networking of smart production systems, there are four main areas to highlight, namely *IT integration, cloud-based applications, efficiency of operations,* and *data management and analytics* [7]:

- **IT integration:** The existing IT infrastructures of most entrepreneurial and business ventures are often very poor and fragmented. For these ventures to successfully implement IoT, they must replace or significantly upgrade these IT infrastructures. New combined solutions are required to be put in place, especially in the aspects of sensor supplies, control systems, business applications, customer-facing applications, and communications network [7]. However, for entrepreneurs and businesses to enjoy the immense future that IoT holds for them, they need to be able to choose the right components, adaptations and integrations to put into these all-encompassing new solutions.
- **Cloud-based applications:** For cloud-based applications to be a force to be reckoned with in the implementation of IoT, entrepreneurial and business ventures need to network cloud-based applications. These give rise to great opportunities in the hosting and efficient use of collected big data. Decentralized networked smart-production systems have specific advantages as previously inconceivable computation power will allow cloud-based applications to deliver access to all vital data anywhere and at any time. This will make it far easier to monitor, collect, distribute, analyze and manage data throughout the network of the global value chain [7]. In addition, it will give rise to the provision of market solutions that are all-encompassing, which will effortlessly and completely integrate all of the processes and components involved in the business value chain, including the end customers. It will also give room for further product innovations.
- **Operational efficiency:** For entrepreneurial and business ventures, the future of IoT holds new and great opportunities for them to achieve high efficiency in operations. If the data gathered from machines and sensors are efficiently analyzed, properly assessed and effectively applied, it will enable innovative decision-making for safety in operations, service deliveries, maintenance as well as faster and better work processes. Moreover, there will be a reduction in costs to customers due to maintenance being executed before a fault develops [7]. Therefore, for entrepreneurial and business ventures to have advantage over their competitors with regard to costs and reliability, they will need to implement IoT in order to have efficient operations [7].

- **Data management and analytics:** IoT will produce data in large quantities, which entrepreneurs and businesses are expected to collect, process and analyze in order to gain competitive advantage and be able to make good decisions and eventually create new insights. For entrepreneurs and businesses to benefit from the great future that IoT holds with respect to data management and analytics, they need to ensure the development of specialized skills in the areas of effective data management and analytics [7]. They also need to set up new business processes based on the information revealed by the data analysis. The entrepreneurial and business ventures that stand out from competitors with regard to data management and analytics as well as ability to set up new business processes will rule the particular business sector [7, 13].

With regard to the horizontal integration of the global value chain networks of the new generation, there are five main areas to highlight, namely *smart logistics, smart supply chains, management of IT security, management of new intellectual property (IP)*, and *optimization of the business model*:

- **Smart logistics:** Presently, entrepreneurial and business ventures are faced with the challenge of integrating autonomous technologies, new services and flexible logistics systems as well as linking, for example, internal production and external service providers [7]. For these businesses to benefit from IoT and gain competitive advantage, they need to become smarter across the new generations of the global value chain network [7, 13]. This applies to both inbound and outbound logistics as well as to logistics within the organization.

- **Smart supply chains:** The bright future of IoT requires that entrepreneurial and business ventures should focus on new models geared toward the needs of the individual customer. They also need to work together with their business partners to develop cooperative models [7]. However, this will place new demands on their supply chains, which these businesses must find ways to accommodate. It is expected that IoT will bring about a "single" database [7], thereby creating a smarter, more effective, more transparent and clearer supply chain right from the customer requirements discovery stage to the delivery stage. It is also expected that IoT will bring about more aligned and united functionality of production and sales, R&D as well as purchasing and procurement [7]. Therefore, entrepreneurial and business ventures that strive to be successful need to integrate the needs of both suppliers and customers into every aspect of their value creation processes.

- **Management of IT security:** Alongside the great things that IoT is bringing come greater demands for data security. Entrepreneurial and business ventures must put risk management and security strategies in place to guard against attacks and build up better operational security throughout the value chain [14], including prevention of unauthorized use of data, products and materials.

- **Management of new IP:** It is expected that entrepreneurial and business ventures will approach this issue individually, tailoring their IP solutions to the specific IP issues raised by their particular IoT development of new cooperation and business models [7–14].

- **Optimization of the business model:** The future of IoT is new business approaches, as opposed to modifications and upgrades to existing models. For entrepreneurial and business ventures to enjoy this benefit, they will need to develop new skills across the organization and implement a new (digital) business model across their entire business [7–14].

Regarding engineering throughout the whole value chain, there are two main areas to highlight, namely *effective management of the lifecycle* and *effective management of innovation*:

- **Effective management of the lifecycle:** For entrepreneurial and business ventures to benefit fully from the future that IoT holds for them, they need to put advanced analytics (e.g. predictive and prescriptive analytics) and AI to good use in processing big data and producing useful indicators in the early stages of their business [7–14]. This will assess and reassess the likelihood of producing useful decisions supported by the data. The future of IoT will make it possible to obtain significantly important data for the management of the business life cycle from anywhere in the world and at any time [7]. It will also make it possible for entrepreneurial and business ventures to better grasp and meet the needs and demands of their customers and to be able to customize the life cycle of products [14].

- **Effective management of innovation:** The future of IoT will give room for the further improvement of the effective management of innovation in areas such as product development and project portfolio management, among others [7]. IoT will also make it possible for entrepreneurial and business ventures to keep track of their ROI (return on investment) from IoT innovations and identify possible risks through the use of global comparative project data for monitoring and improvement [7–14]. Moreover, IoT can be used for advanced R&D.

Regarding exponential technologies, there are two main areas to highlight, namely *corporate venturing* and *learning organizations*:

- **Corporate venturing:** The future of IoT will provide entrepreneurial and business ventures with opportunities for corporate venturing, which involves investing in new developments in the early stages. Corporate venturing will also enable entrepreneurial and business ventures to benefit from disruptive advancements and exponential technologies [7]. Early-stage investments will give rise to developed innovations and long-lasting competitive advantage [14]. Therefore, IoT will create new areas of business that will then turn out to be the core areas of future business.

- **Learning organizations:** The future of IoT will provide entrepreneurial and business ventures with opportunities to become learning organizations if the full potential of IoT is harnessed. This will be vital to the sustainability of entrepreneurial and business ventures.

7.6   Case Studies

This section focuses on two business ventures: LeaderMES (Emerald Information Systems Ltd) and Yamazaki Mazak Corporation.

LeaderMES (Emerald Information Systems Ltd) is a company develops software for use in digitizing production processes in factories [15]. LeaderMES uses IoT to optimize production by streamlining production processes [16]. The company was founded in 2003 and its headquarters are located in Israel [15]. The CEO of is Amir Aloni [17]. One of the company's visions is to reach a broad range of new clients and to supply them with a highly "secure and reliable self-deployed solution" [17]. When LeaderMES came up against one particular challenge, it asked Cisco to proffer an IoT solution. The challenge was to deploy solutions that would significantly reduce installation time and complexity as well as increase security, since LeaderMES systems function in a highly demanding business environment [17]. Cisco devised a solution that included [17]:

- IoT connectivity using a Cisco Industrial Router with a Wi-Fi access point
- a fog application
- a fog application framework
- IoT security (control of networks based on policy) [17].

The business outcomes after deployment of Cisco's solution included [17]:

- increased market opportunity through the application of Emerald LeaderMES to digital manufacturing transformation;
- reduced installation time from four weeks (average) to one day;
- global deployment through remote management and compact size;
- faster time to value with measurable customer impact, optimization of the workforce and reduction of the manufacturing process cycle time [17].

This goes to show the significance of IoT for entrepreneurial and business ventures.

The second case study focuses on Yamazaki Mazak Corporation, which has been vital in the development of the machine tool industry [18]. It is a global leading company that was founded in 1919 [18]. The company president is Takashi Yamazaki [18]. Some of the products that Yamazaki Mazak Corporation offers are multi-tasking machines, horizontal machining centers, double-column machining centers, flexible manufacturing systems and production support software [18]. However, when Yamazaki Mazak Corporation faced a particular challenge, it contacted Cisco to come up with an IoT solution. The challenge was a need for a secure, standard-based means of connecting and deriving value and raw data from machine tools [19]. This was a necessity considering, for example, the need to prevent hacking into the system, a need common to both digital technologies and IoT. The solution proffered by Cisco included [19]:
• IoT connectivity
• an application framework
• a fog application
• real-time analytics.

The business outcomes after deployment of Cisco's solution included [19]:
• expansion in the market opportunity;
• cost consolidation as a result of running the fog application and real-time analytics on the IoT network infrastructure;
• swift time to value with measurable customer impact with respect to improved overall equipment effectiveness (OEE) and increased use of the system.

This case study also goes to show the significance of IoT for business and entrepreneurial ventures.

7.7   Summary

This chapter looked at digital entrepreneurship and IoT. It explained that IoT refers to the interconnection of smart devices, physical devices, buildings and other objects and devices that have embedded technology that enables them to exchange and collect data and to communicate with their internal and external environments [5]. The chapter discussed how IoT is part of Industry 4.0 and how it deals with data streams to and from connected physical devices and centralized repositories, whether or not those devices are intelligent and whether or not they create or process the data themselves [6]. The chapter listed the four main areas of Industry 4.0 where IoT plays a key role: *vertical networking of smart production systems, horizontal integration of the global value chain networks of the new generation, engineering throughout the whole value chain,* and *exponential technologies* [7].

The chapter looked at the state of the service market for IoT, focusing on IoT development areas, IoT as a broader digital innovation, the IT opportunities created when competitors collaborate, the ease of accessibility through plug-and-play digital services, the various skills required for sound IoT solutions and services and security. It then discussed IoT connectivity, IoT consulting, IoT management, IoT enablement and IoT integration as the five main categories of IoT services. Furthermore, it discussed the advantages of IoT for digital entrepreneurship, namely increased competition, accelerated transformation, improved IT and other skills and IT resources, development of segments and creation of more opportunities.

Critically, the chapter discussed the potential future of IoT for digital entrepreneurship with respect to the four main characteristics of Industry 4.0: vertical networking of smart production systems encompassed IT integration, cloud-based applications, efficiency of operations, and data management and analytics; horizontal integration of the global value chain networks of the new generation encompassed smart logistics, smart supply chains, management of IT security, management of new IP and business model optimization; engineering throughout the whole value chain encompassed effective management of the life cycle and of innovation; and exponential technologies encompassed corporate venturing and learning organizations.

Finally, the chapter presented two case studies – LeaderMES (Emerald Information Systems Ltd) and Yamazaki Mazak Corporation. – showing how IoT facilitated solutions to two challenges, significantly reducing installation time and complexity as well as increasing security in factory production process for LeaderMES and making it possible to securely connect and derive value and raw data from machine tools for Yamazaki Mazak Corporation.

In conclusion, IoT is hugely significant for the growth, development and sustainability of business and entrepreneurial ventures, making it crucial for such business to take the necessary steps to implement IoT. If these businesses can map out an IoT strategy, create initial pilot projects, define the competencies required, master data analytics, adapt to the transformation and undertake active ecosystem planning, they should be able to enjoy the full range of benefits that IoT offers.

References

1. BusinessDictionary. Entrepreneurship. (2018) www.businessdictionary.co m/definition/entrepreneurship.html [accessed May 28, 2020].

2. European Commission. Digital Transformation of European Industry and Enterprises; A Report of the Strategic Policy Forum on Digital Entrepreneurship. (2015) http://ec.europa.eu/DocsRoom/documents/9462/attachments/1/translations/en/renditions/native [accessed May 28, 2020].

3. Bharadwaj A, El Sawy O, Pavlou P, Venkatraman N. Digital Business Strategy: Toward a Next Generation of Insights. *MIS Q* (2013) 37:471–82.

4. Nambisan S. Digital Entrepreneurship: Toward a Digital Technology Perspective of Entrepreneurship. *Entrepreneurship Theory and Practice* (2016) doi: 10.1111/etap.12254.

5. Purdy M, Davarzani L. *The Growth Game-Changer: How the Industrial Internet of Things Can Drive Progress and Prosperity.* Accenture (2015).

6. Marks O. *Internet of Things (IoT) Services – Excerpt for Cognizant.* HfS Research Ltd (2016).

7. Schlaepfer RC, Koch M, Merkofer P. *Challenges and Solutions for the Digital Transformation and Use of Exponential Technologies.* Deloitte AG (2015).

8. Davies R. Industry 4.0 – Digitalisation for Productivity and Growth – Briefing. EPRS | European Parliamentary Research Service – PE 568.337. European Union (2015).

9. Smart Action. Fostering IoT entrepreneurship and Innovation through Startups and SME Workshop Report. Publisher: Smart Action Project (2014) (www.smart-action.eu).

10. Cisco. *The Internet of Everything: Unlocking the Opportunity for UK Startups: The Road to Digitalisation.* Cisco International Limited (2014).

11. Fleisch E, Weinberger M, Wortmann F. Business Models and the Internet of Things. Bosch Internet Things Serv Lab (2014).

12. Kende M. ICTs for Inclusive Growth: E-entrepreneurship on the Open Internet. Global Information Technology Report 2015. World Economic Forum (2015) 49–55.

13. Spelman M, Weinelt B, Lacy P, Shah A. *Digital Transformation of Industries – Demystifying Digital and Securing $100 Trillion for Society and Industry by 2025 – Industry Agenda.* World Economic Forum in collaboration with Accenture (2016).

14. Geissbauer R, Vedso J, Schrauf S. 2016 Global Industry 4.0 Survey: What We Mean by Industry 4.0 | Survey Key Findings | Blueprint for Digital Success – Industry 4.0: Building the Digital Enterprise. PwC (2016).

15. IoTONE. LeaderMES (Emerald Information Systems LTD). (2017) https://m.iotone.com/vendor/leadermes-emerald-information-systems-ltd/v1652 [accessed May 28, 2020].

16. Emerald Information Systems – LeaderMES. About. (2017) http://leadermes.com/about/ [accessed April 2, 2018].

17. Cisco Public. IoT: Driving Digital Transformation – Ecosystem Partner Case Study – LeaderMES – C36-737328–00 07/16. Cisco (2016).

18. Yamazaki Mazak Corporation. About Mazak. (2017) www.mazak.com/about-mazak/ [accessed April 2, 2018].

19. Cisco Public. (2016) IoT: Driving Digital Transformation – Connected Machines Case Study – Mazak – C36-737400–00 06/16. Cisco.

20. Van der Straeten J. A Cost Perspective on 3D Printing. pwc Belgium. (n.d.)
    www.pwc.be/en/news-publications/insights/2017/cost-perspective-3d-print
    ing.html [accessed December 30, 2020].
21. Team Blueprint. The Real Cost of 3D Printing. (2020) https://3dprint.com
    /267987/the-real-cost-of-3d-printing/ [accessed December 30, 2020].

8   Digital Entrepreneurship and Blockchain

8.1   Introduction

In 2008, under the name of Satoshi Nakamoto, a whitepaper introduced the protocol for what the author claimed was a needed "electronic payment system based on cryptographic proof instead of trust, allowing any two willing parties to transact directly with each other without the need for a trusted third party" (p. 1) [1]. The resulting cryptocurrency was eventually named Bitcoin [2], while the block "chained" to create the underlying network of transactions became known as "blockchain" (Nakamoto's whitepaper referred only to "block" and "chain," not to "blockchain").

As Vinay Gupta [4], founder of Hexayurt.Capital and CEO of Mattereum[3], pointed out in 2017, after bitcoin "the second innovation was called blockchain, which was essentially the realization that the underlying technology that operated bitcoin could be separated from the currency and used for all kinds of other interorganizational cooperation" [5]. Accordingly, in the last decade, we have diffused interest in the blockchain application across different industries as well as public sector organizations [6–8]. Moreover, although the main interest has been oriented toward the change and innovation that blockchain may bring to the financial sector and banking, a stream of research has investigated its impact on business models in other industries where, for example, organizations are acting as intermediaries creating value from brokerage (see, e.g., [9, 10]). Accordingly, blockchain has also been seen and studied as a source of innovation opportunities and challenges for entrepreneurs [10, 11]. Taking these issues into account, this chapter briefly introduces the main elements of blockchain technology first, before discussing eight companies that apply the technology in different sectors, thus providing insights into the potential of blockchain for digital entrepreneurs.

8.2 Insights into Blockchain

Blockchain technology was brought to life as a result of Bitcoin, which is both a digital currency that was launched in 2009 [12] and an example of a virtual currency. It is a cryptocurrency based on cryptographic algorithms and built on a log of transactions in a blockchain and circulated across networked users. Bitcoin adopts the "distributed ledger" scheme, which is the decentralized fundamental structure of the database used for digital currencies transactions, including Bitcoin, for the storage of all historical transactions [13].

It is worth noting here that the operation of digital currency schemes should include a means of security against attacks on the blockchain. For example, consider the case where an attacker spends a certain amount of money and then tries to reverse that particular transaction. The attacker could broadcast their own version of the blockchain where that particular transaction was not included, meaning that other participants would not know what the valid version of the ledger was prior to the attack. Nevertheless, the purpose behind the design of Bitcoin was to perform three main functions of traditional money. As pointed out, for example, by [14], these three main functions are: (i) to simplify exchange commercially, (ii) to store value by users for future purpose and (iii) to act as the basic unit for measuring the value of goods and services.

Before the invention of Bitcoin and its blockchain, digital currencies were perceived as not being realistic as a result of the simplicity in the way that digital currencies could be replicated. This was referred to as a "double-spend" problem in which every transaction bears a risk [15] related to the sending by a holder of a copy of the original digital transaction to a merchant. This risk was typically faced by deploying a trusted centralized intermediary. However, the adoption of Bitcoin blockchain has transferred to the entire network system both (i) the history of all transactions and their authentication and (ii) the obligation of keeping up to date with every transaction. For Bitcoin, there are nodes (i.e., the users of the network) and these nodes hold a blockchain made up of all the historical transactions carried out on the network. The blockchain performs as a network of computer-generated databases with each consisting of historical Bitcoin transactions. Bitcoin's approach can be grouped into seven categories: *data storage, data distribution, mechanism of agreement, mechanism upgrade, criteria for participation, defense mechanism* and *incentivization scheme* (see a summary in Table 8.1).

Moreover, the Bitcoin network security is dependent on a security protocol called "*Proof of Work*" (PoW). Initially proposed in 1993 by Cynthia Dwork and Moni Naor, this network security protocol is

Table 8.1 *The categories, questions and approaches of Bitcoin*

Category	Question	Approach of Bitcoin
Data storage	How should data be stored?	Data should be stored via the blockchain technology
Data distribution	How should the distribution of new data be?	The distribution of new data should be in a peer-to-peer format
Mechanism of agreement	How should conflicts be resolved?	Conflicts should be resolved via the longest chain rule
Mechanism upgrade	How do the rules change?	The rules change via: • Bitcoin Improvement Proposals (BIPs) for writing the rules • Vote by hashing power for the implementation of the rules
Criteria for participation	Who can submit transactions?	Transaction submission is anonymous and open
Criteria for participation	Who can read data?	Data reading is anonymous and open
Criteria for participation	Who can authenticate transactions?	Transaction authentication is anonymous and open
Defense mechanism	How is bad behavior prevented?	Bad behavior is prevented through the use of proof-of-work
Incentivization scheme	How are block-makers incentivized?	Block-makers are incentivized through block reward, which has to be replaced by transaction fees
Incentivization scheme	How are transaction validators incentivized?	How transaction validators are incentivized is not considered

Source: Adapted from Lewis [16].

a piece of data that is expensive to create in order to meet particular prerequisites and its verification is inconsequential. As to Bitcoin, it should be noted that within a specific period of time, every transaction carried out is recorded and stored into the Bitcoin block, which is subsequently spread to all the participating nodes within the Bitcoin network [17]. The *Hashcash* PoW scheme is used in this case. This Hashcash PoW scheme was introduced in 1997 by Adam Back [17]. Under the Hashcash PoW scheme, each participant adds a piece of data referred to as a "nonce" to the block to form a "block + nonce." This "block + nonce" is then taken and placed in an algorithm referred to as a "hash algorithm" [17]. The hash algorithm then comes up with a mathematical computation in which each participating node tries to provide a solution to using the SHA (Secure Hash Algorithm)-256 hash function [17]. As soon as a solution is provided to the mathematical computation by a node, the particular prerequisites by the PoW scheme are then thought to be met and this now becomes "block + nonce + hash." As soon as this occurs, the "block + nonce + hash" is then included with the Bitcoin blockchain and broadcast to every one of the participating nodes within the network, which is assisted for PoW operations by physically scarce resources. As pointed out by [13], these physically scarce resources are *the hardware* required to run the mathematical computations and the electric power required to run the hardware. This implies that the use of the Bitcoin PoW protocol is highly demanding on resources.

Among the different schemes available, *"Proof of Stake"* (PoS) serves as an alternative to the PoW scheme [17]. PoS is a scheme built on less-costly computations, being dependent on the entities that hold stake within the network. For the authentication and reception of a transaction to occur, some of the coins must be owned by a miner [17]. The probability that a miner is successful in the creation of a new block is dependent on the amount of coin owned and not on the computational power whenever the PoS scheme is used [17]. Although not free from challenges, the PoS scheme has more advantages over the PoW scheme such as a low latency ability. Nevertheless, one of the challenges faced by the PoS scheme is related to centralization, where large stake holdings could attempt to display a level of domination over the network.

Finally, another alternative to the previous schemes is to adopt a hybrid scheme: on the one hand, it employs the PoW scheme for the mining and distribution at the initial stage and this implies that it makes it possible for the distribution of new coins to miners via the network; on the other hand, the PoS scheme provides the cryptocurrency with good energy effectiveness [17]. Furthermore, the generation of a block in this hybrid scheme is dependent on a model referred to as "coinage," which is the multiplication of the total amount of coin a miner owns and the span of ownership the present coin owner has. Hence, the block generation goes to the block with the highest coinage [17]. The low consumption of energy by this scheme is one of its key features.

Table 8.2 highlights the main characteristics of the PoW, PoS and hybrid schemes. It can be seen from Table 8.2 that the PoW scheme has high latency and energy cost in the long run, while both the PoS scheme and the hybrid scheme have low latency and energy cost based on the long run. Finally, it is worth noting that other schemes exist, such as the PBFT (Practical Byzantine Fault Tolerance), which uses the

Table 8.2 *The major characteristics of the Proof of Work, Proof of Stake and hybrid schemes*

Scheme	Low latency	Long-run low energy cost
Proof of Work (PoW)	No	No
Proof of Stake (PoS)	Yes	Yes
Hybrid Proof of Work and Proof of Stake (PoW/PoS)	Yes	Yes

Source: Adapted from Farell [17].

metaphor of Byzantine generals to question the reliability of communications and the integrity of the participants [18].

Taking the above issues into account, blockchain was developed as the main authentication and verification technology behind Bitcoin, where a transaction is initiated when the future owner of the coins (or digital tokens) sends his/her public key to the original owner. The coins are transferred by the digital signature of a hash. Public keys are cryptographically generated addresses stored in the blockchain. Every coin is associated with an address, and a transaction in the crypto-economy is simply a trade of coins from one address to another [19]. In a blockchain, the data of the transactions are stored in a public record that is locked by the members who participate in the network, thus acting like verifiers of its truthfulness [19, 20]. Hence, blockchain technology provides a mechanism to enable transactions that don't need intermediary agents to verify or monitor the integrity of the value exchanged through computer networks [21]. Simply put, blockchain allows businesses to transact among each other without central financial institutions such as banks [21]. Consequently, network members automatically play the role of authenticators that validate and guard the transactions against double-spending through one of the validation systems that we have already discussed, for example the PoW, which actually represents a competition among network members to validate the transaction [21]. Lastly, when the transaction is validated, the public ledger (blockchain record) as well as the users of the network are collectively updated with the status of the newly added transaction. The following points summarize the key attributes of blockchain technology: *decentralization, trust and provenance* and *resilience and irreversibility*.

As for *decentralization*, blockchain technology links the participants together so that they can make transactions and transfer ownership of valued assets among them in a transparent way and without the help of third-party mediators. This leads to an emphasis on *trust and provenance*, for blockchain technology allows verification that the data of a transaction has existed at a specific time in the block. Moreover, because each block in the chain contains information about the previous block, the history, position and ownership of each block are automatically authenticated, and cannot be altered. Considering *resilience and irreversibility*, blockchain resilience derives from its structure since it is designed as a distributed network of nodes (i.e. computers), where each of them stores a copy of the entire chain. Consequently, when a transaction is verified and approved by the participating nodes, it is impossible to alter its data.

Taking these issues into account, what follows illustrates the basic components in blockchain technology [22], where the transaction is composed of the sender, the transaction information and the receiver, and it is secured by an encryption code. The block contains several transactions and the blockchain is constructed of several blocks. However, a blockchain can be either public or private. A key issue of public blockchains is their high capability to uphold the transactional agreements in the network, which gives room for blocks of transactions to be written to the blockchains (*distributed ledgers*) by anyone as well as for the creation of transactions and the ability to send such transactions. Moreover, as said, all these do not require the approval of any third party or intermediary. On the other hand, the limitations of users in private blockchains involve the use of firewalls within the private network. The systemized pattern of private blockchains can be done in such a way that only known participants can include data to the blockchain. Moreover, private blockchains give neither read nor write access to unknown participants.

Examples of public blockchains and private blockchains include *Ripple*, which could be placed between both public blockchains and private blockchains [23] and *Ethereum*, which employs the use of public block-chains [23]. We will now take a look at the "*decentralized database*," which is another key concept of blockchain technology. A decentralized data-base allows both decentralized and secure data exchange. If required, information can be published and distributed across a huge number of computers in an encrypted manner thereby eliminating the ability of a single entity to censor [24]. An example of a decentralized database is the *anonymous decentralized cloud storage system*, which employs block-chain technology in collaboration with other peer-to-peer technology to make it possible for people to use surplus space on hard disks [24].

As a result of the advent of blockchain technology, organizations are now looking for a way to use the features of a decentralized database, which blockchain technology makes possible, for example, for unrelated people to vote over the Internet or using their mobile devices securely [24]. This is due to the ability of a decentralized database to function as a distributed irreversible and encrypted public paper, which can be effortlessly audited as every voter would be able to validate that their vote was counted [24].

Finally, blockchain technology was designed in such a manner as to be independent of any financial institution, such as banks or governments. This makes it more attractive and less prone to regulations. Furthermore, blockchain technology has enhanced the speed of transactions. Since blockchains can automate messages by the addition of code snippets called "smart contracts" that do not involve any human in any way, the speed of payment is much quicker. This also implies that there will be a lower transaction completion time as third parties have been eliminated. Finally, the robustness of blockchain technology makes it possible for data to be stored across a large number of nodes [23], and the higher the number of nodes, the more resilient the data [23].

8.3   Case Studies

At 2016, almost $1.1 billion had been invested in venture capital (VC) to start-up companies for research and development (R&D) of blockchain innovative solutions [25]. Nevertheless, in 2019, according to [26], "The Blockchain Report 2020" [27] published by research company CB Insights found that "cryptocurrency companies received $2.3 billion in VC-backed funding while enterprise blockchain received $434 million" [26]. Moreover, blockchain has already been applied to numerous use cases that span from financial services, trade finance, and smart contracts to healthcare, supply chain, and identity management [28]. Thus, this section aims to provide interesting examples of solutions that utilize blockchain technology and that have received both attention and funds from investors and managed to build start-up companies. The first case belongs to the financial services with a specific focus on the loyalty rewards area. Having established a partnership with Deloitte, *Loyyal* introduced a platform that offers interoperability between loyalty programs and vendors, such as credit card providers or airline companies, through one digital wallet. *Everledger* is the second presented case: it aims to fight insurance fraud and jewelry theft by recording the transaction history and provenance of high-value goods such as diamonds, luxury goods and fine art in the distributed digital ledger of the blockchain. The third case, *GemHealth*, brings innovation to the healthcare industry by offering a radical patient-centric solution that allows the interoperability of healthcare data across the continuum of care so that different stakeholders, such as patients and clinicians, can have access to it. Moving to a focus on the supply chain process, the fourth case describes *Wave*, a platform that can be used by shipping companies for faster, safer and simpler trade finance. Also, in the financial services industry and more specifically in the international payments sector, the fifth case, *Veem*, offers a solution that aims to modernize current business-to-business (B2B) payment processes. Then, *Civic*, the sixth case, is an identity management company that aims to protect consumers from identity theft by alerting them in real-time when a transaction is using their social security numbers. In a similar area, the next case, *ShoCard*, provides blockchain-based solutions to securely store customers' information, which they can use to verify their identities whenever they need to. Finally, the last case study, *Factom*, discusses the profile of a start-up company that aims to build on the advantages of blockchain technology to secure and verify the integrity of the data transacted between and within private as well as public organizations.

8.3.1 Loyyal

Loyyal is a fintech start-up offering a loyalty and rewards platform built with blockchain and smart contract technology. Loyyal can benefit both loyalty program providers and their customers. The start-up aims to unify the currently fragmented loyalty industry by introducing interoperability of data among loyalty programs, thus allowing for multivendor alliances, enabling dynamic issuance and redemption options to each customer while at the same time maintaining consumer privacy [29]. By leveraging the decentralized solution of blockchain technology, the platform offers a personalized added-value service to customers by enabling the creation, redemption and exchange of loyalty points across vendors, programs and industries in near real time and through one digital wallet, ultimately aiming to improve customer experience [30]. Originally founded in 2014 as Ribbit.me, the New York-based start-up was recently rebranded to Loyyal to better reflect the underlying industry and meet the company's business objectives [31].

Loyyal was co-founded by Greg Simon, who is currently the CEO of the start-up and also serves as a founding member and current president of the Bitcoin Association as well as a member of the Dubai Global Blockchain Council [29, 32]. He holds an MBA from Columbia and is a Certified Blockchain Professional. Having worked in the financial services industry for the last fifteen years, Simon aspired to provide customers with a fuller and more personalized experience as "loyalty should be about enriching the individual's life experience, not simply rewarding repeat behavior" [33]. Simon's co-founder Sean Dennis also has a business educational background and a genuine interest in the applications of blockchain and distributed ledger technology [29]. Moreover, according to the chief operating officer (COO) of Loyyal and Chairman of Wall Street of Blockchain, Ron Quaranta, recent studies have shown that current loyalty programs are ranking very poorly in terms of both innovation and customer satisfaction [34]. Loyyal is aiming to "cure" this ailment of the loyalty industry by bringing in a creative and innovative solution that will attract and retain customers by introducing a more personalized experience to the user while at the same time increasing the reputation of financial institutions [34].

Table 8.3 depicts the competitiveness indicators for time-to-market and the growing market demand. The start-up has a large market to tap. There are some competitors in the rewards market, but Loyyal has established strong partnerships that could differentiate it among the others. The enabling infrastructure currently uses the beta version on the Dubai initiative and the developers are aiming for continuous improvements. Furthermore, Loyyal was one of the five start-up companies that Deloitte, one of the largest accounting firms in the world, teamed up in a partnership with in the first quarter of 2016 [35]. By utilizing blockchain technology, Loyyal aims to apply the loyalty network platform in the financial services sector to benefit both individuals and companies; it will result in the unification of the fragmented loyalty industry, near real-time transparency, cost savings, fraud and abuse prevention, and overall enhanced customer retention and satisfaction [30]. For example, following the example by [30], when a hypothetical customer Alice buys her airline tickets from London to Paris, her credit card transfers the awarded points into her digital wallet in a real-time manner. Alice can then instantly use the points she just earned to upgrade her booked room at a local hotel in Paris. Thus, in this example, the customer can enjoy an

Table 8.3 *Loyyal's competitiveness indicators for time-to-market*

Solution	Loyyal
Founded	2014
No. of products	1
Clients	Financial institutions, enterprises and individuals
Partners	Different levels of partnership
Market dimension	Growing
Competitors	Some

enhanced experience while at the same time the airline and hotel companies have gained a satisfied customer who is very likely to return [30]. Loyyal has also joined the Dubai Future Accelerators program, collaborating with Dubai Holding in the industries of food and beverages, hospitality, and real estate [36]. Moreover, Loyyal has launched the Dubai points program which is focused on the tourism industry and aims to incentivize tourists to visit local attractions. By using the Loyyal smartphone app, users earn points every time they perform specific activities such as traveling, visiting museums or staying in hotels. They can then use the earned points to offset the cost of the promoted places of attraction [37].

8.3.2 Everledger

Utilizing distributed ledger technology, Everlegder was created in an endeavor to combat insurance fraud as well as diamond theft, by facilitating diamond certification and tracing of diamond transaction history [38, 39]. The platform can be used by insurance companies, owners and law enforcement to track diamonds' provenance more robustly and reliably, compared to using paper certificates that can easily be lost or modified [39].

Everledger is built on blockchain technology and can track any asset with a unique identification. Since creating the first-of-its-kind global digital ledger, Everledger collects thousands of data points for each recorded diamond and creates a digital fingerprint in the immutable distributed ledger [40]. According to the founder of the company, every single tiny detail of a diamond is recorded in the blockchain, "[a]ll of the angles and the cuts and the pavilions and all of the crown ... as well as the serial number, ... the four Cs" [39] (cut, color, clarity and carat). Leveraging the notion of smart contracts within blockchain technology, Everledger's start-up was founded in 2015 in London by Leanne Kemp.

Having worked for twenty years in emerging technologies and ten years in the jewelry and insurance industry, Kemp hit upon the idea while discussing diamond fraud with insurers and seeking potential solutions to combat the problem [39, 41].

Since the first presentation of Kemp's idea at the Aviva hackathon in 2015 [42], Everledger has won numerous awards, the most prominent being the 2016 best blockchain company at the European Financial Technology Awards and the 2015 Meffy Award for Innovation Fintech [38, 43]. Everledger has also been included in the Forbes Fintech 50 list of the Most Innovative Fintech Companies in 2020 [44]. Furthermore,

Table 8.4 *Everledger's competitiveness indicators for time-to-market*

Solution	Everledger
Founded	2015
No. of products	1
Clients	Insurance companies, law enforcement and individuals
Partners	Different levels of partnership
Market dimension	Growing
Competitors	Few

embedded into the distributed ledger of the blockchain, as of 2017, are around 980,000 diamonds [45].

Table 8.4 illustrates the competitiveness indicators for time-to-market and growing market demand. The start-up is solid with few competitors in the market, who are following a more traditional approach. The company has established strong collaborations in order to grab the attention of the market. Both the law enforcement and the insurance sectors have shown interest in the application, which already looks promising. Moreover, the enabling infrastructure is continuously evolving. In particular, Everledger focuses on introducing transparency into the diamond market. As reported by [46], the system includes three stages:

1. *Establish an electronic identity (ID) by collecting thousands of reference-able data points of each diamond and recording them on the global digital ledger.*
2. *Assign a digital passport to each diamond that will record each transaction history and provenance.*
3. *Detect, guard, and prevent illegal activities associated with diamond fraud and theft.*

Finally, over the years Everledger has developed solutions that aim to extend the industries covered by the company from diamonds to high-value luxury goods, fine art, and wines and spirits [47]. These developments follow the ultimate vision of the start-up, which is to combat counterfeiting, and can be applied in online retail marketplaces such as Amazon and eBay in order to detect the authenticity of the products being sold to customers [39, 40].

8.3.3   Gem Health

Gem Health is a blockchain network that includes players such as Philips [48]. It uses the GemOS enterprise platform, built by start-up Gem, based in Venice, Los Angeles (USA), to support a patient-centric approach to healthcare through blockchain [49]. Moreover, Gem Health enables the collaboration of different stakeholders in the sharing and transferring of healthcare data. Gem Health enables different healthcare operators to have access to the same information with transparency through a universal data infrastructure [48]. By exploiting the dynamics of blockchain technology, Gem Health introduces a robust and flexible healthcare ecosystem that guarantees data integrity and security among collaborating parties [48]. The system represents a decentralized architecture that is tamper-proof and allows for an immutable and secure library of healthcare data [50].

Founded by its current CEO Micah Winkelspecht in 2013, at the time of the writing of this book, Gem has received a total of $20.5 million [48, 51]. As already stated, Gem's focus is on providing enterprise solutions utilizing blockchain technology and the underlying idea of data exchange through a shared infrastructure. Winkelspecht found a gap in the blockchain market as most of the attention has been on applications for the financial industry [48]. According to him, blockchain could be applied to numerous non-financial use cases and this is how his idea about Gem Health was born. Gem Health follows its founder's goal of introducing a patient-centric model for healthcare to ensure the security of clinical data. He believes that it is about time to leave behind the idea of silos and separate views and move forward to a more united world of data regarding patient care [48]. In Table 8.5 the time-to-market competitiveness indicators appear to be high, with growing market demand. The company is in continuous development aiming to provide more pioneering solutions for enterprises in the field of care. Moreover, the enabling infrastructure is ready and the demand is really high.

Table 8.5 *Gem's competitiveness indicators for time-to-market*

Solution	Gem
Founded	2013
No. of products	4
Clients	Enterprises and individuals
Partners	Different levels of partnership
Market dimension	Growing
Competitors	Very few

As anticipated at the beginning of this section, Gem has a partnership with Philips Healthcare focusing on further R&D of the Gem Health platform [48, 49]. The healthcare application is aiming to fill an important gap in the market where, for many years, both patients and clinicians yearned for a digital shared unified patient record [50]. Medical record repositories and closed bookkeeping create significant obstacles in the effective facilitation of health services offered to patients. This is because data exchange and collaboration among different healthcare providers – private or public – are not entirely feasible. This becomes quite clear in cases where a patient relocates or gets sick while traveling abroad. Gem Health facilitates electronic health record (EHR) interoperability, replacing the classic paper patient record; through the EHR, physicians, clinicians, patients and payers can have access to the same shared data. The application is illustrated through the following example adapted from [50].

Adam faints and hits his head while hiking in Oregon. As his primary doctor is unavailable, his friends drive him to the emergency room where he is accepted by Dr Yang. Through his wearable device, Adam can grant read access to Dr Yang to his medical records, latest laboratory results as well as the list of current and previous medications. In that way, Gem Health enables information exchange among different parties so that all users are connected to a universal library of health data across the continuum of care [50].

The potential use cases of Gem Health span from wellness applications, electronic medical records and global patient ID software to medical inventory management, rehabilitation incentive programs, billing and claims processing, targeted to both users and healthcare providers [49]. Finally, as stated, Gem Health runs on GemOS, which is the infrastructure that supports the implementation of the decentralized servers, the applications and the platform. In other words, it is the technology that can be used to implement blockchain networks in healthcare.

8.3.4   Wave

Innovation in the trade finance sector is considered crucial nowadays as this particular area is facing a huge amount of challenges and competition from newly founded fintech companies entering the industry. Having graduated from Barclays TechStar Accelerator Program in 2015 and created a partnership with the bank [52, 53], Wave, which also claims to be the first company to execute a global trade transaction through blockchain technology [54], nowadays is especially focused on replacing "paper across industries like shipping, banking, and insurance among others" [55]. By dematerializing paper documents, Wave aims to reduce costs in supply chain management and eliminate downtime, disputes and fraud, thus offering simpler, safer and faster trade finance. The application makes it feasible to connect all carriers, banks, traders and any other parties involved in the international trading supply chain into one decentralized network [55, 56].

OGY Docs developed Wave. It was founded in 2014 by current CEO Gadi Ruschin, who has twelve years' experience in the international trade sector of the shipping industry [57–59]. The rest of the team of the Tel Aviv-based company includes Or Garbash, the chief technical officer (CTO) of the start-up, and Yair Sappir, vice president R&D, both of whom are experts in information security [55]. According to Garbash, the trade finance sector can be transformed globally as blockchain solution technologies can successfully outperform pen-and-paper processes that have been utilized by shipping companies for almost two centuries, and make sure that no fraud or falsified documents are being used along the way [60]. The first global trade transaction utilizing the Wave application was executed between Ornua, formerly known as the Irish Dairy Board that owned, among others, the brand Kerrygold cheese, and the Seychelles Trading Company [61].

In Table 8.6 the time-to-market competitiveness indicators appear to be medium, as Wave performed the first pilot transaction in the market. There is relatively growing demand, but the company needs more team members and partners. The start-up has announced that it will continue R&D of the application with some select trade finance clients. The Wave platform can have applications in almost all industries, as the majority of companies are involved in imports and exports at some level. Currently, trade transactions involve a high number of participants in the process, such as banks, insurance companies and

Table 8.6 *Wave's competitiveness indicators for time-to-market*

Solution	Wave
Founded	2014
No. of products	1
Clients	Enterprises
Partners	Different levels of partnership
Market dimension	Growing
Competitors	Few

government customs inspectors, and a significant amount of paperwork has to be signed and transferred between one another. Lack of trust is a huge challenge among the parties involved in every trading process. By replacing documents with electronic versions that are stored in the distributed ledger of the blockchain, Wave allows all involved parties to view, transfer titles and submit shipping documents and other original trade documentation through a secure decentralized network [55]. Unlike regular electronic files, such as PDFs, documents saved in the blockchain have to be approved by all involved parties and any changes can be detected immediately [60]. As a result, the application advances trust between participants as well as eliminating the risk of documentation fraud, reducing errors in documents and, most importantly, increasing the speed of the overall document transfer process [60]. Since the seventeenth century, nothing has actually changed in the processes of the shipping industry; shippers have been using the same producers to sell, ship and deliver goods. Wave aims to optimize the antiquated methods of global trade finance and to revolutionize the supply chain process. It has replaced the printed bill of lading (BOL – a document that includes information about the shipment and, more specifically, about the type of goods being transferred, their quantities and their destination) with an electronic version of the document that will be stored in the blockchain and that all interested parties can have access to [57].

8.3.5   Veem

Digitalization has seen electronic payments reach unprecedented diffusion, often giving the impression of having taken over the world; nevertheless, the B2B payment landscape seems still to be living in the past. As reported by [62] in 2015, according to a report of the US Association for Financial Professionals (AFP), paper checks were the predominant method of payment for 97 percent of the considered organizations, most of them small and medium businesses (SMBs) [62]. The scenario of payments has evolved since then and the only US B2B market is estimated to reach $23.1 trillion in 2020 [63, 64]. However, in B2B there are still inefficiencies due to, for example, paper-based invoicing [65], when "[17] percent of deposited checks are image deposits, 93 percent of image deposits are by businesses, and 71 percent of businesses are capable of making electronic payments" according to a 2019 report by Behalf [63] (p. 7). As a result, businesses are facing numerous difficulties and challenges including lack of transparency, inability to track their transactions, and slow processing times. Having recognized this need for urgent modernization of the B2B payment process, Veem (formerly Align Commerce) aims to change the payment process by combining blockchain technology with traditional banking transfers and treasury operations [62]. As its mission states, Veem aims "to revolutionize the legacy financial payment system by offering enterprise-level financial services and negotiating power to the small businesses who need it most" [66]. Thus, the company offers a solution that can significantly improve customer satisfaction as well as provide a "frictionless" and ultimately simple business experience [67].

Having started as Align Commerce and raising $12.5 million in funding through Silicon Valley venture firm Kleiner Perkins Caufield & Byers (KPCB) [68], Veem still aims to revolutionize the global B2B payment industry. Founded in early 2014 in San Francisco by the current CEO Marwan Forzley, former general manager of Western Union and founder of eBillme, and Aldo Carrascoso, now CEO of InterVenn Biosciences [69], the start-up comprises a big team of 101–250 people [69].

Going after the small business market, Veem aims to change the legacy financial payment system and offer an innovative solution that will significantly simplify cross-border payments. As a two-sided payment network, by exploiting blockchain, the platform is designed to reduce times and high transaction costs and offer a better overall customer experience, also allowing third parties to integrate Veem's global payments service through application programming interfaces (APIs) [70].

In Table 8.7 the time-to-market competitiveness indicators show that the company is stable and ready to tap into a large market as it has received funding from a wide range of investors [67, 68]. Also, the platform is already available in nearly 100 countries around the world [71] and the demand is growing.

Table 8.7 *Veem's competitiveness indicators for time-to-market*

Solution	AlignCommerce
Founded	2014
No. of products	1
Clients	Enterprises
Partners	Different levels of partnership
Market dimension	Growing
Competitors	Few

Currently, cross-border payments are both time-consuming and expensive for small businesses as usually, when a company sends a payment to a vendor overseas, the money needs to pass through several intermediaries till it reaches the destination bank. These cooperating intermediary banks are charging additional fees for their services, which are translated into more costs for the company that initiated the payment. Thus, Veem aims to renew cross-border payments by offering a solution that small businesses can use to pay their vendors at a much lower cost than before. The main difference from currently used processes is that Veem bypasses any intermediaries in the process, reduces forms and fees, and offers much simpler transactions characterized by transparency and high security. This is achieved by utilizing blockchain technology and the idea of a digital distributed ledger [62, 70]. With Veem, a company can send a payment in euros and the vendor can receive the money in US dollars. Both parties are still using traditional bank accounts, but the platform converts the euros into Bitcoins and sells the digital currency at an exchange rate for the desired currency of the recipient [68]. Another interesting feature of the platform is that it offers timely information about the transaction and both parties can track at any moment the status of the ongoing payment. Similar to package tracking on UPS or FedEx websites, with Veem both the sender and the receiver can track all money movements, from invoice generation to completion of the payment process [62]. In summary, the platform offers a distinctive feature in the cross-border payment system, tracking payments through a dashboard [62] with a simple design that is easy to grasp, that being a key issue considering that "even 'mom and pop' businesses must embrace globalization to compete with incumbents, grow their businesses and innovate," as pointed out by Forzley [67].

8.3.6   Civic

Nearly a year after the launch of Civic, in 2016, 13.1 million fraud victims were recorded in the USA with more than $112 billion having been stolen by fraudsters during the previous six years, according to [72], discussing the security firm Javelin's report "2016 Identity Fraud: Fraud Hits an Inflection Point." The 2020 edition of the Javelin report points out that the total identity fraud figure reached $16.9 billion in 2019 [73]. As hacks and data breaches are continuously increasing, identity theft is a crucial issue that needs to be tackled, also considering the emergence of new areas of attention such as real-time person-to-person (P2P) payments [73, 74]. Thus, attempting to combat this ongoing serious problem, Civic offers an identity management service ecosystem to protect people from identity theft [75]. The identity protection application ensures, for example, that a user's personal information and, more importantly, social security number are secure, not compromised and not used by someone attempting to impersonate him or her [76]. The company conducted its token sale in 2017 [75]; since then the Civic (CVC) token allows for secure and low-cost access to identity verification through the blockchain [77]. By leveraging blockchain technology through the use, since 2017, of identity.com's open-source, blockchain-based ecosystem [78] to verify credentials, Civic prevents identity replication and blocks access to a user's data from unauthorized people and software agents [75, 79].

Based in San Francisco, USA and currently comprising a team of nearly thirty people [75, 80], Civic was co-founded in 2015 by both Jonathan Smith, an expert in banking and security and the current CTO of the company, and South African entrepreneur and CEO of the start-up Vinny Lingham, former co-founder of the gift card application Gyft [81], which was sold for over $50 million in 2014 [82]. Lingham had been working for several years in the e-commerce industry when he noticed that, although hacks of digital information have been on the rise, there was still no universal solution [79]. As a result, the idea of developing and implementing a global solution for fighting identity fraud came along. Nowadays, Civic has announced that its solution Civic Wallet, which is currently in private beta, is the "first and only non-custodial crypto wallet to offer a $1 million (USD) digital currency provided by Coincover" [83], this latter being among the leading brands in crypto security [84].

In Table 8.8 the time-to-market competitiveness indicators show that the company is solid as, since its early days, it has created strong partnerships with big investors such as Digital Currency Group and Social

Table 8.8 *Civic's competitiveness indicators for time-to-market*

Solution	Civic
Founded	2015
No. of products	2
Clients	Individuals and enterprises
Partners	Different levels of partnership
Market dimension	Growing
Competitors	Some

Leverage, and is continuously seeking more partners and clients from a variety of industries [85], as also shown by the this overview of the company's activities and solutions. Recognizing that there is a very large market to tap into, the start-up has adopted a very good strategy by offering the Civic Secure Identity application for free to consumers as well as with initiatives such as that related to the Civic Wallet, where eligible participants who pre-register to be in the waitlist for the campaign launch of the app "can get up to 25,000 CVCs in rewards, and early access to the next generation identity and payment network" [86].

Although there are some competitors in the market, Civic offers a proactive feature of alerting the user in real time, an element that is missing from similar applications. Characterizing its applications as proactive, Civic differentiates itself from other competitors in the market by detecting transactions in real time, meaning that the user is alerted the exact moment that his or her personal information is being used. The user is notified by email, text or a pushup notification on their smartphone. At this point, the user can immediately either accept or deny the transaction, in case they suspect fraudulent activity. Thus, Civic can prevent fraud before it actually happens [82]. The application uses a two-way authentication process between users and financial institutions so that both parties can be sure that they are communicating with each other and no fraudster has compromised the transaction [72]. Users can download the Civic Secure Identity app for free as well as the abovementioned Civic Wallet, which, for security reasons, offers its users credit report alerting, $1 million fraud coverage in case of fraudulent activity, through the Coincover Cryptocurrency Protection Guarantee, and twenty-four /seven fraud call support [79].

8.3.7   ShoCard

In the current digitized world, where smart handheld devices are the norm, people need easy, simple and secure ways to verify their identities upon request. The situation gets even more crucial in cases of identity theft and fraud where such acts bring huge losses to individuals, institutions, businesses and merchants. For example, the airline industry requires secure and customer-friendly identity verification systems for people to be able to clear security check-in and to board airplanes. Having proven its merit to secure Bitcoin transactions over the Internet, blockchain can be the ideal technology to provide people with a secure and simple way to use digital identity card platforms, which consumers can use through a mobile app built on the top of the public Blockchain data layer. Taking these issues into account, ShoCard aims to leverage the security features of blockchain technology to provide a personal digital identity that can replace traditional methods such as passports, driving licenses, and user names and passwords [87, 88]. The start-up, based in Palo Alto, CA, USA, was acquired in March 2020 by Ping Identity, a company headquartered in Denver, Colorado, USA, that provides cloud-based identity management software for both private and public sector organizations [87, 89]. Beside suggesting likely future developments of ShoCard by Ping Identity, the rest of this subsection provides a summary of the company's characteristics, to show the insights that it can provide to other prospective digital entrepreneurs interested in the same domain of application of blockchain technology.

With a desire to have a consumer-friendly and secure method to verify personal identity, Armin Ebrahimi and Jeff Weitzman founded the start-up in 2015. Their motivation was to offer an application that people can use in order to verify their identities, whenever necessary, without sharing their personal and sensitive information with the verifiers [87]. As pointed out by Jeff Weitzman in an interview, the company has created "a digital identity card that is as easy to use as a driver's license but it's so secure that a bank can rely on it" [90]. The basic concept is to use blockchain infrastructure to encrypt and store personal identification data, where it cannot be altered or falsely modified, in order that it can be used to verify someone's biometric data (such as, e.g., fingerprint, facial, iris and voice data) when required [87, 91]. The founders' vast experience in scalable platforms, online services, mobile development and digital advertising, gained from working at big technology firms such as Yahoo! and AOL, AT&T and Verizon, has enabled them to successfully establish ShoCard to achieve their vision of having an identity for a mobile world [87, 88, 90]. According to the founders of ShoCard, the trend of people using their digital assets in their daily life will continue to prevail because of the increased crossover between digital life and physical life. Thus, there is an emerging need for a solution that enables easy and secure access to the desired resources and ShoCard was developed to fill this gap [87]. The developers at ShoCard are looking to use blockchain for online identity by providing a simple and intuitive mobile application that people can use in conjunction with biometric data (fingerprints and face recognition information). The goal is to provide the ultimate user authentication while protecting users' private information. Such a solution can open the door for many use cases such as login services without the need for a username and password, digital signature, financial transaction authentication to prevent fraud, and governmental transactions to protect people's sensitive information [92].

Table 8.9 *ShoCard's competitiveness indicators for time-to-market*

Solution	ShoCard
Founded	2015
No. of products	1
Clients	Travel industry and other industries where identity verification is a necessity to enable access
Partners	ATM and travel technology providers
Market dimension	Growing
Competitors	Few

As shown in Table 8.9, which provides competitiveness indicators for the company, ShoCard has partnered with SITA, a travel technology provider, and together they aim to utilize blockchain to enable a single secure travel identification across borders [93]. They are developing a prototype that uses a mobile app and face recognition technologies to keep private information safe in the blockchain network. Broadly, the idea is eventually for travelers to generate a "Single Travel Token" containing all their travel documents [93].

Thus, when needed, the traveler and her/his data can be quickly and securely verified by the concerned stakeholders such as airlines, airports and other agencies, by reading the data from the dedicated blockchain network without compromising the traveler's information privacy. Finally, in 2019, ShoCard entered into a partnership with Alhamrani Universal (AU), the largest ATM provider in Saudi Arabia, to develop a biometric ATM prototype for allowing customers in that region "to use their blockchain-based App and faces instead of personal identification numbers to withdraw money from cash points" [94, 95].

8.3.8   Factom

Trust is considered one of the most important factors in today's business world [96]. Securing the integrity of the data used in business and government transactions necessitates massive investments to audit and verify financial or governmental records. This situation poses a considerable reduction in efficiency and return on investment (ROI), which affects the prosperity of organizations [97]. Taking these issues into account, Factom, a technology company, has a vision to harness the power of blockchain and its ability to secure data and make it verifiable and independently auditable, in order to provide platforms that can be used by organizations to ensure that their data are secured and cannot be manipulated or falsely altered [98, 99]. In 2018, the company released the Factom protocol as open-source, while in 2017, with more than $8 million raised in a Series A led by Tim Draper, of Draper Associates, the company built the Factom Harmony, a "Blockchain-as-a-Service platform" for data provenance and integrity solutions, "all without cryptocurrency exposure or costly infrastructure" [98–100]. Thus, Factom Harmony provides its customers with different connect and integrate solutions to verify the integrity of the data being used in the organization's business processes as well as the integrity of data generated from Internet of Things (IoT) devices, including users' entries, identity, reputation, origin and manufacturer [98, 101, 102].

Factom is located in Austin, Texas, USA and was founded in 2014 by a team that includes Peter Kirby, David Johnston, Paul Snow, Tiana Laurence, Brian Deery and Abhisek Dobhal. The team is the perfect example of combining a wide range of expertise that covers entrepreneurship, leadership and management as well as a passion for blockchain technology [99, 103].

Table 8.10 shows the competitiveness drivers on a time-to-market basis. The information in Table 8.10 demonstrates the advanced development of the technologies behind Factom's products and the growing demand of the market based on the value that can be acquired by having trustworthy systems with immutable data. Moreover, the continuously growing interest in secured applications and data coupled with the advantages provided by Factom's solutions means that the time-to-market competitiveness measures look very high.

Factom Blockchain based its idea on the fact that although Bitcoin's blockchain is the most trusted and immutable database that has ever existed on the Internet, "it is not very useful for non-Bitcoin transactions"

Table 8.10 *Factom's competitiveness indicators for time-to-market*

Solution	Factom
Founded	2014
No. of products	3
Clients	Enterprises and governmental organizations
Partners	Different levels of partnership
Market dimension	Growing
Competitors	Very Few

[96]. Furthermore, a token is needed to provide an incentive to participants in decentralized systems, increase cooperation and create network value [104]. Thus, the goal of a Factom token is "to move transactions off the Bitcoin blockchain" and create "artificial scarcity to reduce spam" [104]. Accordingly, Factom has developed a data layer on top of Bitcoin's blockchain, allowing users to have full access to the features offered by the blockchain technology without having to deal with the complexity associated with the cryptocurrency [104]. As mentioned in the 2018 company whitepaper, Factom's goal is to create a "faster, cheaper, and bloat-free way to develop blockchain based applications" [96].

In summary, the company could be considered, together with the other organizations discussed in this chapter, an interesting case for other digital entrepreneurs willing to enter the same market with other blockchain-based solutions.

8.4   Summary

This chapter showed the potential of blockchain for digital entrepreneurs by introducing its main elements and presenting eight companies that apply the technology in different sectors, thus providing insights for new ventures. Alongside this can be added a perspective regarding the likely future innovations within the field of blockchain.

Blockchain, Business, Board: these three words are bound together for a reason. Nowadays, companies across the world are facing some major IT challenges, where the latest one might reshape the global market and economy as we know them, and *Blockchain* is still among the technologies contributing to that change. Yet, the blockchain, as shown by the examples provided in this chapter, is far more than a technology, and this brings us to the second term, *Business*. Blockchain is not only about keeping a ledger of currency transactions; it goes beyond that and the perspective we propose in this chapter wants to explore how business can leverage blockchain in several industries: financial institutions, insurance companies and healthcare are some of the areas which could be improved by adopting and implementing blockchain-based technologies. In the last twenty years, it has been clear that the IT sector is one of the most important business units for any company that wants to compete, improve and progress in the new digital economy. Blockchain needs to be studied and embraced by the business world since this technology does not relate to the IT world alone: it's a cross-industry technology that is going to be implemented in a variety of fields.

It therefore seems necessary to understand how business and technology can work together, in order to make sure that, when this innovation takes place, everyone will be ready to change, adapt and adopt it quickly. As also shown by the companies discussed in previous sections, this technology could turn into a differentiating factor for adopting businesses, enabling them to process transactions and share information with more efficiency, security and reliability. Managers should not convert to blockchain initiatives right away. However, as shown by the executives of the companies presented here, a strong strategy is fundamental for every established company or new venture that wants to understand whether blockchain is transformative or not. The time is right for pilot projects, experiments and proof-of-concepts that show and make it possible to see how this technology works and may create value. This leads us to the third word that makes up the perspective we are proposing here: *Board*. There is a need for bringing the business world together as potential users, customers and investors to discuss and discover the technology's potential and this can be done when all stakeholders are brought together to explore the many different technology implementations. Those are the reasons behind the *Blockchain, Business, Board* perspective, which aims to guide businesses, entrepreneurs and researchers to see, for example, how business models could evolve in line with the blockchain technology innovation.

Taking the above issues into account, education seems to be one of the key drivers of digital innovation and entrepreneurship (as also discussed in Chapter 4), and that's one of the main pillars of the perspective proposed here. Education refers not only to learning by studying but also to learning by discussing and sharing insights with technology influencers and academics. This is also what this chapter has tried to develop with its discussion of blockchain companies and start-ups that could provide insights for readers interested in developing further blockchain initiatives.

References

1. Nakamoto S. Bitcoin: A Peer-to-Peer Electronic Cash System. (2008) https://bitcoin.org/bitcoin.pdf [accessed December 25, 2020].
2. Tapscott D, Tapscott A. *Blockchain Revolution: How the Technology behind Bitcoin Is Changing Money, Business, and the World*. Penguin (2016).
3. Mattereum. Mattereum – For Truth in Trade. (2020) https://mattereum.com/ [accessed May 24, 2020].
4. Crunchbase. Vinay Gupta. (2019) www.crunchbase.com/person/vinay-gupta-5#section-overview [accessed May 24, 2020].
5. Gupta V. A Brief History of Blockchain. *Harvard Business Review – Technology* (2017) Feb. 28 https://hbr.org/2017/02/a-brief-history-of-blockchain [accessed May 24, 2020].
6. Grover, P., Kar, A.K. and Janssen, M. Diffusion of blockchain technology: Insights from academic literature and social media analytics, *Journal of*

Enterprise Information Management (2019) 32(5):735–757. doi: https://doi.org/10.1108/JEIM-06-2018-0132

7. Casino F, Dasaklis TK, Patsakis C. A Systematic Literature Review of Blockchain-Based Applications: Current Status, Classification and Open Issues. *Telemat Informatics* (2019) 36:55–81. doi: https://doi.org/10.1016/j.tele.2018.11.006.

8. European Union Blockchain Observatory and Forum. Map. (2020) www.eublockchainforum.eu/initiative-map [accessed May 24, 2020].

9. Morkunas VJ, Paschen J, Boon E. How Blockchain Technologies Impact Your Business Model. *Business Horizons* (2019) 62:295–306. doi: https://doi.org/10.1016/j.bushor.2019.01.009.

10. Weking J, Mandalenakis M, Hein A, Hermes S, Böhm M, Krcmar H. The Impact of Blockchain Technology on Business Models – A Taxonomy and Archetypal Patterns. *Electron Markets* (2019) doi: 10.1007/s12525-019-00386-3

11. Larios-Hernández GJ. Blockchain Entrepreneurship Opportunity in the Practices of the Unbanked. *Business Horizons* (2017) 60:865–74. doi: https://doi.org/10.1016/j.bushor.2017.07.012.

12. Zohar A. Bitcoin under the Hood. *Communications of the ACM* (2015) 58:104–13.

13. BitFury Group. Proof of Stake versus Proof of Work – White Paper. (2015) September 13 (Version 10):1–26.

14. Code F. The Dangers Linked to the Emergence of Virtual Currencies: The Example of Bitcoins. *Focus (Banque de France)* (2013) 10 (December 5):1–6 www.banque-france.fr/sites/default/files/medias/documents/focus-10_2013-12-05_en.pdf [accessed December 25, 2020].

15. EVRY. Blockchain: Powering the Internet of Value. (2016) www.finyear.com/attachment/637653/ [accessed April 27, 2020].

16. Lewis A. *A Gentle Introduction to Blockchain Technology*. Brave New Coin (2015).

17. Farell R. An Analysis of the Cryptocurrency Industry. *Wharton Research Scholars Journal* (2015) 130:1–23.

18. Sayadi S, Rejeb S Ben, Choukair Z. Blockchain Challenges and Security Schemes: A Survey. In: *2018 Seventh International Conference on Communications and Networking (ComNet)* (2018) 1–7.

19. Kale V. Blockchain Computing. In: *Digital Transformation of Enterprise Architecture*. CRC Press – Taylor & Francis Group (2020) 446.

20. Dorri A, Kanhere SS, Jurdak R. Blockchain in Internet of Things: Challenges and Solutions. *arXiv preprint arXiv:1608.05187* (2016) 1608.

21. Kiviat TI. Beyond Bitcoin: Issues in Regulating Blockchain Transactions. *Duke Law Journal* (2015) 1:569–608.

22. Froystad P, Holm J. Blockchain: Powering the Internet of Value. (2015) www.finyear.com/attachment/637653/ [accessed April 27, 2020].

23. Lewis A et al. *Understanding Blockchain Technology*. Asian Insights Office DBS Group Research (2016).

24. Wright A, De Filippi P. Decentralized Blockchain Technology and the Rise of Lex Cryptographia. (2015) doi: http://dx.doi.org/10.2139/ssrn.2580664.

25. Hileman G. State of Blockchain Q1 2016: Blockchain Funding Overtakes Bitcoin. (2016) May 11 www.coindesk.com/state-of-blockchain-q1-2016 [accessed June 1, 2020].

26. Ghosh M. Funding in Cryptocurrency and Blockchain Is Moving from the U.S. to China. (2020) April 9 https://jumpstartmag.com/funding-in-cryptocurrency-and-blockchain-is-moving-from-the-u-s-to-china/ [accessed June 1, 2020].

27. CB Insights. The Blockchain Report 2020: Financing, Themes, Coronavirus, & The Year Ahead. (2020) www.tagonline.org/wp-content/uploads/2020/05/CB-Insights_Blockchain-Report-2020.pdf [accessed December 25, 2020].

28. Bogart S, Rice K. The Blockchain Report: Welcome to the Internet of Value. Needham Company, LLC (2015).

29. Loyyal. About Us. (2018) www.loyyal.com/ [accessed May 5, 2020].

30. Fromhart S, Therattil L. *Making Blockchain Real for Customer Loyalty Rewards Programs*. Deloitte Development LLC (2016).

31. EconoTimes. Blockchain Startup Ribbit.me Rebrands as Loyyal. (2016) www.econotimes.com/Blockchain-Startup-Ribbitme-Rebrands-As-Loyyal-200254 [accessed May 5, 2020].

32. de Leon P. Startup Loyyal Uses Blockchain Tech to Keep Customers, Well, Loyal. (2017) www.entrepreneur.com/article/292332 [accessed May 5, 2020].

33. Simon G. Banks Should Be Experience Providers, and Blockchain Can Help. (2016) July 23 (article originally posted MoneySummit June 29, 2016) www.linkedin.com/pulse/banks-should-experience-providers-blockchain-can-help-gregory/ [accessed May 5, 2020].

34. PYMNTS. Loyalty Programs, The Blockchain Way. (2016) www.pymnts.com/blockchain/2016/topic-tbd-loyalty-programs-blockchain-loyyal/ [accessed May 5, 2020].

35. Deloitte. Deloitte Continues Growing Major Blockchain Initiative, Teaming with Five Technology Companies and Announcing 20 Prototypes in Development. (2016) May 3 www2.deloitte.com/mt/en/pages/about-deloitte/articles/mt-pr2016-008-deloitte-blockchain-initiative-with-five-tech-companies-and-20-prototypes-in-development.html [accessed May 5, 2020].

36. Loyyal. Loyyal Selected to Participate in the Inaugural Dubai Future Accelerators Program. (2016) https://medium.com/@Loyyal/loyyal-selected-to-participate-in-the-inaugural-dubai-future-accelerators-program-81f92fa7308e [accessed May 5, 2020].

37. Parker L. Loyyal Helps Make Dubai the Global Leader in Blockchain Technology. (2016) October 11 http://bravenewcoin.com/news/loyyal-helps-to-make-dubai-the-global-leader-in-blockchain-technology/ [accessed May 5, 2020].

38. Everledger. About Us – We Are the Digital Transparency Company. (2019) www.everledger.io/about [accessed May 7, 2020].

39. Lomas N. Everledger Is Using Blockchain to Combat Fraud, Starting with Diamonds. (2015) June 29 https://techcrunch.com/2015/06/29/everledger/ [accessed May 7, 2020].

40. Price R. This London Startup Could Make Diamond Theft a Thing of the Past – and That's Just the Start. (2015) August 28 www.businessinsider.com

.au/everledger-ledger-diamonds-blockchain-tech-theft-fraud-2015–8 [accessed May 7, 2020].

41. Peverelli R, de Feniks R. Everledger: Blockchain-Based Diamond Fraud Detection. (2016) March 16 www.digitalinsuranceagenda.com/featured-insurtechs/everledger-blockchain-based-diamond-fraud-detection/ [accessed May 7, 2020].

42. Wiggers K. Everledger Raises $20 Million to Track Assets with Blockchain Tech. (2019) September 24 https://venturebeat.com/2019/09/24/everledger-raises-20-million-to-track-assets-with-blockchain-tech/ [accessed May 7, 2020].

43. Estimeo. Everledger. (2020) www.estimeo.com/p/everledger [accessed May 7, 2020].

44. Novack A, Kauflin J. The Forbes Fintech 50: The Most Innovative Fintech Companies In 2020. (2020) February 12 www.forbes.com/fintech/2020/#7 b004b3a4acd [accessed May 7, 2020].

45. Natarajan H, Krause S, Gradstein H. Distributed Ledger Technology (DLT) and Blockchain – FinTech Note No. 1. International Bank for Reconstruction and Development / World Bank (2017).

46. Walport M. Distributed Ledger Technology: Beyond Block Chain – A Report by the UK Government Chief Scientific Adviser. Government Office for Science (UK) (2016).

47. Everledger. Industry Solutions. (2019) www.everledger.io/industry-solutions/ [accessed May 7, 2020].

48. Prisco G. The Blockchain for Healthcare: Gem Launches Gem Health Network with Philips Blockchain Lab. (2016) April 26 https://bitcoinmaga zine.com/articles/the-blockchain-for-heathcare-gem-launches-gem-health-n etwork-with-philips-blockchain-lab-1461674938 [accessed May 9, 2020].

49. Gem. Health. (2018) https://enterprise.gem.co/health/. [accessed May 9, 2020].

50. Burniske C, Vaughn E, Shelton J, Cahana A. How Blockchain Technology Can Enhance EHR Operability. ARK Investment Management LLC (2016).

51. Crunchbase. Gem. (2020) www.crunchbase.com/organization/gem#sec tion-overview [accessed May 9, 2020].

52. Barclays. Blockchain Revolution in Trade Finance. (2016) September 30 www.barclayscorporate.com/insights/innovation/blockchain-revolution-in-t rade-finance/ [accessed May 10, 2020].

53. Finextra. Barclays Signs Contracts with Six Accelerator Graduates. (2016) September 16 www.finextra.com/newsarticle/29448/barclays-signs-contracts-with-six-accelerator-graduates [accessed May 10, 2020].

54. Kelly J. Barclays Says Conducts First Blockchain-Based Trade-Finance Deal. (2016) September 7 www.reuters.com/article/us-banks-barclays-block chain/barclays-says-conducts-first-blockchain-based-trade-finance-deal-id USKCN11D23B [accessed May 10, 2020].

55. Wave. The Digital Courier. (2020) http://wavebl.com/ Accessed 10 May 2020

56. Andreasyan T. Barclays and Fintech Start-Up Wave Pioneer Blockchain Trade Finance Transaction. (2016) September 7 www.fintechfutures.com/2016/09/barclays-and-fintech-start-up-wave-pioneer-blockchain-trade-fina nce-transaction/ [accessed May 10, 2020].

57. Rizzo P. Wave Brings Blockchain Trade Finance Trial to Barclays. (2015) October 15 www.coindesk.com/wave-blockchain-trade-finance-barclays [accessed May 10, 2020].

58. AngelList. (2018) Wave (OGYDocs Inc) – The Key to Paperless Trade. https://angel.co/company/wavebl [accessed May 10, 2020].

59. The Blockchain Summit. Speakers & Panelists. In: *Blockchain Summit Conf. Thursday, March 23* (2017). https://the-blockchain-summit.events.co.il/peo ple/3411-gadi-ruschin [accessed May 10, 2020].

60. Shamah D. Israeli Start-Up's Bitcoin-Based Tech Raises a Mast for Shippers. (2015) November 3 www.timesofisrael.com/israeli-start-ups-bitcoin-based-tech-raises-a-mast-for-shippers/ [accessed May 10, 2020].

61. Global Banking & Finance Review. (2016) Barclays and Wave Complete World First Blockchain Trade Finance Transaction. (2016) September 9 www.globalbankingandfinance.com/barclays-wave-complete-world-first-b lockchain-trade-finance-transaction/ [accessed May 10, 2020].

62. Parker L. Align Commerce Could Modernize the B2B Payments Industry with Bitcoins Blockchain. (2015) November 24 http://bravenewcoin.com/n ews/align-commerce-could-modernize-the-b2b-payments-industry-with-bit coins-blockchain/ [accessed May 13, 2020].

63. Behalf. Cutting Edge B2B Payment Trends in 2020 and the Cloud Impact. Behalf (2019).

64. Financial IT. Preparing for 2020: The Impact of the Cloud on B2B Payments. (2019) November 18 https://financialit.net/news/payments/pre paring-2020-impact-cloud-b2b-payments [accessed May 13, 2020].

65. Srinivas V, Schoeps J-T, Ramsay T, Wadhwani R, Hazuria S, Jain A. *2020 Banking and Capital Markets Outlook: Fortifying the Core for the Next Wave of Disruption*. Deloitte Center for Financial Service (DCFS) (2019).

66. Veem. Our Mission. (2019) www.veem.com/about-us/ [accessed May 13, 2020].

67. Lunden I. Veem, Formerly Align Commerce, Gets $24 M from GV, Others for Its Venmo for SMBs. (2017) March 8 https://techcrunch.com/2017/03/ 08/align-commerce-veem-24-million/ [accessed May 13, 2020].

68. Rizzo P. KPCB Leads $12.5 Million Round for Blockchain Firm Align Commerce. (2015) November 17 www.coindesk.com/blockchain-kpcb-align-commerce-12-5-million-series-a/ [accessed May 13, 2020].

69. Crunchbase. Veem. (2020) www.crunchbase.com/organization/goveem [accessed May 13, 2020].

70. Veem. Technology to Help You Pay and Get Paid. (2019) www.veem.com /how-it-works/ [accessed May 13, 2020].

71. Veem. Send to and from These Countries / Send to These Countries. (2019) www.veem.com/where-to-send-receive-wire-transfers/ [accessed May 13, 2020].

72. Shapshak T. Identity Service Civic Launches, Offers $1 M ID Theft Insurance. (2016) July 19 www.forbes.com/sites/tobyshapshak/2016/07/19/identity-service-civic-launches-offers-1m-id-theft-insurance/ [accessed December 25, 2020].

73. Tedder K, Buzzard J. 2020 Identity Fraud Study: Genesis of the Identity Fraud Crisis. (2020) April 7 www.javelinstrategy.com/coverage-area/2020-identity-fraud-study-genesis-identity-fraud-crisis [accessed December 25, 2020].

74. Kraus E. 2020 Javelin ID Fraud Study Points to Dramatic Rise in Real-Time P2P Fraud. (2020) April 27 www.fisglobal.com/ja-jp/insights/what-we-thin k/2020/april/2020-javelin-id-fraud-study-points-to-dramatic-rise-in-real-ti me-p2p-fraud [accessed December 25, 2020].

75. Crunchbase. Civic. (2020) www.crunchbase.com/organization/civic#sec tion-overview [accessed May 18, 2020].

76. Barrett B. A New Service Alerts You When Someone Uses Your Social Security Number. (2016) July 19 www.wired.com/2016/07/new-service-alerts-social-security-numbers-used/ [accessed May 18, 2020].

77. Civic. The Token Sale Has Ended! (2017) https://tokensale.civic.com/ [accessed May 18, 2020].

78. Identity. Decentralized Identity Verification. (2020) www.identity.com/ [accessed May 18, 2020].

79. Civic. To Give People Control and Security Over Their Digital Identity. (2020) www.civic.com/company/ [accessed May 18, 2020].

80. Civic. Meet the Team. (2020) www.civic.com/company/team/ [accessed May 18, 2020].

81. Crunchbase. gyft. (2020) www.crunchbase.com/organization/gyft#section-overview [accessed May 18, 2020].

82. Redman J. Civic's $1 Million Identity Fraud Protection. (2016) https://news .bitcoin.com/civic-identity-fraud-protection/ [accessed May 18, 2020].

83. Youngs B, Henley S. Civic and Coincover Announce the First-of-Its-Kind Crypto Wallet With a $1 Million Protection Guarantee. (2020) March 31 www.businesswire.com/news/home/20200331005187/en/Civic-Coincover-Announce-First-of-its-Kind-Crypto-Wallet-1 [accessed May 18, 2020].

84. Coincover. Coincover Is the #1 Brand in Crypto Security. (2020) www .coincover.com/about-us [accessed May 18, 2020].

85. Rizzo P. Vinny Lingham Leaves Gyft, Raises $2.75 Million for Identity Startup. (2016) January 27, updated January 28 www.coindesk.com/gyft-founder-raises-2–75-million-for-id-startup-civic/ [accessed May 18, 2020].

86. Civic. Civic Wallet FAQs. (2020) www.civic.com/civic-wallet-faqs/ [accessed May 18, 2020].

87. ShoCard. ShoCard – Acquired by Ping Identity (March 2020). (2020) www .linkedin.com/company/shocard-inc [accessed May 19, 2020].

88. Crunchbase. ShoCard. (2020) www.crunchbase.com/organization/shocard-inc [accessed May 19, 2020].

89. Crunchbase. Ping Identity. (2020) www.crunchbase.com/organization/pin g-identity-corporation [accessed May 19, 2020].

90. Dillet R. ShoCard Is a Digital Identity Card on the Blockchain. (2015) May 5 https://techcrunch.com/2015/05/05/shocard-is-a-digital-identity-card-on-the-blockchain/ [accessed May 19, 2020].

91. Shrier D, Wu W, Pentland A. Blockchain & Infrastructure (Identity,Data Security) – Part 3. *MIT Connection Science* (2016) May:1–19.
92. Shocard. Identity for a Mobile World. (2016) www.sita.aero/globalassets/d ocs/events/2015-sita-innovation-day/shocard-armin-ebrahimi.pdf [accessed June 1, 2020].
93. Dillet R. ShoCard and SITA Want to Store Your ID Details on the Blockchain to Authenticate Travelers. (2016) May 25 https://techcrunch .com/2016/05/25/shocard-and-sita-want-to-store-your-id-details-on-the-bl ockchain-to-authenticate-travelers/ [accessed May 19, 2020].
94. ShoCard. Alhamrani Universal & ShoCard Develop Biometric ATM for Saudi Arabian Market. (2019) February 27 www.globenewswire.com/news-release/2019/02/27/1743463/0/en/Alhamrani-Universal-ShoCard-Develop-Biometric-ATM-For-Saudi-Arabian-Market.html [accessed May 19, 2020].
95. Porter D. Alhamrani Universal & ShoCard Develop Biometric ATM for Saudi Arabian Market. (2019) March 4 https://bitcoinsbrain.com/news/busi ness/alhamrani-universal-shocard-develop-biometric-atm-for-saudi-arabian -market/ [accessed May 19, 2020].
96. Snow P, Deery B, Lu J, Johnston D, Kirb P. Factom: Business Processes Secured by Immutable Audit Trails on the Blockchain. Whitepaper. Factom (2014) https://raw.githubusercontent.com/FactomProject/FactomDocs/ma ster/Factom_Whitepaper.pdf [accessed December 25, 2020].
97. Bible W, Raphael J, Taylor P, Oris Valiente I. Blockchain Technology and Its Potential Impact on the Audit and Assurance Profession. Deloitte Development LLC (2017).
98. Factom. The Factom Story. (2019) www.factom.com/company/about-us/ [accessed May 21, 2020].
99. Crunchbase. Factom. (2020) www.crunchbase.com/organization/factom [accessed May 21, 2020].
100. Factom. Factom Inc. Announces Next Generation of Harmony. (2019) June 4 www.factom.com/company/news/press-release/factom-inc-announces-next-generation-of-harmony/ [accessed May 21, 2020].
101. Factom. Internet of Things with Factom. (2019) www.factom.com/solu tions/iot-use-cases/ [accessed May 21, 2020].
102. Factom. Solutions to Make Your Applications Stand Out. (2019) www .factom.com/solutions/ [accessed May 21, 2020].
103. AngelList. Factom – A Blockchain Innovations Company Transforming the Way Organizations Interact with Data. (2018) https://angel.co/company/fac tom-for-profit [accessed May 21, 2020].
104. Factom. Factom Blockchain. (2019) www.factom.com/factom-blockchain/ [accessed May 21, 2020].

Part III

Industries

9   Fintech

9.1   Introduction

Financial technology, or "fintech," has been characterized as the most important, innovative and revolutionary change that has happened in the financial services sector in the last decade as it is radically transforming the way we make payments, transfer funds, borrow as well as manage and protect our money [1, 2]. By leveraging emerging technologies, fintech firms aim to provide a wide range of services to organizations and individuals including money transfer and payments, financial planning, savings and investments, borrowing and insurance, introducing challenges and growing competition to banks and financial institutions.

Three major participants exist in the fintech ecosystem: governments, banks and financial institutions, and entrepreneurs (Figure 9.1). Technology leaders and start-ups also have an important role in this ecosystem. While the governments' critical role is to implement "friendly" policies that ease the development of the ecosystem, banks contribute expertise while entrepreneurs provide innovation. Functioning independently but also through collaborating together, the players of the ecosystem stimulate technological innovations as well as create growth opportunities for sub-segments of the industry, thus contributing to a thriving business environment [3]. The idea of open innovation, where all players of the ecosystem collaborate together, as discussed in Chapter 2, has been wholeheartedly embraced by the fintech industry where investment banks are collaborating through their incubators, accelerators and their respective labs, with new, upcoming start-ups and already established firms as well as entrepreneurs aiming to develop their innovative ideas into solutions that could efficiently tackle existing complex problems [1].

Nowadays, fintech firms are becoming increasingly interested in adopting and combining innovative business models with new and promising consumer technologies, such as mobile and cloud computing, in order to

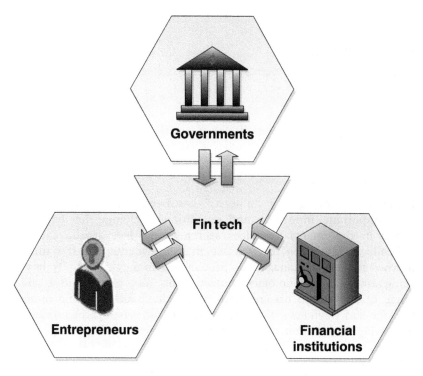

Figure 9.1 Major participants in the fintech ecosystem
Source: [3].

introduce new services to the market, disrupt the existing financial services industry and offer unique customer experience. While back in 2015
only one in seven individuals was using online financial services, already
in 2017 one in three actively online consumers are using two or more
fintech services, thus showing that fintech has reached early mass adoption [4].

A big wave of new entrants has been seen entering the sector, ranging
from small start-ups and young entrepreneurs to big technology firms [4].
Although many new and innovative ideas have already been introduced in
the fintech market, it is estimated that financial technology still has huge
unexplored potential able to dramatically change and reshape the current
financial services sector [2]. Looking forward, it is expected that the
evolution and future of financial services lie in data sharing, open application programming interfaces (APIs), the application of biometrics as
well as the use of artificial intelligence (AI) and robotics [4].

9.2 Macro Analysis of the Fintech Industry

Having intensely reduced the profits of banks, fintech firms are characterized as lean, flexible and highly innovative, requiring almost no physical infrastructure and utilizing agile processes and customer-oriented approaches in combination with the latest technologies in order to offer new services and solutions to their customers [5]. Constituting the intermediate between the bank and the customer, fintech firms both redesign already existing products and create completely new solutions based on processes and algorithms that eliminate the need for any human intervention. It is estimated that most of the already established fintech companies are operating in the incoming and outgoing payments sector, focusing on the use of financial services through smartphones and tablets [5].

As an example, which provides a useful starting point for subsequent research by interested readers, take the year 2019 [6]. From a global perspective, as seen in Figure 9.2, the average adoption of fintech services was 64 percent, with China and India being the global leaders and Russia following in third place [6]. According to Ernst & Young [6], as depicted in Figure 9.3, ranking first among the most commonly used fintech services in 2019 was money transfers and payments (75 percent), followed by insurance (48 percent), savings and investments (34 percent), budget and financial planning (29 percent) and borrowing (27 percent). Still today, web banking, that is, conducting money transfers online, constitutes the financial service used by the majority of digital active individuals around the globe.

Globally in 2019, there was an overall slow start in investments in the fintech sector dropping from $120 billion in 2018 to $38 billion (Figure 9.4). Nevertheless, in the USA, for example, according to KPMG [7], mergers and acquisitions (M&A) for fintech activity seem to be oriented toward further growth in the coming years with median size risen to $265 million in H1 2019, while venture capital (VC) investment reached a new high due to three late-stage megadeals raised by SoFi ($500 million), Carta ($300 million) and Affirm ($300 million) [7].

Although the geopolitical and macroeconomic environment may impact investors, optimism still rules the fintech market, mainly reflected by the recognition of governments and lawmakers of the importance of fintech innovation along with its remarkable contribution to the economy as a whole. For example, several countries, such as Hong Kong, continue to keep a regulatory sandbox program through which companies can test innovative products and services in a "safe space" without having to worry about any regulatory consequences [7, 8]. Furthermore, the UK has already established connections ("bridges") with Australia, Singapore,

Figure 9.2 Consumer fintech global adoption in 2019, across twenty-seven markets (average 64 percent)
Source: Adapted from [6].

	2019	2017	2015
Money transfer and payments	75%	50%	18%
Insurance	48%	24%	8%
Savings and investments	34%	20%	17%
Budgeting and financial planning	29%	10%	8%
Borrowing	27%	10%	6%

Figure 9.3 Comparison of the most common categories of fintech services used around the world, 2015–19
Source: Adapted from [6].

China, Hong Kong and South Korea, aiming to reduce regulatory barriers between them and support fintech growth, thus creating a very positive climate among these countries of the world [8, 9]. What follows is a deeper look at the economies of the Americas, Europe and Asia Pacific on the basis of [7]:

- **Americas:** In 2019, investments in the Americas touched $21.0 billion across 545 deals [7], with 7 of the top ones among them in the USA [7]. Nevertheless, Canada sees a relevant growing interest in fintechs and their capacity to attract investments, especially through the activity of US investors, as shown by the acquisitions of Solium Capital and Wave

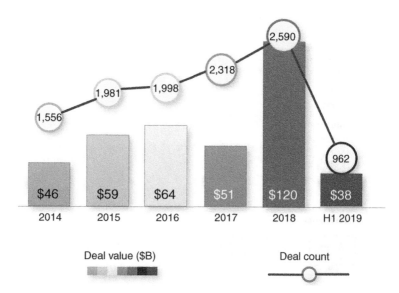

Figure 9.4 Total global fintech investment, 2014–end H1 2019
Source: Adapted from [7], which uses data from the PitchBook
database, including data on VC, private equity (PE) and M&A.

Capital by US companies [7]. Another example is the role of Toronto's
Creative Destruction Lab as one of the members of the Libra
Association gathered by Facebook (also including, among others,
Uber and Spotify) for the governance of the Libra cryptocurrency [7].
Moreover, investments in fintechs in Latin America are showing interesting phenomena. Among them, it is worth mentioning the rise of
a new fintech unicorn. Based in Argentina, Prisma Medios de Pago is
a payments company that has followed "a buyout of a 51 percent stake
in the company by US-based Advent International" [7] (p. 27). Also
worthy of mention is the launch in Brazil of the new payment platform
BanQi by Airfox (based in Boston, USA) in partnership with the retail
company Via Varejo, whose Casas Bahia stores it uses [7].

• **Europe:** In Europe, fintech investment touched $13.2 billion with 307
deals in H1 2019; thus, it seems that investment interest in European
fintechs is still strong, although there has been some slowdown in the
last years. Characterized as one of the most important fintech capitals
around the world, the UK is still attracting relevant investments,
including six of the top ten fintech deals in Europe, notable among
them Greensill Capital (receiving $800 million investment from the
SoftBank Vision Fund), payment company WorldFirst (acquired by

Ant Financial for $717 million) and the British banking start-up OakNorth (with a $440 million investment again led by the Softbank Vision Fund, with Clermont Group providing the remaining money) [7]. Then, TransferWise (a global money transfer company) released $292 million worth of private shares to BlackRock, Lead Edge Capital, Lone Pine Capital, and Vitruvian Partners [7]. The UK has a "fintech-friendly" policy with tax incentives and governmental programs that aim to support fintech innovation and cultivate a nourishing environment both for early start-ups that have innovative and radical ideas and for entrepreneurs who are interested in entering the financial services industry [2]. Nevertheless, Singapore's progressive initiatives and China's surging fintech activity are challenging the UK's long-term position as the leading market in the world, while the Brexit vote in 2016 created a big wave of uncertainty in the market that will hold until the situation is resolved [1]. In other European countries, such as Germany, the Nordic countries, Spain and France, significant endeavors have taken place with the development of fintech hubs including labs, accelerators and incubators as well as with the establishment of partnerships between banks, financial institutions and firms, ultimately aiming to support fintech innovation and enhance entrepreneurial activity within the sector [1, 7].

- **Asia Pacific:** In this area, fintech investment activity reached a new level of $3.6 billion across 102 deals in 2019. Once boosted by China [8, 10], other countries began to undertake relevant activities in fintech investment in the Asia Pacific area. According to [7], the top deals, as of H1 2019, included, besides four deals in China and one in Korea (a $200 million investment by the Blockchain Exchange Alliance to expand the cryptocurrency trading platform Bithum [11]), "Australia (AirWallex: $100 million), Indonesia (Akulaku: $100 million), Vietnam (Momo: $100 million) and Singapore (GoBear: $80 million)" [7] (p. 63). Extremely important for Asia's fintech growth are the several governmental partnerships that have taken place over the years, such as the fintech cooperation agreement of Singapore with Australia, which aim to build bridges between different countries that could lead to fruitful collaborations and be highly beneficial for the success of their respective fintech sectors [8].

Looking forward, "insurtech" (*insurance technology*) and "regtech" (*regulatory technology* for compliance with regulations, and protection from employee and customer fraud) still attract funding after being predicted to be the next big investment trends within the fintech industry; however, regtech together with cybersecurity, "wealthtech" (*wealth technology* to enhancing the wealth-management process[12]) and "proptech" (*property and technology* for managing commercial and residential property and in general for the real estate markets[13]) are worth considering for growth in the future [7, 8]. Moreover, areas such as AI, cognitive learning and data analytics technologies seem to be attracting growing attention from investors in the field. In more detail, robo-advisors, digital platforms offering financial planning advice to customers with almost no human supervision, have already been introduced by financial institutions and have gathered strong investment power in the USA in recent years. As AI and modern technologies are evolving rapidly, robo-advisory is expected to have a profound impact on the processes of financial institutions by improving efficiencies as well as risk selection and assessment. For these reasons, it is expected to be one of the strongest upcoming trends in fintech in the next few years [6–8, 14]. Furthermore, investment in blockchain technologies for application on financial technologies, which created a huge buzz over the last few years, although still considered relevant [6, 7], is nowadays displaying a slight deceleration with investors moving from a "fear of missing out" attitude [7] (p. 16) to making "more mature investment decisions" [7].

9.3   Digitalization in the Fintech Industry

Digitalization, that is, the process of integrating digital technologies into everyday life by converting everything into digital form [15], has radically transformed every aspect of business and society [16–18]. Several sectors, such as the hotel industry, journalism and transportation services, have been severely influenced or even completely changed by the impact of digitalization with numerous opportunities to be grabbed but also important challenges to be tackled [19]. Digitalization has transformed the financial sector, posing significant challenges but also providing several benefits to organizations, as follows:

- **Challenges.** The digital disruption has introduced a vast amount of challenges, especially for traditional banks that have seen their margins shrinking and their costs increasing exponentially. Furthermore, the emergence of new technologies in the fintech industry has intrigued hundreds of start-ups and businesses to enter the market offering alternative solutions and innovative services that can potentially jeopardize current financial institutions by diminishing their traditional operations and making their current banking processes obsolete. As a result, traditional banks and financial institutions are being "forced" to fundamentally change their thinking, embrace innovation, adopt new business models as well as redesign the whole customer experience life cycle in order to stay competitive and retain their customers during the digital revolution [5, 19, 20].

- **Opportunities:** In the financial sector, digitalization has created new markets and segments filled with solutions, innovative products and services aiming to satisfy the needs of individuals and enterprises. The emergence of new digital technologies, characterized as game changers, for example cloud computing, blockchain, AI and the Internet of Things (IoT), is enabling innovation and offering tremendous potential and opportunities for entrepreneurs and small businesses. By leveraging the dynamics of these modern technologies, banks have the opportunity to open new sources of revenue while new fintech entrants have the chance to develop pioneering solutions that could disrupt the current market, scale quickly and achieve high revenues. Furthermore, the digital revolution is creating great opportunities for both fintech companies and incumbent firms to collaborate with traditional financial institutions, enabling them to gain access into funds and accelerator programs as well as to participate in sharing knowledge and novel ideas in one open innovation ecosystem [19–21].

Taking these issues into account, the rest of the chapter considers a selection of start-ups as examples of digital entrepreneurship in fintech, with a focus on the insurtech and realtech domains.

9.4   Case Studies

This section presents two cases studies that describe the innovation practices of companies in fintech, focusing on insurtech and realtech as domains of application. Following the model adopted in my previous publications (see, e.g., [16]), each innovation is described, highlighting its key characteristics and information about its developers, then this introduction is complemented by the main company competitiveness indicators for time-to-market as well as user value in terms of perception, such as the user experience and the "wow" effect.

9.4.1   Metromile

Metromile is a pay-per-mile insurance start-up that belongs to insurtech, a fintech sub-segment focused on creating innovations as well as addressing challenges and opportunities in the insurance industry. Having adopted a unique business model and having redefined the industry with its innovation and technology offerings, the insurance provider introduced a novel solution targeted to people who drive low mileages but still pay huge amounts of money on car insurance, to help them save money by paying more affordable rates [22–25]. Drastically lowering the costs of insurance for drivers, the San Francisco-based company identifies low-risk drivers by collecting data that were not available to insurance providers before. Through its smartphone application, Metromile logs the miles of the car so that an individual who drives their car less than the average, and thus is prone to fewer accidents, pays a smaller fee than they would pay with a normal insurance program [22–24, 26].

9.4.1.1 Development Founded in 2011 in California by Stanford graduate and current CEO Dan Preston, Metromile aims to provide a completely new model of car insurance by making car ownership easier and more affordable to drivers while at the same time providing high-quality customer experience [24]. The start-up is composed of a small team of nine people, including David Friedberg, co-founder and current chairman of the board, who has been working with big technology companies, such as Google, since 2006, and also Carrie Dollan, the chief financial officer (CFO), who has a strong business background and several years' experience in the financial services industry [25].

Having raised the surprising amount of $191.5 million in funding in early 2016, the pioneer car insurance provider, which has just acquired Mosaic Insurance, a carrier [27], plans to underwrite its own insurance policies and manage its claims in-house without having to rely on or collaborate with other insurance companies. Being the leader in the pay-per-mile insurance sector and being equipped with years of technology expertise, the insurtech start-up plans nationwide expansion by extending its operations to additional cities in the USA as well as continuing to build and improve on the features of its application [22, 24]. Table 9.1 depicts

Table 9.1 *Metromile's competitiveness indicators for time-to-market*

Solution	Metromile
Founded	2011
No. of products	1
Clients	Individuals
Partners	Different levels of partnership
Market dimension	Growing
Competitors	Very few
Enabling infrastructure	Ready

the competitiveness indicators for time-to-market and the growing market demand. The enabling infrastructure is ready and the demand is very high as very few competitors exist in the market.

9.4.1.2 Application Traditionally, insurance providers charge their fees based on people's driving habits and location. As a result, people who don't use their car much end up paying the same fees as people who drive several hours per day covering thousands of miles [23, 26]. Offering a smartphone application, Metromile provides a novel solution to low-mileage people by measuring the miles of the car through a small wireless device, called Pulse, which can be installed by the driver on the board diagnostics of the car. Available both for Android and iOS smartphones, the application provides multiple functionality including access to several types of information such as previous trips, the health of the car, the location where the driver parked, tips for optimizing fuel efficiency as well as best times to commute to avoid heavy traffic. The car locator function has been characterized as the best feature of the application: it provides exceptional functionality such that many drivers have been able to use it to locate their stolen vehicles [23, 24, 26].

Having established a partnership with Uber in 2015, Metromile provides the option to professional drivers to pay under a different insurance scheme when they are using their car for personal purposes. Recognizing when the driver is working, the consumer pay-per-mile application understands when the car is covered by Uber's insurance program and logs only the mileages covered for personal use. As a result, Metromile significantly reduces insurance costs for drivers who mostly use their car professionally [26].

Table 9.2 shows a good level of perceived *user value* for the Metromile solution as user feedback is very positive, the solution exhibits great novelty and the "wow" effect is high.

Table 9.2 *User value indicators for Metromile*

Fast learning	Medium
User interface	Positive
User experience	Positive
Process impact	Medium
User feedback	Positive
"Wow" effect	High

9.4.2   Compass

Valued at more than $1 billion, Compass is a New York-based real estate start-up that focuses on broker listings for both rental and sale of properties by merging data analytics with real estate agents [28, 29]. Aiming to transform the existing antiquated real estate industry, Compass claims to reduce friction and time when seeking to rent or buy property as well as to facilitate a transparent and efficient experience both for real estate agents and for customers [30].

Having disrupted the market by introducing a game-changing solution, Compass combines proprietary search technology and analytics with the expertise of thousands of highly qualified real estate agents that hold years of industry experience [31]. Claiming an annual sales run of $7 billion, Compass has received significant attention both from investors and from the public; it is considered a rare "unicorn" case among its competitors in the fintech industry as it has achieved extremely high revenues, almost $180 million in 2016, and rapid growth in more than ten regions of the USA [28, 32].

9.4.2.1 Development

Founded in 2012, this real estate technology-driven brokerage encompasses a team of people with exceptional educational and industry backgrounds. Co-founder Israeli Ori Allon, the current chairman of Compass, has already sold two of his previous established technology start-ups, for which he had developed the underlying search technology, to Google and Twitter; Allon's co-founder, Robert Reffkin, is the current CEO of the company, holds an MBA from Columbia and previously worked at Goldman Sachs as well as McKinsey consulting firm [33, 34].

Having raised almost $210 million in funding to date, the real estate company, currently established in 30 cities in the USA and equipped with more than 1,400 real estate agents and employees, has plans to expand its business in the near future by opening more offices in the USA while also improving its technology for analyzing the real estate market [28, 29, 32]. Having attracted most of the top brokers and best employees in the industry, the tech start-up has been following an aggressive recruitment approach that has created strong rivals in the already intensely competitive industry [31, 33].

In Table 9.3 the time-to-market competitiveness indicators appear to be high, with a solid company and growing market demand. The company has received funding from a wide range of investors such as Wellington Management and Co, IVP, Thrive Capital and Founders Fund [35].

Table 9.3 *Compass's competitiveness indicators for time-to-market*

Solution	Compass
Founded	2012
No. of products	1
Clients	Individuals
Partners	Different levels of partnership
Market dimension	Growing
Competitors	Many
Enabling infrastructure	Ready

9.4.2.2 Application Compass offers a solution for both sides of the equation, consumers and agents. The tech-driven start-up doesn't use advertisements to generate revenues; instead, it makes a profit by charging a small percentage on the transactions that take place through its platform [28]. Compass's real estate listing application enables individuals to rent, buy and sell properties. The application provides real-time national property data available to potential interested buyers and renters as well as agents. For people looking to sell, buy or rent a property, Compass has designed an intuitive, user-friendly application that includes a vast variety of features such as search by neighborhood, number of bedrooms or price range, as well as view advanced analytics such as year-by-year analysis, negotiability and days on the market. The platform aims to provide a seamless user experience by presenting only verified listings and charging much less than the average real estate firms [30, 31].

Regarding the brokers' use, the application can save huge amounts of time by reducing much of their tedious work, enabling them to create flyers almost automatically and instantly send emails about new listings in order to advertise properties [36]. According to co-founder Allon, the platform helps "agents triangulate the value of properties, develop property-specific marketing ROI [return on investment] plans, predict how the market will respond to new properties entering the market. We are bringing the science to what has for too long been only an art" [31]. The real estate platform derives its data from multiple sources and merges them in one central database where machine learning algorithms execute the data analysis [31].

Table 9.4 depicts the measure of *user value* of the Compass solution. The platform has received very positive feedback from users as the

Table 9.4 *User value indicators for Compass*

Fast learning	Medium
User interface	Positive
User experience	Positive
Process impact	Medium
User feedback	Positive
"Wow" effect	High

interface looks promising, including a simple design that is easy to grasp and use.

9.5   Summary

This chapter introduced the world of financial technologies – called fintech – describing the digital revolution that has reshaped the finance sector and completely transformed the way we protect, borrow and manage our money. By delineating the players of the fintech ecosystem, constituting governments, financial institutions and banks as well as start-ups and technology companies, it briefly explained the role and impact of every participant in the ecosystem, highlighting the need for collaboration and sharing of ideas, knowledge and innovation.

Furthermore, the chapter provided an in-depth global macro analysis of the fintech industry by focusing on three regions – the Americas, Europe and Asia – analyzing the geopolitical and macroeconomic factors that affected the amount of fintech deals, investments and venture capital during 2019. The chapter concluded by discussing the future investment trends for the industry, including the growth of insurtech and the evolution of modern technologies such as biometrics, cognitive learning and data analytics as well as AI applications. It also discussed the profound impact of digitalization on the fintech industry by analyzing the great opportunities that have emerged for firms, banks and financial institutions as well as the critical challenges that the digital disruption has posed. The last section of the chapter presented two case studies of companies whose innovative solutions have attracted considerable attention both from the public and from investors. Belonging to very upcoming and growing sub-segments of fintech, namely insurance (insurtech) and real estate (realtech), the start-ups were discussed in detail, including the main characteristics of their solutions, interesting information on the backgrounds and motivations of the members of the founding teams along with their plans for the future. Furthermore, each solution was accompanied by the main company competitiveness indicators for time-to-market as well as indicators of user value in terms of perception, such as the user experience and the so-called wow effect.

References

1. Gulamhuseinwala I, Kotecha V. UK FinTech on the Cutting Edge: An Evaluation of the International FinTech Sector. Ernst & Young (2016).
2. Fülöp A, Lachowski A, Martyniuk D, Stasczak S, Spionek A, Bartosiak A. Fintech in CEE: Chartering the Course for Innovation in Financial Services Technology. Deloitte, UK Department for International Trade (2016).
3. Diemers D, Lamaa A, Salamat J, Steffens T. Developing a FinTech Ecosystem in the GCC: Let's Get Ready for Takeoff. Strategy&, PwC (2015).
4. Bull T, Chen S, Gulamhuseinwala I, Hatch M, Lloyd J. EY FinTech Adoption Index: The Rapid Emergence of FinTech. Ernst & Young (2017).
5. Drummer D, Jerenz A, Siebelt P, Thaten M. FinTech – Challenges and Opportunities: How Digitization Is Transforming the Financial Sector. McKinsey & Company (2016).
6. Chen S, Chiselita D. Global FinTech Adoption Index 2019 – As FinTech Becomes the Norm, You Need to Stand Out from the Crowd. EYGM Limited (2019).
7. Pollari I, Ruddenklau A, Armstrong J, Bedri B, Chia TY, Deol E, Gobbo F, Milligan D, Packman B, Lazlo P, Pyle A, Rae A, Raviv M, Ruark R, Scally A, Stark-Goddard L, Steidl-Küster S, Thoume C, Zhang T. The Pulse of Fintech 2019: Biannual Global Analysis of Investment in Fintech. KPMG International Cooperative (2019). https://assets.kpmg/content/dam/kpmg/xx/pdf/2019/07/pulse-of-fintech-h1-2019.pdf [accessed January 3, 2021].
8. Fortnum D, Mead W, Pollari I, Hughes B, Speier A. The Pulse of Fintech Q4 2016 – Global Analysis of Investment in Fintech. KPMG (2017).
9. Horton C. Are the Fintech Bridges Working? (2019) www.raconteur.net/finance/uk-fintech-bridges [accessed May 3, 2020].
10. Mittal S, Lloyd J. The Rise of FinTech in China – Redefining Financial Services. Asian Insights Office DBS Group Research, Ernst & Young (2016).
11. Suberg W. South Korea: Bithumb Exchange Operator Gains $200 Million from Japanese Investment Fund. (2019) https://cointelegraph.com/news/south-korea-bithumb-exchange-operator-gains-200-million-from-japanese-investment-fund [accessed May 3, 2020].
12. Jones A. Wealthtech: A Game Changer for Wealth Management. (2019) https://internationalbanker.com/brokerage/wealthtech-a-game-changer-for-wealth-management/ [accessed May 3, 2020].
13. Lecamus V. PropTech: What Is It and How to Address the New Wave of Real Estate Startups? (2017) https://medium.com/@vincentlecamus/p

roptech-what-is-it-and-how-to-address-the-new-wave-of-real-estate-start ups-ae9bb52fb128 [accessed May 3, 2020].

14. PwC. Opportunities Await: How InsurTech Is Reshaping Insurance. pwc .com/InsurTech (2016).

15. IGI Global. What Is Digitalization. (2018) www.igi-global.com/dictionary/ digitalization/7748 [accessed May 29, 2020].

16. Morabito V. *The Future of Digital Business Innovation.* Springer International (2016).

17. Morabito V. *Trends and Challenges in Digital Business Innovation.* Springer (2014).

18. Tilson D, Lyytinen K, Sørensen C. Digital Infrastructures: The Missing IS Research Agenda. *Information Systems Research* (2010) 21:748–59.

19. Hess M, Hess R. Digitisation. (2020) www.swissbanking.org/en/topics/digi tisation [accessed April 10, 2018].

20. Skan J, Dickerson J, Masood S. The Future of Fintech and Banking – Digitally Disrupted or Reimagined? Accenture (2015).

21. Williams D, Ogle S, Wintermeyer L. Capital Markets: Innovation and the FinTech Landscape – How Collaboration with FinTech Can Transform Investment Banking. Ernst & Young (2016).

22. Chapman L. Metromile Raises $192 Million to Take on Car Insurance Business. (2016) www.bloomberg.com/news/articles/2016–09-21/metromile-raises-192-million-to-take-on-car-insurance-business [accessed May 3, 2020].

23. Huckstep R. Metromile &Telematics – It's Car Insurance, but Not as We Know It! (2015) https://dailyfintech.com/2015/06/04/metromile-telematics-its-car-insurance-but-not-as-we-know-it/ [accessed May 3, 2020].

24. Metromile. Metromile Announces $191.5 M in Funding; Acquires Insurance Carrier. (2016) www.prnewswire.com/news-releases/metromile-announces-1915m-in-funding-acquires-insurance-carrier-300331552.html [accessed May 3, 2020].

25. Metromile. About Us – Metromile. (2018) www.metromile.com/about-us/ [accessed May 3, 2020].

26. Constine J. Metromile Launches Uber Car Insurance Where Drivers Only Pay for Personal Miles. (2015) https://techcrunch.com/2015/01/28/metro mile-launches-uber-car-insurance-where-drivers-only-pay-for-personal-mil es/ [accessed May 3, 2020].

27. Lunden I. Pay-per-Mile Insurance Startup Metromile Raises $191.5 M, Acquires Mosaic Insurance. (2016) https://techcrunch.com/2016/09/21/pa y-per-mile-insurance-startup-metromile-raises-191-5m-acquires-mosaic-in surance/ [accessed May 3, 2020].

28. Frier S. Compass Earns $1 Billion Valuation as New Unicorns Become Rarer. (2016) www.bloomberg.com/news/articles/2016–08-31/compass-said-to-win -1-billion-valuation-as-new-unicorns-become-rarer [accessed May 3, 2020].

29. Roof K. Compass Raises $75 Million at $1 Billion+ Valuation for Real Estate Listings. (2016) https://techcrunch.com/2016/08/31/compass-raises-75-million-at-1-billion-valuation-for-real-estate-listings/ [accessed May 3, 2020].2020

30. McAlone N. This $800 Million Startup Just Launched an App to Make Buying a Home Easier. (2016) http://uk.businessinsider.com/compass-real-estate-startup-launches-new-app-2016–7 [accessed May 3, 2020].

31. Titlow JP. Why This Real Estate App Is Making New York Brokers Nervous. (2015) www.fastcompany.com/3047603/why-this-real-estate-app-is-making-new-york-brokers-nervous [accessed May 3, 2020].

32. Barzilay O. Compass Launches the Pinterest of Real Estate. (2017) www.forbes.com/sites/omribarzilay/2017/03/28/compass-launches-the-pinterest-of-real-estate/#787d0100b066 [accessed May 3, 2020].

33. Fairley J. Why Rivals Fear This Real Estate Agency. (2017) https://thebridgebk.com/why-rivals-fear-real-estate-agency/ [accessed May 3, 2020].

34. Compass. About Us. (2018) www.compass.com/about/ [accessed May 3, 2020].

35. Rosbrow-Telem L. Real Estate Platform Compass Becomes Billion-Dollar Startup after Raising $75 Million. (2016) www.geektime.com/2016/08/31/real-estate-platform-compass-becomes-billion-dollar-startup-after-raising-75-million/ [accessed April 10, 2018].

36. Brown E, Kusisto L. Real Estate Is Latest Target for Would-Be Disrupters. (2017) www.wsj.com/articles/real-estate-is-latest-target-for-would-be-disrupters-1487327401 [accessed May 3, 2020].

10 Manufacturing

10.1 Introduction

Before we thoroughly define "macroeconomics," we need to first look at the definitions of *business* and *manufacturing*. Every entrepreneurial venture can be referred to as a business. This implies that a business is not fully an entrepreneurial venture but an entrepreneurial venture is a business. Therefore, a business is an organized effort that consists of the supply of goods and services to consumers in order to make a profit. Businesses vary in size with regards to the number of employees, the volume of sales and its nature. With regard to nature, a business could be a manufacturing business, a service business or one of a host of other types.

This brings us to the definition of manufacturing. Manufacturing can be generally defined as the process of the transformation of raw materials, parts or components into finished goods or products for sale to customers whose expectations and requirements the goods or products meet. This process of transformation of raw materials, parts or components into finished goods or products is referred to as production. The employment of labor (man) and machine, as the case may be, is vital in manufacturing. The environment within which business thrives is made up of several factors, including organizational orientation, internal power relationships, sociocultural factors, global factors, government policies and a host of other factors. These factors can be categorized into internal factors, otherwise referred to as microeconomic factors (micro factors), and external factors, otherwise referred to as macroeconomic factors (macro factors). Macro factors refer to factors like global trends, government regulations and policies, economic nature, sociocultural factors as well as international relationships with other economies.

This now brings us to "macro analysis." Macro analysis, which can also be referred to as macroeconomic analysis, refers to how the economic activities of the existing firms, the government economic policies and technological advancement can affect the overall output, price levels, employment rate and growth rate of an economy. It is made up of models that help to clarify how higher economic growth rates are achieved within a specific period of time. These models also help to clarify how both internal and external economic stability is maintained. Macro analysis can also be defined as the analysis of the economic structure as well as performance and the government's economic policies and technological advancements and how they affect the economy. Economists are hugely interested in the factors that play a role in the economic growth of a country, as such economic growth brings about more job opportunities and affordable prices of goods and services, thereby raising the standard of living of the people in a country. In spite of the wide disagreement among macroeconomists about the part that economic regulations and policies play in the rate of growth of the economy in the short run, a large number of them agree on factors that affect the rate of growth of the economy in the long run. Let's now take a critical look into a macro analysis of the manufacturing industry.

10.2   Macro Analysis of the Manufacturing Industry

The microenvironment of manufacturing industries consists of forces or factors that are operational in the larger macroenvironment. These forces determine the opportunities as well as the threats posed to the manufacturing industries. The macro forces are not as controllable by the industry as the micro forces. These macro forces are political and regulatory forces, technological forces, global forces, natural forces as well as sociocultural forces. The political and regulatory forces consist of the authority exercised by the legislative, executive and judiciary political institutions (arms of government). They help to direct, structure, develop and regulate business activities. Technological forces are the systematic applications of scientific innovations and knowledge to practical tasks. However, since technological innovations are fast-growing and developing, it is important to keep pace with this growth and development; thus, companies should be ready to implement such new technological innovations to improve their businesses. The global forces consist of the reality of viewing businesses on a global perspective especially with regard to business and managerial practices that are required to thrive in the global economy. The sociocultural forces consist of people's attitudes to work as well as the role of marriage, religion, family and education in business growth and development. As stated earlier, political and regulatory forces, technological forces, global forces, natural forces as well as sociocultural forces are the macro forces and it is of utmost importance to note that these forces determine the level of success or failure of the manufacturing industry in any country and the world at large. We will now discuss these forces one after the other.

10.2.1 Political and Regulatory Forces

Political and regulatory forces play a huge role in determining the level of success or failure of the manufacturing firm and all other firms in general. Furthermore, if government regulations are favorable to manufacturing firms, there is higher productivity and a higher level of sales made; as such, if manufacturing firms could improve this, it would have a hugely positive effect on the economy of nations. For example, if the government were to come up with a regulation that restricted the importation of clothes manufactured by firms in other countries into a country, this would improve support for locally made clothes (clothes made by manufacturing firms in the particular country). It would also motivate the manufacturing firms in such a country to improve on the quality of delivery, such that investors would be drawn into the manufacturing firms. Moreover, the government would also be willing to pump revenue into the manufacturing firms.

In addition, it is worthy of note that new government regulations can bring about changes in three different dimensions: the level of *stringency*, the level of *information* and the level of *flexibility* [1]. The level of stringency of any regulation is a measure of the degree of compliance required by the manufacturing firms as well as the inconvenience or obligation imposed by such regulations on the manufacturing firms. The level of stringency can also be said to be the minimum level of compliance inconvenience that is required to achieve the desired result of the stipulated regulation. For any government regulation to achieve the desired result, the level of stringency can be tightened, either *by increasing the regulation's level of stringency gradually* or *by increasing the level of stringency at once*, in order to achieve the desired result [1].

The first way (increasing the regulation's level of stringency gradually) implies that the level of stringency is increased over a specific period of time depending on the compliance of the manufacturing firms. This is further illustrated in Figure 10.1, where point 1 represents the point at which the regulation was adopted while point 2 represents the desired result, which implies the highest level of stringency of the regulation. Also, Figure 10.1 shows a linear variation between the level of stringency of the regulation and the time required to attain the highest (fulfilling) point of the regulation.

STRINGENCY LEVEL

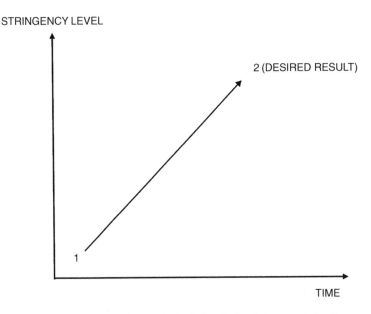

Figure 10.1 Increasing the regulation's level of stringency gradually

The second way (increasing the level of stringency at once) forces immediate full compliance with the regulation and could serve to disrupt the operations of manufacturing firms. This is illustrated in Figure 10.2, where point 1 represents the point at which the regulation was adopted while point 2 represents the desired result, which implies the highest level of stringency of the regulation. Also, Figure 10.2 shows a very sharp variation between the level of stringency of the regulation and the *time* required to attain the highest (fulfilling) point of the regulation.

Also, the level of information is the measure of the promotion of information in the marketplace as a result of government regulation [1]. Regulation can give rise to better information or awareness of the manufacturing and marketing processes of products. In addition, the level of flexibility of a regulation can be said to be the total number of available *paths* of implementation for the manufacturing firms in order to comply with the regulation [1]. This dimension of regulation gives room for manufacturing firms to decide on the path of implementation to take for optimum compliance with the regulation. This helps to reduce the burden of compliance on the manufacturing firms.

Furthermore, Figure 10.3 illustrates the level of flexibility required to achieve the desired result of the regulation. We can see two paths: path

STRINGENCY LEVEL

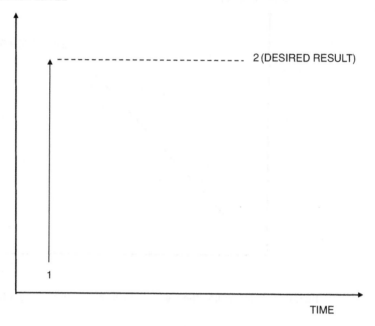

Figure 10.2 Increasing the regulation's level of stringency at once

A and path B. Note that both paths A and B start from point 1, which represents the point at which the regulation was adopted, and that both paths A and B end at point 2, which represents the desired result. There are several paths to achieving the desired result but Figure 10.3 shows only these two.

10.2.2 Technological Forces

Technological forces play a huge role in determining the level of success or failure of the manufacturing firm and all other firms in general. The effect of the forces of technology on manufacturing firms with regard to production can be viewed as leading to increased output (production) with the same resources [2]. This can be achieved in the following ways:

- *The production time* is reduced with the same production output and the same amount of resources being used.
- *The production output* is increased within the same time frame and with the same amount of resources.

FLEXIBILITY LEVEL

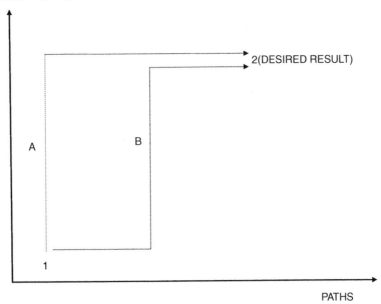

Figure 10.3 Flexibility level required to achieve the regulation's desired result

- *The production cost* is reduced with the same production output.
- *The production output* is increased at the same cost.

It is worth noting that the four ways indicated above are relative to both the old technologies (OT) and the new technologies (NT).

Figure 10.4 shows that the production output (PO) was achieved within a shorter period of time using NT instead of OT.

Moreover, Figure 10.5 shows the increase in PO within the same time frame when moving from OT to NT. PO1 represents the OT PO while PO2 represents the NT PO. From Figure 10.5, it is obvious that the production output point PO2 and the production output point PO1 were achieved within the same time frame, represented by T1. This signifies that a higher production output (PO2) was achieved for the new technologies (NT) while a lower production output (PO1) was achieved for the old technologies (OT) within the same period of time (T1).

Consider now Figure 10.6; it shows the reduction in production cost with the same production output. From Figure 10.6, it is obvious that the

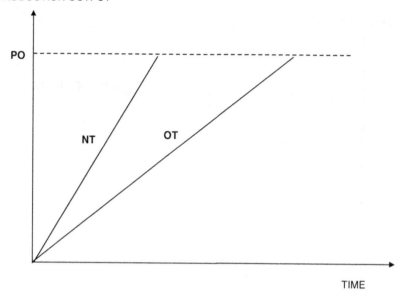

Figure 10.4 PO and time for OT and NT

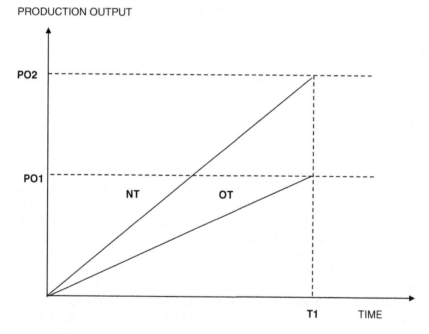

Figure 10.5 The increase in PO within the same time frame from OT to NT

PRODUCTION OUTPUT

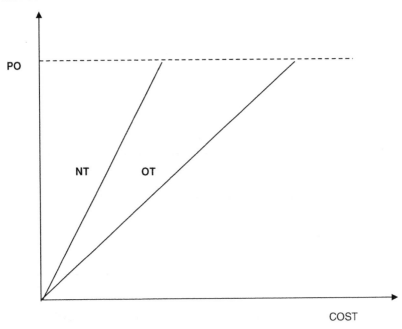

Figure 10.6 PO and cost for OT and NT

production output point PO was achieved with a lower cost for the new
technologies (NT) than the old technologies (OT).

In addition, Figure 10.7 shows the increase in production output (PO)
with the same cost with regard to the old technologies (OT) and the new
technologies (NT).

In Figure 10.7, again, the point PO1 represents the production output
point for the old technologies (OT) while point PO2 represents the production output point for the new technologies (NT). From Figure 10.7, it
is obvious that the production output point PO2 and the production output
point PO1 were achieved with the same cost, represented by C1. This
signifies that a higher production output (PO2) was achieved for the new
technologies (NT) while a lower production output (PO1) was achieved for
the old technologies (OT) with the same cost (C1). However, it is worth
noting that for the new technologies to better the old technologies for
production and other processes for manufacturing firms, such manufacturing firms have to carry out an analytic process to compare the old

PRODUCTION OUTPUT

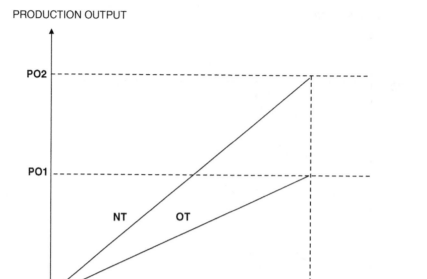

Figure 10.7 The increase in PO with the same cost from OT to NT

technologies and the new technologies to be adopted in order to ascertain better effectiveness of the new technologies in comparison to the old technologies.

10.2.3 Global Forces, Natural Forces and Sociocultural Forces

Global forces – such as exchange rate, import and export levels as well as foreign investments – play an immense role in determining the level of success or failure of the manufacturing firm and all other firms. For example, some manufacturing firms purchase raw materials from other countries, and these purchases are affected by the exchange rate. If the exchange rate increases then it might be a bit difficult for manufacturing firms to produce, as the cost of production will increase, leading to lower production rates or closing up of such firms as there might be a decrease in demand if finished product prices increase. Moreover, natural forces such as the weather and natural hazards such as volcanoes, tornadoes, earthquakes and so on also play an important role in determining the level of success of manufacturing firms. Severe natural forces can lead to large losses and maybe even put an end to manufacturing firms.

Finally, sociocultural forces such as people's attitudes to work, marriage, religion, family and education play a huge role in the success or failure of manufacturing firms. Workers' attitudes to work determine the levels of effectiveness and productivity of manufacturing firms; for instance, a manufacturing firm will not be able to produce effectively if its workers are lackadaisical (not very productive), and the reverse is true if they are extremely hardworking. Also, some manufacturing firms employ only their relatives and family members and this could affect the level of productivity of such a firm. In addition, some manufacturing firms are controlled by the sons or daughters of the owner of such firms, as the firms are passed down the lineage, and this could affect the effectiveness of such firms positively or negatively. It is worth noting that all these forces discussed so far could impact negatively or positively on manufacturing firms. Manufacturing firms are thus encouraged to critically analyze the forces that may be within their control, especially the technological and sociocultural forces.

10.3 Importance of Digitalization to the Manufacturing Industry

As also seen in the previous chapters of this book, data and technology are fast bringing huge transformation to every facet of our lives. They interrupt the existing state of affairs by creating new means of getting things done. However, various companies, especially those in the industrial sector, are looking at ways to best implement and make use of these existing digital technologies in order to obtain maximum benefits from them. As we have seen in the previous chapters, these technologies include the smartphone, tablets, computers and the Internet. Thus, service delivery, production and virtually all aspects of life are affected by the digitalization enabled by those technologies. Consequently, considering the manufacturing sector, digitalization could have an immense impact on the processes of production, including:

- **Lowering the cost of production:** The manufacturing sector is witnessing lower production cost and this has a huge effect on the overall cost of goods after production because the higher the cost of production, the higher the cost to the market. Also, digitalization has made it possible for the industry to shift tasks that are labor-intensive to emerging economies.
- **Reshaping the manufacturing sector for good:** Digitalization is fast reshaping existing business models, increasing market reach and

lowering barriers for manufacturing industries across the globe. Consider the VoIP (Voice over Internet Protocol), for example. Skype has been of immense benefit to manufacturing industries as they can get their message across to over 500 million Skype users across the globe [6]. This has made it possible for existing business operators worldwide, especially in the manufacturing sector, to introduce their own VoIP models [6].

- **Building brands:** As a result of the emergence of digitalization, companies, especially those within the manufacturing sector, have also changed the way they build their brands and products as well as their modes of communication and provision of services to their customers. They now rely more on digitalization to build such brands [3]. Online "subscribers" are adopting purchase attitudes, with a consequent growth of items bought online by customers who researched them using the web or digital channels.
- **Shaping modes of operation:** Digitalization has had a great impact on the modes of operation of the manufacturing industries. It has been a vital force in determining how companies within this sector organize and operate in order to gain competitive advantage. For example, digitalization has brought about the redefinition of the office space model [6].
- **Reducing unemployment:** Digitalization had the greatest effect on employment in the emerging digitized manufacturing sector across the globe [4]. For example, in East and South Asia as well as Latin America, over 4 million jobs were created in 2011 due to the developments in digitalization [4].
- **Increasing productivity:** As a result of digitalization, the manufacturing sectors across the globe have witnessed increases in productivity.
- **Raising efficiency rates:** As a result of digitalization, which is creating much faster ways of getting things done, the manufacturing sector across the globe has witnessed a higher rate of efficiency. This, however, makes the cost of production a lot less than without digitalization.

Taking these issues into account, the future of digitalization holds a lot for the future global economy, including:

- The potential value that can be generated through deployment of digital technologies in factory settings by 2025 is US$3.7 trillion [5].
- Annual global spending on digitalization by 2020 is estimated to be US$500 billion [5].
- The expected incremental revenue to be derived from digitalization by 2020 is US$300 billion [5].
- There are estimated to be 50 billion devices connected through the Internet by 2020 [5].

Table 10.1 *Impact of digitalization on GDP in 2011*

Region	GDP impact (US$ billions)
East Asia and the Pacific	55.8
Western Europe	31.5
Latin America and the Caribbean	27.0
North America	25.3
Middle East and North Africa	16.5
Commonwealth of Independent States	11.8
South Asia	9.4
Africa	8.3
Eastern Europe	7.0
TOTAL	192.6

Source: Adapted from [4].

Thus, digitalization is not just important for the manufacturing sector; it is having an immense impact on global and national economies as well [4].

According to Table 10.1, the biggest impact of digitalization on GDP in 2011 was in the region of East Asia and the Pacific, at US$ 55.8billion. Even the region with the smallest impact of digitalization on GDP, Eastern Europe, still recorded US$7 billion in 2011. And the impact of digitalization on GDP across the global economy in 2011 was a whopping US$192.6 billion [4].

10.4   Case Studies

This section focuses on two manufacturing companies: Canon Incorporated and Ernst & Young (EY).

Canon Incorporated was co-founded on August 10, 1937 by Takeshi Mitarai, Takeo Maeda, Goro Yoshida and Saburo Uchida [7]. It has its headquarters in Ohta-ku, Tokyo, Japan. The present chairman and chief executive officer (CEO) is Fujio Mitarai [7]. The company is known for manufacturing professional imaging equipment and production printing [8]. The company is founded on three guiding principles, the San-ji ("Three Selfs"): self-motivation, self-management and self-awareness [7]. As of December 31, 2019, the company had a common stock of 174,762 million yen, a total number of 25,740 employees (as of March 31, 2020), 361 consolidated subsidiaries (as of December 31,

2019), non-consolidated net sales of 1,539,271 million yen (2019) and consolidated net sales of 3,593,299 million yen (2019) [7].

Furthermore, the company produces high-image-quality and performance industrial equipment, which include a 3D machine vision system that incorporates both optical and image-processing technologies in order to help industries, as well as society, grow [8]. It is worthy of note that the company's fast growth has been a result of digital innovations, leading it to be ranked third overall in US patents in 2016 [9]. This case is worth considering by digital entrepreneurs especially interested in developing applications or tools suitable to complement the offering of incumbents as Canon or else support the digitalization of the offering by companies in manufacturing that, once leaders in a "physical" product market, now have to act as new ventures in businesses close to those of Canon.

The other case study concerns a company called Ernst and Young (EY) founded in 1989, with its headquarters in London, UK. The company's purpose is to build a better working world through its own actions and by engaging like-minded individuals and organizations [10]. EY offers services that include assurance, financial advisory, legal, tax advisory, and consulting. The company has offices in 700 different locations across 150 countries in the world and around 280,018 employees (as of 2019) as well as global revenues of US$1.8 billion [11]. Considering digital entrepreneurship, EY believes that entrepreneurs make a huge difference, have recognized the potential embedded in entrepreneurs [12]. As a consequence, EY encourages companies, especially in the manufacturing industry, to go digital. EY has some distinct digital offerings that reflect the challenges that manufacturing companies encounter as a result of digitalization. They are [5]:

- **Digital enterprise strategy:** EY believes that it can help its clients to design and deliver a totally new and fully developed business model that will work well as a result of digitalization.
- **Digital experience transformation:** EY puts programs together that focus on digital enablement by combining purpose, abilities, people as well as experiences to make provision for transformation.
- **Digital innovation:** EY helps its clients to set up a model that will drive the experiences in businesses, products and services.
- **Digital supply chain and operations:** EY helps to launch new ways in which products and services can be manufactured and distributed.

We will now take a look at one of the solutions provided by EY on the basis of the discussion provided by [5] and illustrated as follows (by first identifying the client's challenge, indicating what EY did to overcome it and showing the results obtained):

- **The client's challenge**: "The client had a diversified set of traditional manufacturing businesses that spanned corporate, trade and consumer interests, so they faced a true digital challenge. The client lacked a digital culture and direct e-commerce to measure success, and had a large number of different web and mobile properties with very different brands and designs but virtually no measurement infrastructure" [5]. Thus, EY was asked to create a customer-focused, data-driven digital presence and a virtuous cycle of continual improvement for the client.
- **What EY did**: EY created a comprehensive analytics program that drove intelligent design decisions across all major properties. It included: (i) implementation of analytics and tag management across forty to fifty separate domains; (ii) creation of a success framework based on the integration of behavioral analytics data and before-after voice-of-the-customer (VoC) data to measure the true incremental rise of digital experience; (iii) measurement of the "actual dollar values" and key behaviors pointing out online success; (iv) digital marketing optimization; (v) creation of a cycle of site analysis, testing recommendations, and "creative implementation" [5].
- **The results obtained**: According to [5], the results included: (i) improved key use cases by as much as 50 percent over two years; (ii) universal agreement on the value of key web activities, with consequent changes in brand and digital focus; (iii) US$10 million in revenue from changes to the website, with a 65–75 percent increase in effective event engagement.

This goes to show the effect of guided digitalization actions, in this case facilitated by EY, on a client manufacturing company. This case is worth considering by digital entrepreneurs especially interested in developing new ventures proposing advisory frameworks for boosting digitalization in manufacturing or else developing complementary applications or tools suitable to support actions such as those described here.

10.5 Summary

This chapter outlined the effects of macroeconomic factors on manufacturing and, thus, how undertaking *macroeconomic analysis* can helps especially manufacturing firms achieve higher economic growth. By understanding how macro forces – political and regulatory forces, technological forces, global forces, natural forces as well as sociocultural forces – affect their business and the wider national and global economies, manufacturing companies can make adjustments to their processes to best work within and around these forces. This is of primary importance because manufacturing is the principal industry when it comes to determining the growth and development of any economy globally [13].

Moreover, the chapter looked at digitalization and how it is fast bringing huge transformation to every facet of our lives. It discussed the importance of digitalization for the manufacturing industry, in terms of lowering production cost, reshaping how brands are built, and increasing productivity and efficiency. It also noted the huge impact on GDP of digitalization of the manufacturing sector, which affects the economies of nation across the globe.

Finally, the chapter looked at two case studies – Canon Incorporated and Ernst & Young (EY) – two incumbent companies whose actions and offerings can nonetheless provide insights for digital entrepreneurs into what are the opportunities for new ventures in manufacturing. In conclusion, then, digitalization is key to the existence of the manufacturing sector in any nation, which in turn drives the growth and development of each nation's economy.

References

1. Stewart LA. The Impact of Regulation on Innovation in the United States : A Cross-Industry Literature Review. *Information Technology and Innovation Foundation* (2010) 1–29.
2. Alcorta BL. The Impact of New Technologies on Scale in Manufacturing Industry: Issues and Evidence. UNU/INTECH Working Paper No. 5 (1992).
3. Morabito V. Digital Business Identity. In: *Trends and Challenges in Digital Business Innovation SE – 7*. Springer International (2014) 133–44.
4. El-Darwiche B, Friedrich R, Koster A, Singh M. Digitization for Economic Growth and Job Creation: Regional and Industry Perspectives. Strategy&, PwC (2013).
5. Kuchler M, Cederlöf ST. Digitalization in Industrial Products: Harnessing the Power of Digital. EYGM Limited (2016).
6. Sabbagh K, Friedrich, R, El-Darwiche B, Singh M., Koster, A. Digitization for Economic Growth and Job Creation: Regional and Industry Perspectives. Chapter 1.2. The Global Information Technology Report 2013. World Economic Forum (2013) 35–42.
7. Canon. Corporate Profile. (2020) http://global.canon/en/corporate/information/profile.html [accessed May 30, 2020].
8. Canon. Industry. (2019) http://global.canon/en/business/industry.html [accessed May 30, 2020].
9. Canon Inc. U.S.A. Canon U.S.A to Exhibit Award-Winning Projectors and Innovative Solutions at the InfoComm Show. (2017) www.prnewswire.com/news-releases/canon-usa-to-exhibit-award-winning-projectors-and-innovative-solutions-at-the-2017-infocomm-show-300470278.html [accessed May 30, 2020].

10. EY. Who We Are – Builders of a Better Working World. (2018) www.ey.com /en_gl/who-we-are [accessed May 30, 2020].
11. EY. Global Review 2019 – How Can We Create Long-Term Value for a Better Working World? (2020) www.ey.com/en_ch/global-review/2019 [accessed May 30, 2020].
12. EY. Entrepreneurship – Fueling Our Future through Entrepreneurship (2019) www.ey.com/en_uk/entrepreneurship [accessed May 30, 2020].
13. Manyika J, Sinclair J, Dobbs R, Strube G, Rassey L, Mischke J, Remes J, Roxburgh C, George K, O'Halloran D, Ramaswamy S. Manufacturing the Future: The Next Era of Global Growth and Innovation. McKinsey & Company (2012).

11 Fashion

11.1 Introduction

The fashion industry has adopted digital technology in innovative ways both to remain viable and to change the way consumers seek fashion products such as accessories, clothing and jewelry [1]. Nowadays, technology is creating omni-channel experiences for consumers who are actively engaged as digital shoppers in the fashion industry [2]. In a fast-paced fashion market, brands are adapting to consumer trends and need to remain relevant [3]. The need to design and develop products at a rapid pace has led to the adoption of 3D technology, thus reducing the time to market [4]. As we have also seen in previous chapters, the intent behind innovative products or services could be to meet and satisfy requirements or needs expressed by consumers, or to introduce novel services that could make people's lives easier and more interesting, as done by Instagram, Uber and Airbnb. The services provided by such firms were not a necessity for people, but now people use them extensively in their daily lives throughout the world. Such innovative ideas have created a digital disruption that transformed the way traditional firms conduct their businesses and made it compulsory for them to appreciate the digital transformation and embrace the opportunities offered by the Internet and the emerging technologies [9]. One of the major digital trends in the fashion industry is wearable technology [5]. According to reports, one in four adults in the USA owns a wearable device [6–8]. Devices are now available for heart rate and overall fitness monitoring in the form of bras and bracelets. Also, fashion technology has gone further by producing handbags for charging smartphone batteries [10]. Arguably, the need to provide an extra level of appeal for consumers and widen the target market has led to the multi-functionality of fashion products. Fashion customers are now adopting mobile commerce as a new way of shopping while getting re-targeted by smart agents with similar products and ads based on their shopping behavior. The explosion of mobile shopping has created a novel technique for gathering big data about consumers' behavior as well as a new understanding of the products they care about. Furthermore, the digitalization of fashion would connect online and offline buying patterns and would not necessarily alienate the latter. Although fashion is rapidly going online, experts perceive that immersive consumer shopping behavior will grow both offline and online. Specifically, immense growth is expected for digital changing rooms, virtual fashion shows, and personalization for online shopping.

There is a sense of urgency among fashion retailers and manufacturers not just to grow production but to improve upon it as well. Consumer awareness is swiftly escalating about the methods with which products are being designed and developed; thus, organizations are adapting their strategic operations to be more environmentally compliant. More recently, there is a shift to green suppliers such as using natural dyes and fabric materials. Additionally, fashion companies are pursuing the goal of sustainability by utilizing smart manufacturing options [11]. As discussed in Chapter 7, advances in the Internet of Things (IoT) are providing an enormous level of data that are useful for the design, production, manufacturing and sale of fashion products and services. It was estimated that, in 2017, 8.4 billion "things" were connected to the Internet, which signified a 31 percent increase from 2016, and it is expected to reach 20.4 billion by 2020 [12, 13].

The digital revolution is also making a significant impact on fashion week events. Instagram and other social media such as Snapchat have been adopted by fashion designers with enormous implications that could see, for example, the replacement of fashion editorial teams existing within many fashion brands as well as media incumbents [14]. Moreover, platforms such as Instagram and Snapchat are likely to eventually be employed as e-commerce portals in the future [15]. For example, considering luxury fashion designers, Burberry became the precursor of fashion digitization when it started streaming its runshows [16]. In addition, it created mobile applications for its customers to test various outfits irrespective of their locations. The availability of streaming big data and analytics is providing fashion organizations with insights into hyper-personalization, tracking customer trends, and aligning customer experience. Another luxury brand adopting digital technology to transform its in-store experience is Harrods, which has developed a number of novel high-resolution stairwell displays at the flagship Knightsbridge, London store [16]. Likewise, Adidas has created a store wall that displays collections of its products in three dimensions; this allows customers to view product designs from various angles [16]. These days, dressing rooms are equipped with augmented reality facilities as well as social media features. L'Oréal is adopting augmented reality features in its "special kiosks" that allow customers to test makeup virtually, simply by taking a picture [16]. Section 11.2 discusses the novel facets of the digitization of the fashion industry, including innovation in business models, innovation in product development, and an orientation toward green and ethical fashion [5].

11.2   The Novel Facets of the Fashion Industry Digitization

Nowadays, digital transformation has significantly impacted the fashion industry and created innovative opportunities for interaction among organizations, stakeholders and customers. Experts suggest that digital technologies have increased information availability and usage and enhanced interactive communication.

Table 11.1 summarizes the different ways in which organizations are impacted by digitization. Taking these issues into account, what follows analyzes the changes brought about by digital trends in the fashion

Table 11.1 *How organizations are impacted by digitization*

Organizational impacts of digitization	Description
Restructuring customer interaction and business transactions	Digitization is restructuring the ways in which customer interactions are carried out and managed. It is creating new paths for executing marketing strategies and influencing customers at scale. Some of the tools for fostering interaction between customers and organizations include social media strategies, digital marketing, and big data analysis tools.
Varying stages of the digital experience of clients and customers	Organizations and their customers demonstrate varying stages in terms of their digital aims and objectives. For example, advanced practitioners of digital technologies are relatively focused on enhancing their customer relationships. On the other hand, early adopters are mainly concerned with improving their business opportunities and boosting sales through digitization.
Lack of resources and capabilities to drive a digital strategy	Many organizations pursuing the adoption of digitization require the expertise of partners with capabilities in providing digitized services. Experts with a track record of digital capabilities, including local expertise, are in huge demand.

Source: Adapted from [17].

industry to *business models, innovative product development,* and the orientation to *green and ethical fashion,* in line with the arguments outlined, in particular, by [5].

11.2.1 Business Model Innovation

Digitization in the fashion industry is affecting the production, packaging, communication and distribution of products and services. Within the e-commerce ecosystem, new online business models are being created, especially by luxury brands.

The business models within e-commerce ecosystems are customer subscription, social merchandising, mass customization, shared consumption and innovative marketing [5]. The following subsections briefly discuss each in turn.

11.2.1.1 Customer Subscription Nowadays, customers are subscribing to monthly club systems of various fashion brands to ascertain their style preferences [5]. The club systems are designed to display a list of products that customers can purchase for a fixed rate every month. Through this "monthly subscription" technique, customers can choose to spend a consistent amount of money on fashion clothing and accessories. The financial value proposition of this approach implies a considerable reduction in transaction costs for customers. Besides, it allows fashion brands (particularly retailers) to maximize profits as a result of the consistent revenue streams. A remarkable example of the customer subscription approach is Shoedazzle [5, 18].

11.2.1.2 Social Merchandising Social merchandising is a model founded on comments, reviews, posts and user-generated content through social media platforms. In the decision-making processes of many fashion brands, big data extrapolated through user-generated content have become a key factor [5]. Customers are now prone to seek the opinion of other people about the best product to purchase as well as the reliability of the sources they buy from. Customers also investigate the quality of service of potential sellers through the advice of other buyers and their feedback on level of satisfaction. Fashion brands often utilize consumer feedback for innovative production [19]. The websites of most fashion brands display the comments, ratings and frequency of purchase of their customers to gain the attention of other potential buyers with the aim of positively influencing their purchase decisions. Brands like Macy's allow customers to share looks that synthesize various items to enhance the viral outcome of their sales [5, 19].

11.2.1.3 Mass Customization   Mass customization involves the combination of mass production with custom-made tailoring, as in the case of Levi Strauss & Co. (Levi's in what follows) which in 1994 introduced this business model when the "original spin" jeans for women were launched [5]. The mode of operation back then involved measuring customers in store, electronically transferring their details to Levi's factory then mailing the customized jeans to the respective customers. Thus, mass customization works through a process known as modularity [5]; in this case, the organization develops specific production modules that can be amassed in different innovative ways [5]. In the fashion industry, one of the significances of mass customization is that clothing products are perfectly designed to suit customers at a relatively low cost, also allowing companies to be distinguished from their competitors. Additionally, mass customization includes the customers in the design of the products, by selecting their colors, material types, styles and sizes [5]. Moreover, it allows the customer to discount the cost of having to get the clothes altered to fit when making a purchase. Brand loyalty is another benefit of mass customization, and it also avails an organization of quality information about the fashion taste of their customers [5].

11.2.1.4 Shared Consumption   Shared or collaborative consumption [5] delineates the platforms that allow consumers to share, rent or exchange fashion products beyond their standard financial capacity. In this process, fashion sellers may dispose of assets depreciating; while buyers are able to acquire the assets at a price significantly lower than retail. Covetique was a good example of this business model [5]. As a secondary market for pre-owned luxury goods, Covetique allowed sellers to send their products to its online platform to be held on consignment pending their sales. On the other hand, platforms like Lyst assist customers in monitoring the time it takes for an item displayed on the runway to become readily available. Lyst also has the functionality to execute filtering to allow customers to associate with like-minded people to keep updated about relevant fashion trends that suit their tastes [5].

11.2.1.5 Innovative Marketing   In the area of marketing techniques, traditional players such as newspapers and magazines have now been relegated by most fashion brands. Fashion blogs are gaining traction as the foremost marketing technique due to the avalanche of new tools and considerably low cost. Also, fashion blogging is fast becoming a lucrative career, making bloggers quasi trendsetters and influencers. Advantages of fashion blogging include time effectiveness and fashion forecasting. Fashion brands such as H&M and American Apparel are massively building direct relationships with personal style, beauty and fashion blog-gers, thereby reducing marketing costs and saving time [5].

11.2.2 Innovative Product Development

The transformation of fashion goods into technological products has led to a new wave including smart textiles and wearable technologies [20, 21]. Before now, it was mainly sportswear that was designed with high-tech fabrics to enhance the comfort and performance of athletes [21]. Nevertheless, recent trends have seen the escalation of wearable gadgets and smart watches such as the Fitbit products, Apple Watch and Google Glass (or simply "Glass"), indicating a massive culture shift [5]. OLED is one of the foremost technologies used, as it allows the printing of light-emitting materials onto any device and media, thereby allowing the development of bright fabrics [5, 22]. The integration of textile fibers and computer systems to store and share data from the human body for social and health purposes is also a growing technological fashion trend. Some tech-nology-driven fashion materials have been developed to measure individuals' vital signs using specific clothing [21] and also to power mobile phone batteries, solar panels and MP3 players [5].

According to statistics available at [23], global revenues from wearable technology devices have been on the rise steadily since 2016 and are estimated to surge further from 2018 to 2022, as shown in Figure 11.1. Innovation in the fashion industry is also demonstrated by 3D printing capabilities, which involve making three-dimensional physical objects from a digital file. The technique used for 3D printing is relatively quicker than other fashion tasks such as weaving textiles, and it creates new opportunities for customized clothing [4]. Many fashion designers are now utilizing laser beams to combine various parts of reprocessed plastic powder into shape, to create smooth clothing from 3D printers. A good example of 3D printing is the N12 bikini created by fashion brand Continuum without any traditional sewing input [5]. As 3D printing makes a huge impression in fashion, engineers at San Francisco have developed an "Electroloom" that behaves like a 3D printer for fabrics through the use of polyester and cotton sprayed on a template to create smooth clothing [24].

Moreover, as designers have embraced the technology of clothing fabrication, conventional fashion design procedures are shifting toward high-tech techniques to create novel production methodology. One of the key tools used to create 3D models is Computer Aided Design (CAD); this tool replaces the traditional approach of drawing fashion designs on

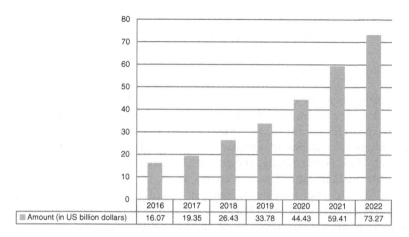

Figure 11.1 Steady global sales revenue growth of wearable devices, 2016–2022 (in US$ billions)
Source: Adapted from [23].

paper. Digital technology has drastically advanced the current state of the fashion industry by reducing the time usually involved in traditional tailoring; it is now possible to produce accurate three-dimensional measurements using 3D scanners within seconds. Lately, a digital fashion service, Bodi.Me, has been making use of 3D body scanners to enable customers to easily match their sizes to purchased outfits based on sizing information retrieved from registered fashion organizations [25]. Arguably, the combination of 3D body scanners and 3D clothing printing could stimulate the creation of fashion products that perfectly suit every individual customer.

11.2.3 Green and Ethical Fashion

Green fashion is a new trend taking place within the fashion ecosystem, and it is leading to a new rise in craftsmanship [5]. The combination of the ethical, eco-friendly and local crafting aspect of fashion clothing demonstrates a huge concern for the environment as well as sustainable cost-effective production. Green and sustainable fashion has experienced a steady rise in the last decade, paving the way for pioneers such as the Danish luxury brand NOIR and Stella McCartney, both of whom are founded on ethical philosophies and the need for sustainable fashion [5]. Ethical and green fashion creation entails biological tissues and a certified production chain, and stresses the need for locally made materials for the purpose of decreasing carbon emissions. Moreover, there exists a tendency for luxury fashion brands to play the ethical way in the production of cosmetics and other fashion accessories, too [5]. Moreover, organizations such as LVMH have invested early in sustainable clothing companies like Edun, founded in 2005 by Bono, the vocalist of rock band U2, and his wife Ali Hewson [26]. Nevertheless, there is an ongoing debate about the long-term cost benefits of green fashion sustainability over the desire to use such products by fashion enthusiasts. While emphasizing the need for fashion clothing produced under certified ethical standards suitable to the needs of the environment, established brands, as well as the digital entrepreneurs interested in fashion, should also consider how best to optimize the mass acceptability of their products. Still, there is a growing level of *transparency* in the fashion community as consumers are now more curious about how their clothes are made and by whom. Such occurring levels of curiosity can move the fashion industry into more transparency [27, 28]. The greater the transparency of the supply chain, the higher the tendency to identify the human and socioeconomic abuses that existing unethical practices could potentially diminish. Experts argue that transparency is the start of the revolution of the fashion industry. The data that fashion brands, retailers, suppliers, governments and multi-stakeholder organizations are willing to share with the masses on the techniques used to make clothing are extremely notable [27, 28]. As consumers become more aware and engaged about the fundamental techniques of various clothing designs, the better should become the creativity of fashion brand developers, designers and their overall impact.

11.3 Fashion Industry Digitization and Enabling Technologies

As previously stated, organizations in the fashion industry have accepted the use of digital technology to facilitate their business processes, to a large extent. With the aid of digital tools readily available on the Internet, they can create efficient systems for gathering customer data to make better business decisions, improve the shopping experience and sustain their brand equity. This section reviews some relevant technology-based tools; it also highlights a few real-world examples to show how they relate to existing innovative business models making waves in the fashion industry.

11.3.1 Platforms for Virtual Fitting Rooms

Platforms for virtual fitting rooms were developed to enable online shoppers to "try on" the clothing items they intend to buy. Without virtual fitting rooms, the rates of return for online clothing purchases are extraordinarily high, which has a huge negative impact on the operational costs of fashion retailers. To minimize this challenge, there are three major tools being used in the fashion industry that are also worth considering by digital entrepreneurs: the Webcam Social Shopper (WSS) platform, Rakuten Fits.me and interactive mirrors [19]. These tools are shown in Figure 11.2 and discussed in the following sections.

11.3.1.1 Webcam Social Shopper (WSS) Platform   Developed by Zugara, a Los Angeles-based organization, WSS is designed to integrate augmented reality and motion picture technologies combined with the functionalities of online social networks to offer virtual fitting room capabilities

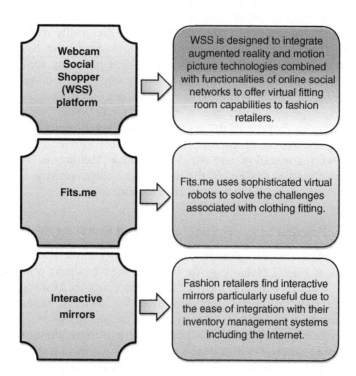

Figure 11.2 Platforms for virtual fitting rooms
Source: Adapted from [19].

to fashion retailers [19]. As a result, online shoppers' webcams can be transformed into a realistic virtual mirror, which enables online shoppers to select clothes from the store shelves and get a better feel of how the items would fit their size as well as their style.

Additionally, online shoppers can share their digital pictures with friends to elicit their opinion on the suitability of their desired clothing item, where various channels like online social network platforms can be used to share them.

11.3.1.2 Rakuten Fits.me   Rakuten Fits.me uses virtual robots to solve the challenges associated with clothing fitting [29]. A robot mannequin ("Fitbot") is the core component of the virtual fitting room, which uses artificial muscles to imitate diverse human shapes and body types [19]. The Fitbot works at high speed and in high resolution while executing swiftly through its different body shapes at the call of multiple instances [19–29]. After the system has recorded the measurements of each customer, the dress pictures, based on each customer's body shape, are then displayed by an online fashion retailer. Hence, customers are able to view the range of dresses in any preferred size before deciding to place their orders [19].

11.3.1.3 Interactive Mirrors   Also known as "virtual mirrors," interactive mirrors are technological devices founded on visual computing technology based on the concept of "augmented reality" (AR) [30], thus allowing traditional retail stores to exemplify AR capability [19, 31]. Moreover, fashion retailers find interactive mirrors particularly useful due to the ease of integration with their inventory management systems, which also use the Internet. As a result of their integrated capabilities, interactive mirrors have the ability to capture the images of customers and merge them on the mirror along with specific articles of the clothing searched by the customers [32]. With virtual mirrors, customers can assess whether various clothing items look good on, and then their experiences can be shared with friends and followers on different online social networks.

11.4   Case Studies

This section presents case studies that illustrate the digital explorations of fashion-tech-oriented organizations that enable them to accomplish their strategic goals to become strong and successful in the digital competitive environment. The chosen case studies are Ermenegildo Zegna, Smithfield Case and Uniqlo.

The first case study is based on a case history by [19]. Ermenegildo Zegna, an Italian luxury fashion house, is a digitally driven retail fashion organization leading the way in luxury fashion products. It was the foremost brand specializing in menswear, with business operations in China. The major enabling digital technologies of Ermenegildo Zegna include a Web environment, personal subscription, a virtual fitting room platform and Social Web integration platforms. China is a big market for Ermenegildo Zegna with more than 70 sales centers in the region [19]. To establish its digital retailing strategy, the company carries out major operations through www.zegna.com, a Web-based platform that utilizes customer subscription features to reinforce the brand identity with bespoke products. Thus, Ermenegildo Zegna is a customer-centric organization using web-based subscription features to gather relevant information about its numerous customers, for example their fashion taste, measurements and product delivery address. To store all information pertaining to customers, Ermenegildo Zegna designed a unique dynamic profile for each customer to facilitate their active engagement and improve their overall online experience. Furthermore, the organization has adopted the design and implementation of a virtual fitting room platform (the above-discussed Rakuten Fits.me) to assist its customers in visualizing whether or not the clothing adequately fits their measurements. Ermenegildo Zegna has also integrated an email newsletter system on its Web-based platform; through this means, customers can opt in to receive information about the latest products, services, deals, job openings and events. Events can be streamed live through mobile apps, in an engaging manner. Another key functionality of the web-based platform is the use of customer subscription resources to execute the Zegna World Pass, a private elite access to exclusive benefits as well as customizable services.

POINT OF ATTENTION: The success of Ermenegildo Zegna is attributed to its strong family-based values. Besides those, the company demonstrates quality of service, authenticity, accountability and, most importantly – vision. Also, the organization's leaders' preparedness to adapt to the needed changes in a fast-advancing tech-driven world motivated their willingness to evolve their business processes to suit the ever-changing digital society.

The second case study is also adapted from [19]. Smithfield Case was a London-based start-up founded in 2011 by Alex Valls and Jose Ojeda

[33] and then sold to The Chapar, its main UK competitor, in early 2013 [34]. The start-up exemplified a subscription business model that used a customer-oriented approach for the purpose of easing the stress experienced by fashion customers. The enabling technology drivers of Smithfield included a Web environment and customer subscription resources. The company was relatively innovative in its approach to presenting its products to its customers. For example, during the registration phase on the platform, customers were required to fill in a detailed questionnaire with their address, fashion style, measurements and overall shopping preferences [19].

POINT OF ATTENTION: Smithfield Case actively used digital technology to allow its customers to experience a photo-realistic web portal, thus playing a significant role in their brand loyalty. It also extended the functionality of digital technology to enhance its rewards program, with customers able to earn several points just by making sure that their profile was updated as well as taking simple surveys. Based on this case study, it is evident that start-ups in the fashion industry should use data as a key resource to make smart decisions regarding the actual needs of their customers.

Moreover, the web-based store was in charge of collecting information concerning customers' search and browsing behavior; then, the organization used such information to send customers specific fashion products based on their known preferences. Customers were allowed to try the products before deciding which to buy and which to return to Smithfield. The organization offered the flexibility for customers to pay only for the products they decided to keep as well as the required delivery fees. On the other hand, the organization used to gift its customers with free deliveries and collections during weekends and evenings if they lived around the central metropolitan area of London [19].

The third case study concerns Japanese company Unique Clothing Warehouse (Uniqlo), whose first store opened in 1984 in Hiroshima. As of January 2018, it has more than 1,300 stores in 15 countries across Asia, Europe and the USA and is the biggest chain in Asia with nearly 800 stores [35, 36]. The growth of Uniqlo was made possible through technological innovation as well as expanding its product variations under a "fast fashion" business model in the retail sector [37, 38]. Following a fast fashion model as a response to changes in the fashion industry [39] means for Uniqlo that its customers are drawn to the brand based on the high-quality and cost-effective clothing it provides; it gives customers a sense that they are buying a lifestyle rather than just fashion items. According to the founder of Uniqlo, Tadashi Yanai, "Uniqlo is not a fashion company, it's a technology company" [40]. Accordingly, Uniqlo is well known for its three exclusive innovations. Firstly, the HEATTECH brand, which concerns innerwear including tights, long johns, sleeves, leggings and camisoles, uses a specially designed fabric to capture the moisture created by the body to re-emit heat [41, 42]. Uniqlo's second innovative product, AIRism, is a smart, breathable, smooth and anti-odor base layer designed to release heat as well as moisture in order to adapt to any condition [43, 44]. AIRism uses the "Cupro" fiber, which is produced in Japan by Asahi Kasei and is "made from regenerated cotton linters" [45].

POINT OF ATTENTION: Uniqlo has been successful over the years working in innovation at the fabric level. Yet, the company may consider various options to address its fast fashion business model, especially in retail where the challenge is to integrate physical stores and virtual stores to create an omni-channel experience [35]. One of the options available is adoption of the "virtual robot" previously discussed in this chapter. For example, Uniqlo could use the functionality of virtual "fitting" robots to its advantage to drive its corporate and innovation plans into the future.

Although Uniqlo's rapid growth is based on its technology-driven business model, it faces significant brand and business challenges, as pointed out by [35]. One such challenge is the product shift from price to quality, also considering issues such as size and fit, especially for international expansion; thus, the company must further take into account the actual differences among global customer groups [35]. Consequently, Uniqlo has to adapt the results of the standardization of its products through advanced production techniques and fabrics, adjusting them to fit the unique clothes sizes and body shapes required by each country. Finally, Uniqlo faces the challenge of further leveraging digital: on the one hand, to cover the whole online customer journey; on the other hand, to use analytics for collecting retail data, analyzing consumers patterns and identifying strategies for improving sales through mobile as well as other digital platforms and systems that nowadays act as key "touch-points" [35].

11.5 Summary

The fashion industry is currently engaging with digital technology to stay competitive through the design and creation of customized products for varying levels of customers. Unarguably, digital technology has turned the fashion industry inside out, influencing the development of promising digital experiences across multi-platforms. One of the significant changes in the fashion industry is the integration of omni-channel approaches aimed at providing an excellent experience or a "wow" factor to gain customer loyalty and consistent support. The days when fashion brands communicated to their target audience mainly by means of billboards, magazines or television appear to be fading at a faster pace than expected. The fashion industry is relatively slow-moving in adapting to novel technology advances; most such advances have been in quicker and smarter machines for factory use only. Nevertheless, this chapter has highlighted a few ways in which 3D technology can assist fashion organizations to produce better and faster models of their clothing as well as gaining a faster time-to-market. However, one of the key challenges of implementing 3D technology is the extreme dependence on highly technical designers. More often than not, the technical designer plays the role of creative designer and pattern designer too, which is relatively overtasking and burdensome, resulting in fewer quality designs and less production output. To solve this challenge, organizations are forced to add to their overhead and payroll by recruiting technical, creative and pattern designers for 3D projects, and to a great extent this process is not practicable because digital technology should provide the feasibility for organizations to achieve more with fewer resources. In this regard, the concept of "3D as a service" is highly recommended to allow designers to work on any design solutions and create instances of their designs that can then be uploaded on a decentralized and distributed application and made accessible to all stakeholders of the particular project. Moreover, this would allow for seamless internal review, data sharing and availability as well as avoidance of unnecessary data duplication and redundancy.

For a long time, online fashion retailers have struggled with high return rates due to ineffective tools for remotely assisting customers in determining their actual sizes and adequate fit measurements. Standardized sizing measures have proved fruitless as they try to fit online shoppers into rigid frames. Moreover, the high return rates are not predominately due to size alone; other factors such as color, fabric texture and overall user experience have been attributed to relatively high customer return rates. Thus, this chapter discussed the practicality of using virtual fitting rooms to allow online shoppers to adequately assess the size fit as well as the style suitability before making their purchases. Furthermore, because virtual fitting rooms can also allow customers to take snapshots of how the clothing they intend to purchase fits them in size and style, such snapshots can be shared with friends on online social networks to gain second opinions before the final purchase. Hence, with such measures in place, there is a huge potential for fashion retailers to experience reduced return rates as they continue to integrate new features of virtual fitting rooms on their online stores.

Overall, the chapter suggested that key ongoing developments in the digitalization of the fashion industry have led to changing business models and the adoption of novel technological tools and techniques. Consequently, fashion brands as well as digital entrepreneurs especially interested in fashion industry innovation need to completely and consistently embrace the much-needed review of the existing business models to maximize the positive impact of these new waves of digitalization.

References

1. Mihaleva G, Koh C. Evolution of Fashion Design in the Era of High-Tech Culture. *International Journal of Fashion Technology and Textile Engineering* (2016) 10:2447–51.
2. Verhoef PC, Kannan PK, Inman JJ. From Multi-channel Retailing to Omni-channel Retailing. Introduction to the Special Issue on Multi-Channel Retailing. *Journal of Retailing* (2015) 91:174–81. doi: 10.1016/j.jretai.2015.02.005.
3. Shankar V, Venkatesh A, Hofacker C, Naik P. Mobile Marketing in the Retailing Environment: Current Insights and Future Research Avenues. *Journal of Interactive Marketing* (2010) 24:111–20. doi: 10.1016/j.intmar.2010.02.006.
4. Spahiu T, Grimmelsmann N, Ehrmann A, Shehi E, Piperi E. On the Possible Use of 3D Printing for Clothing and Shoe Manufacture. In: *Proceedings of the 7th International Conference of Textile, 10–11 November, Tirana, Albania.* (2016) 1–7.
5. Pratt A, Borrione P, Lavanga M, Ovidio MD, Florence V. International Change and Technological Evolution in the Fashion Industry. In: Agnoletti M, Carandini A, Santagata W (eds.) *Essays and Researches: International Biennial of Culture and Environmental Heritage.* Badecchi and Vivaldi (2012) 359–76.
6. EMarketer. Wearable Usage Will Grow by Nearly 60% This Year – Almost Two in Five Internet Users Will Use Wearables by 2019. (2015) www.emarketer.com/Article/Wearable-Usage-Will-Grow-by-Nearly-60-This-Year/1013159 [accessed May 31, 2020].
7. Adams A, Shankar M, Tecco H. 50 Things We Now Know about Digital Health Consumers. (2016) https://rockhealth.com/reports/digital-health-consumer-adoption-2016/ [accessed April 30, 2020].

8. Wellable. Survey: Nearly 25% of Americans Own a Wearable Device. (2017) http://blog.wellable.co/2017/01/04/survey-nearly-25-of-americans-own-a-wearable-device [accessed May 31, 2020].

9. Gulati R, Soni T. Digitization: A Strategic Key to Business. *Journal of Advances in Business Management* (2015) 1:60–7.

10. Hartmans A. I Tried a Pair of High-Tech Luxury Purses – Here's What It Was Like. (2017) www.businessinsider.com.au/mezzi-luxury-purses-handbags-are-filled-with-tech-review-2017-2#/#mezzis-bags-retail-anywhere-from-195-to-495-the-most-inexpensive-bag-is-a-small-zippered-clutch-while-the-priciest-bag-is-a-roomy-travel-tote-that-can-hold-your-laptop-1 [accessed May 31, 2020].

11. Peters A. 5 New Solutions for the Fashion Industry's Sustainability Problem. (2016) www.fastcompany.com/3055925/5-new-solutions-for-the-fashion-industrys-sustainability-problem [accessed May 31, 2020].

12. Tata Consultancy Services. Internet of Things: The Complete Reimaginative Force TCS Global Trend Study – July 2015. TCS (2015).

13. Gartner. Gartner Says 8.4 Billion Connected "Things" Will Be in Use in 2017, Up 31 Percent from 2016. (2017) www.gartner.com/en/newsroom/press-releases/2017–02–07-gartner-says-8-billion-connected-things-will-be-in-use-in-2017-up-31-percent-from-2016 [accessed May 31, 2020].

14. Kay K. Does the Fashion Industry Still Need Vogue in the Age of Social Media? (2017) www.theguardian.com/fashion/2017/jul/08/does-fashion-industry-need-vogue-in-instagram-age [accessed April 30, 2020].

15. Lordahl E. Is Social Selling the Future of eCommerce? (2017) www.conversocial.com/blog/is-social-selling-the-future-of-ecommerce [accessed May 31, 2020].

16. Raut S. Digital Transformation in the Fashion Industry. (2017) http://customerthink.com/digital-transformation-in-the-fashion-industry/ [accessed May 31, 2020].

17. Hoong V. The Digital Transformation of Customer Services – Our Point of View. Deloitte Touche Tohmatsu Limited (2013).

18. Bergstein R. Shoedazzle Didn't Fail. In Fact, It's A $100 M Company. (2017) www.forbes.com/sites/rachellebergstein/2017/04/21/shoedazzle-didnt-fail-in-fact-its-a-100m-company/ [accessed May 31, 2020].

19. Batista L. New Business Models Enabled by Digital Technologies:. A Perspective from the Fashion Sector – Study Report for the EPSRC RCUK DE Research Project NEMODE (New Economic Models in the Digital Economy). NEMODE (2013).

20. Gaddis R. What Is the Future of Fabric? These Smart Textiles Will Blow Your Mind. (2014) www.forbes.com/sites/forbesstylefile/2014/05/07/what-is-the-future-of-fabric-these-smart-textiles-will-blow-your-mind/#1d98d8ac599b [accessed May 31, 2020].

21. Pavlinić DZ. The Potential of Wearables Related in Smart Textiles. *Sigurnost* (2017) 59:219–26. doi: https://hrcak.srce.hr/index.php?show=clanak&id_clanak_jezik=276052

22. Sankaran S, Sridhar R. Energy Modeling for Mobile Devices Using Performance Counters. *2013 IEEE 56th International Midwest Symposium on Circuits and Systems (MWSCAS)* 441–44.

23. Statista. Wearable Device Revenue Worldwide 2016–2022 (in billion U.S. dollars) | Statistic. (2017) www.statista.com/statistics/610447/wearable-device-revenue-worldwide/ [accessed May 31, 2020].

24. Lomas N. Electroloom Is a 3D Fabric Printer in the Making. (2015) https://techcrunch.com/2015/05/18/electroloom-is-a-3d-fabric-printer-in-the-making/ [accessed May 31, 2020].

25. Crunchbase. Bodi.Me. (2018) www.crunchbase.com/organization/bodi-me#section-overview [accessed May 31, 2020].

26. Wood Z. LVMH Takes a Stake in Bono's Clothing Line. (2009) www.theguardian.com/business/2009/may/14/edun-fashion-bono-louis-vuitton [accessed May 31, 2020].

27. Fashion Revolution. Transparency Is Trending. (2019) www.fashionrevolution.org/transparency-is-trending/ [accessed May 31, 2020].

28. Ditty S. Fashion Transparency Index 2017. Fashion Revolution CIC (2017).

29. Lunden, I, Lomas N. Rakuten Buys Virtual Fitting Room Startup Fits.Me in A Fashion Commerce Play. (2015) https://techcrunch.com/2015/07/12/rakuten-buys-virtual-fitting-room-startup-fits-me-in-a-fashion-commerce-play/ [accessed May 31, 2020].

30. Azuma RT. A Survey of Augmented Reality. *Presence Teleoperators and Virtual Environments* (1997) 6:355–85. https://doi.org/10.1162/pres.1997.6.4.355.

31. Bodhani A. Shops Offer the E-tail Experience. *Engineering & Technology* (2012) 7:46–9. doi: 10.1049/et.2012.0512.

32. Raphael R. Interactive "Magic Mirrors" Are Changing How We See Ourselves – And Shop. (2017) www.fastcompany.com/3066781/can-interactive-mirrors-change-consumer-behavior-retailers-are-bet   [accessed May 31, 2020].

33. Crunchbase. Smithfield Case. (2018) www.crunchbase.com/organization/smithfield-case [accessed May 31, 2020].

34. PitchBook. Smithfield Case. (2018) https://pitchbook.com/profiles/company/54514–72 [accessed May 31, 2020].

35. Martin Roll. Uniqlo: The Strategy Behind the Global Japanese Fast Fashion Retail Brand. (2018) https://martinroll.com/resources/articles/strategy/uniqlo-the-strategy-behind-the-global-japanese-fast-fashion-retail-brand/ [accessed May 31, 2020].

36. Uniqlo. Our Story. (2020) www.uniqlo.com/sg/corp/ourstory.html [accessed May 31, 2020].

37. Choi EK. Paradigm Innovation through the Strategic Collaboration between TORAY & UNIQLO: Evolution of a New Fast Fashion Business Model. IIR Work Pap WP#11–01 (2011).

38. Choi EK. The Rise of Uniqlo: Leading Paradigm Change in Fashion Business and Distribution in Japan. *Enterprises and History* (2011) 85–101.

39. Bhardwaj V, Fairhurst A. Fast Fashion: Response to Changes in the Fashion Industry. *The International Review of Retail, Distribution and Consumer Research* (2010) 20:165–73. doi: 10.1080/09593960903498300.

40. Finnigan K. The Plain Truth: Uniqlo Boss Tadashi Yanai Explains His Plans for World Domination. (2016) www.telegraph.co.uk/fashion/brands/the-plain-truth-uniqlo-boss-tadashi-yanei-explains-his-plans-for/ [accessed May 31, 2020].

41. Uniqlo. Women's HEATTECH Thermal Clothing. (2020) www.uniqlo.com/uk/en/women/innerwear-and-loungewear/innerwear [accessed May 31, 2020].

42. Uniqlo. Men's HEATTECH Thermal Clothing. (2018) www.uniqlo.com/uk/en/men/innerwear-loungewear/innerwear [accessed May 31, 2020].

43. Uniqlo. AIRism – Women. (2020) www.uniqlo.com/us/en/women/airism-collection [accessed May 31, 2020].

44. Uniqlo. AIRism – Men. (2018) www.uniqlo.com/us/en/men/airism-collection [accessed May 31, 2020].

45. Uniqlo. A Second Skin. (2016) www.uniqlo.com/sg/timeline/detail/201602 13224/ [accessed May 31, 2020].

12 Conclusion

12.1 Digital Entrepreneurship: The Way Forward

This book aimed to offer a picture of the state-of-the-art around digital entrepreneurship, and to do so looked at different aspects that comprise this domain. For instance, it identified that digital firms lie at the intersection of physical and digital economies and that digital ventures come in different types, such as large enterprises, SMEs, start-ups and spin-offs. It explained how the sharing of ideas and resources among different actors in the open innovation ecosystem could accrue benefits for all of them. Thus, it identified innovation as an integral part of entrepreneurship, and looked at how a strategy trend in large organizations is to innovate through the acquisition of start-ups and/or the creation of innovation hubs to sustain their competitive advantage in the market.

To better understand entrepreneurship, the book explored the different forms that digital innovation has taken in various industries. For example, merging the advantages brought by ICTs with the current financial process has yielded what we today call "fintech." Similar cases exist in almost every industry: "insurtech," "fashiontech," "manutech" and so on. Particular interest was paid to fintech because it has reshaped the finance sector and transformed the way we protect, borrow and manage our money. Chapter 9 discussed the profound impact of digitalization on the fintech industry by analyzing the great opportunities that have emerged for firms, banks and financial institutions as well as the critical challenges that the digital disruption has posed. A similar phenomenon can be seen in the digitalization of the manufacturing industry, as covered in Chapter 10. Digitalization has reshaped the manufacturing sector for good, building brands, increasing productivity, and efficiency. One last example of the impact of digitalization in industry presented in this book concerns the fashion industry. Chapter 11 described a few ways in which 3D technology can assist fashion organizations to produce better and faster models of their clothing as well as gaining a quicker time-to-market. One of the critical challenges of implementing 3D technology, however, is the extreme dependence on highly technical designers.

To identify how entrepreneurship can be achieved, the book explored different tactics used, one being digital marketing. Digital marketing is playing a significant role in the entrepreneurship arena. This book analyzed some of the most prominent and effective digital tactics used by companies to attract and retain customers, gain exposure, enhance brand awareness and increase sales: email marketing, social media marketing, search advertising and affiliate marketing. More importantly, it explored how businesses can use web analytics to measure and track the efficiency of digital marketing campaigns and uncover interesting patterns.

Another aspect of entrepreneurship that is relevant is education. The importance of having productive entrepreneurial education stems from its contribution to economic growth and provision of job opportunities for young graduates. This book discussed how effective entrepreneurial education could help in developing successful entrepreneurs. It observed the essential elements in planning and running entrepreneurship education, including financial management, big data analysis, digital marketing, creativity and innovation. As to these issues, it considered open innovation to be the essential enabler for successful digital entrepreneurship, requiring productive collaboration among all involved parties.

12.2   Final Remarks

The adoption and deployment of digital technologies for entrepreneurial purposes offer remarkable opportunities to digital firms, but, at the same time, they pose several challenges. The following paragraphs summarize what are believed to be critical challenges that start-ups and organizations need to consider when embarking on an entrepreneurship journey.

Security: Digital threats can result in a wide variety of implications for organizations, such as operational, financial, legal, IP and reputation risks [10]. Cybercrime-related risks are at the top of the list of global business risks creating significant concerns for digital entrepreneurs as they use digital platforms and infrastructures as means to offer their products and services to customers. While large enterprises may have the financial resources to implement strong security measures, small businesses and SMEs face a significant threat regarding cybersecurity. Most of the critical and personal data of customers are stored in the cloud, and several new security threats appear every day. Therefore, a digital firm should ensure that a robust security strategy is followed to retain the trust of its current customers and not lose new ones [6, 9, 11].

Financial challenges: Access to funding constitutes a significant problem for digital entrepreneurs and will transpire in different stages and in different periods. Although there are numerous accelerator and incubator programs to aid start-ups, digital firms should plan their funding strategy far ahead of their launch. Crowdfunding is a prevalent practice for raising business finance, though it also comes with some challenges. For example, there are several crowdfunding platforms available, all created for the same purpose but targeted at different audiences. Start-ups that have decided to use crowdfunding as a means of raising business funds should research diligently to find the platform that fits their needs.

Human resources: Finding the right talents who possess the right skills, expertise and mindset is one of the most critical aspects of the success of a start-up. Not having the right team on board is one of the top reasons why start-ups fail today [4, 12]. Digital ventures are dealing with skills shortages as they are all competing for the same underdeveloped pool of STEM graduates who are in high demand from millions of businesses around the world. As we have seen in this book, entrepreneurs are looking for "five-legged sheep," that is, individuals who can successfully do almost everything. The success of the digital firm depends highly on the skills, expertise and knowledge of the workforce that it has employed, thus the human capital management aspect of the company should be at the top of its list of priorities [2].

Increased competition: Digital changes have introduced one major challenge that digital firms need to face: increased competition in the market [8]. Acknowledging that rapid technological advancements, as well as globalization, have resulted in a highly competitive environment, entrepreneurs are intensifying their endeavors toward retaining their customers by developing new innovative products or by shifting their focus from products to services, ultimately looking to gain a strategic competitive advantage. In a world where technology changes rapidly and new digital platforms and tools keep emerging, digital entrepreneurs should be aware of their market competition and seek innovative methods to retain their customers as well as gain new ones [7].

Finally, the other side of entrepreneurship is collaboration with large organizations. Large organizations seek talent and agility, among other benefits, from collaborating with entrepreneurial start-ups. To meet these expectations, big firms have to support open innovation development by considering the following factors, which we provide as a concluding set of recommendations, complementing the main arguments developed in this volume:

- **Clear strategy**:

  A clearly defined vision as well as goals, expectations and performance indicators need to be set and planned to avoid surprises farther along the open innovation journey [1].

- **Top management support**:

  It is essential to align the firm's overall strategic goals with the expected outcomes of collaborating with entrepreneurial start-ups in an innovation ecosystem [1].

- **Budget commitment**:

  When planning financial commitment for open innovation, it is crucial to consider the budget needed for proofing the concept as well as for commercializing the innovative product and/or service [1].

- **Sustainable innovation ecosystem**:

  Big corporations need to collaborate on establishing co-investment schemes. Such collaboration can guarantee sustainable access to resources and funds, which will be reflected in a smart ecosystem where open innovation and knowledge transfer can thrive [5].

- **Promotion of an entrepreneurial culture**:

  Large organizations should embrace the culture of entrepreneurship by adopting agile decision-making processes, a knowledge-sharing mentality and a risk-taking attitude [1, 3, 5].

- **Creation and promotion of the network effect**:

  Start-ups seek to be suppliers for their partners. Having access to partners' extended networks is vital for broadening the ecosystem and promoting open innovation [1].

References

1.   Accenture. Harnessing the Power of Entrepreneurs to Open Innovation. Accenture (2015).
2.   Accenture. The Promise of Digital Entrepreneurs. Accenture (2014).
3.   Ades C et al. Implementing Open Innovation: The Case of Natura, IBM and Siemens. *Journal of Technology Management and Innovation* (2013) 8(SPL. ISS.1):12–25.
4.   CBInsights. The Top 20 Reasons Startups Fail. (2019). www.cbinsights.com /research/startup-failure-reasons-top/ [accessed May 27, 2020].
5.   Debackere K et al. *Boosting Open Innovation and Knowledge Transfer in the European Union*. Directorate-General for Research and Innovation. European Union (2014) ISBN 978–92–79–37867-6. doi:10.2777/72620.
6.   Deloitte. Doing Business in the Digital Age: The Impact of New ICT Developments in the Global Business Landscape. Deloitte (2012).

7. Ernst&Young. The Digitisation of Everything. EY (2011).
8. Finkelstein S. Internet Startups: So Why Can't They Win? *Journal of Business Strategy* (2001) 22(4):16–21.
9. Hair N et al. Market Orientation in Digital Entrepreneurship: Advantages and Challenges in a Web 2.0 Networked World. *International Journal of Innovation and Technology* (2012) 9(6):1250045.
10. Lloyd's. Managing Digital Risk: Trends, Issues and Implications for Business. Lloyd's (2010).
11. OECD. Key Issues for Digital Transformation in the G20. OECD (2017).
12. Salamzadeh A, Kesim H. Startup Companies: Life Cycle and Challenges. In: 4th *International Conference on* Employment, Educ*ation and* Entrep*reneurship* (EEE), *Belgrade, Serbia, August* (2015)

Index